CW00446580

Spon's Asia Pacific Construction Costs Handbook

JOIN US ON THE INTERNET VIA WWW, GOPHER, FTP OR EMAIL:

WWW: http://www.thomson.com
GOPHER: gopher.thomson.com
FTP: ftp.thomson.com   A service of I(T)P®
EMAIL: findit@kiosk.thomson.com

Spon's Asia Pacific Construction Costs Handbook

Edited by
DAVIS LANGDON & SEAH INTERNATIONAL

Second edition

E & FN SPON
An Imprint of Chapman & Hall

London · Weinheim · New York · Tokyo · Melbourne · Madras

Published by E & FN Spon,
an imprint of Chapman & Hall, 2–6 Boundary Row, London SE1 8HN

Chapman & Hall, 2–6 Boundary Row, London SE1 8HN, UK

Chapman & Hall GmbH, Pappelallee 3, 69469 Weinheim, Germany

Chapman & Hall USA, 115 Fifth Avenue, New York, NY 10003, USA

Chapman & Hall Japan, ITP-Japan, Kyowa Building, 3F, 2-2-1 Hirakawacho, Chiyoda-ku, Tokyo 102, Japan

Chapman & Hall Australia, 102 Dodds Street, South Melbourne, Victoria 3205, Australia

Chapman & Hall India, R. Seshadri, 32 Second Main Road, CIT East, Madras 600 035, India

First edition 1994
Reprinted 1994
Second edition 1997

© 1994, 1997 E & FN Spon

Printed and bound in Hong Kong by Dah Hua Printing Press Co.,Ltd.

ISBN 0 419 22040 2

Apart from any fair dealing for the purposes of research or private study, or criticism or review, as permitted under the UK Copyright Designs and Patents Act, 1988, this publication may not be reproduced, stored, or transmitted, in any form or by any means, without the prior permission in writing of the publishers, or in the case of reprographic reproduction only in accordance with the terms of the licences issued by the Copyright Licensing Agency in the UK, or in accordance with the terms of licences issued by the appropriate Reproduction Rights Organization outside the UK. Enquiries concerning reproduction outside the terms stated here should be sent to the publishers at the London address printed on this page.

The publisher makes no representation, express or implied, with regard to the accuracy of the information contained in this book and cannot accept any legal responsibility or liability for any errors or omissions that may be made.

A catalogue record for this book is available from the British Library

Contents

PART THREE : COMPARATIVE DATA

Preface

In 1994, the Editors published the first Asia Pacific Construction Costs Handbook which covered fifteen countries. In this edition, three countries in the Asia Pacific region - Sri Lanka, Taiwan and Vietnam - not previously covered in the last volume have been included. Future volumes will no doubt add to the list of countries.

This book is designed to be a convenient reference. Its purpose is to present coherent snapshots of the economies and construction industries of the Asia Pacific region; it also places this information in an international context with the inclusion of the United Kingdom and USA. It is not a substitute for local knowledge and professional advice. It will, however, be extremely useful as an introduction to a country and its construction industry for clients, consultants, contractors, manufacturers of construction materials and equipment and others concerned with development, property and construction in the region.

Davis Langdon & Seah International
1996

Acknowledgements

The contents of this book have been gathered together from a variety of sources - individuals, organizations and publications. Construction cost data and general background information on local construction industries is based on contributions from a network of professional colleagues and associates worldwide. These include:

• Australia	Davis Langdon Australia
• Brunei	Davis Langdon & Seah : Brunei
• China	Davis Langdon & Seah China Ltd
• Hong Kong	Davis Langdon & Seah Hong Kong Ltd
• Indonesia	Davis Langdon & Seah Indonesia PT
• Japan	Futaba Quantity Surveyors : Japan
• Malaysia	Davis Langdon & Seah Malaysia
• New Zealand	Knapman Clark & Co Ltd : New Zealand
• Philippines	Davis Langdon & Seah Philippines Inc
• Singapore	Davis Langdon & Seah Singapore Pte Ltd
• South Korea	SsangYong Engineering & Construction Co Ltd
• Sri Lanka	Mrs Chitra Weddikkara, University of Moratuwa and Mrs Sriyanie de Silva, Institute for Construction Training and Development (ICTAD) : Sri Lanka
• Taiwan	Davis Langdon & Seah Hong Kong Ltd
• Thailand	Davis Langdon & Seah (Thailand) Ltd
• United Kingdom	Davis Langdon & Everest : London
• United States of America	R S Means Company Inc : United States of America
• Vietnam	Davis Langdon & Seah : Vietnam

Much of the statistical data is from World Bank Development Reports, the *Economist World in Figures* and official published statistics. The background on individual countries has come from local sources, national yearbooks, annual reports and *Economist Intelligence Unit Reports*.

Important sources of general and construction industry data have been various embassies, high commissions, trade missions, statistical offices, and government departments in the UK and overseas. Information on international contracting is largely based on surveys undertaken by *Engineering News Record* magazine. Data on exchange rates and consumer price indices come mainly from the *Financial Times* or International Monetary Fund publications.

Specific acknowledgements and sources are given where appropriate in each country. The research and compilation of this book were undertaken by Davis Langdon Consultancy and Davis Langdon & Seah International. Special acknowledgements are due to Dr Patricia Hillebrandt.

How to use this book

This book is in three parts - Part One: Regional Overview; Part Two: Individual Countries; and Part Three: Comparative Data. The seventeen countries covered in the book are listed in the Contents. The United Kingdom is outside the region but is included for comparative purposes.

Part One: Regional Overview

Part One comprises an essay - The construction industry in the Asia Pacific region - which describes the current situation and main trends in the construction industries covered in this publication.

Part Two: Individual Countries

In Part Two the seventeen countries are arranged in alphabetical order, and each is presented in a similar format under the following main headings:

- *Key data* provides main national, economic and construction indicators.
- *The construction industry* outlines the structure of the industry, tendering and contract procedures plus the regulations and standards.
- *Construction cost data* includes data on labour and material costs, measured rates for items of construction work and approximate estimating costs per square metre for different building types.
- *Exchange rates and inflation* presents data on exchange rates with the pound sterling, US$ and Japanese yen, and includes data on the main indices of price movements for retail prices and construction.
- *Useful addresses* gives the names and addresses of public and private organizations associated with the construction industry.

Part Three: Comparative Data

To allow comparison between countries covered in the book, Part Three brings together data from Part Two and presents them under three main headings:

- *Key national indicators* including financial and demographic data.
- *Construction output indicators* including output per capita.
- *Construction cost data* including labour and material costs and costs per square metre.

Abbreviations

LENGTH

kilometre	km
metre	m
decimetre	dm
millimetre	mm
yard	yd
foot	ft
inch	in

AREA

hectare	ha

VOLUME

kilolitre	kl
hectolitre	hl
litre	l
millilitre	ml

WEIGHT (MASS)

tonne	t
kilogram	kg
gram	g
hundredweight	cwt
pound	lb
ounce	oz

FORCE

kilonewton	kN
newton	N

not available	n.a.

Conversion factors

LENGTH

Metric		Imperial equivalent
1 kilometre	1000 metres	0.6214 miles
		1093.6 yards
1 metre	100 centimetres	1.0936 yards
	1000 millimetres	3.2808 feet
		39.370 inches
1 centimetre	10 millimetres	0.3937 inches
1 millimetre		0.0394 inches

Imperial		Metric equivalent
1 mile	1760 yards	1.6093 kilometres
	5280 feet	1609.3 metres
1 yard	3 feet	0.9144 metres
	36 inches	914.40 millimetres
1 foot	12 inches	0.3048 metres
		304.80 millimetres
1 inch		25.400 millimetres

AREA

Metric		Imperial equivalent
1 square kilometre	100 hectares	0.3861 square miles
	10^6 square metres	247.11 acres
1 hectare	10 000 square metres	2.4711 acres
		11 960 square yards
1 square metre	10 000 square centimetres	1.1960 square yards
		10.764 square feet
1 square centimetre	100 square millimetres	0.1550 square inches
1 square millimetre		0.0016 square inches

Imperial		Metric equivalent
1 square mile	640 acres	2.5900 square kilometres
		259.00 hectares
1 acre	4840 square yards	0.4047 hectares
		4046.9 square metres
1 square yard	9 square feet	0.8361 square metres
1 square inch		6.4516 square centimetres
		645.16 square millimetres

VOLUME

Metric		**Imperial equivalent**
1 cubic metre or	10 hectolitres	1.3080 cubic yards
1 kilolitre	1000 cubic decimetres	35.315 cubic feet
	1000 litres	
1 hectolitre	100 litres	3.5315 cubic feet
		21.997 gallons
1 cubic decimetre	1000 cubic centimetres	61.023 cubic inches
or 1 litre	1000 millilitres	0.2200 gallons
		1.7598 pints
		0.2642 US gallons
		2.1134 US pints
1 cubic centimetre	1000 cubic millimetres	0.0610 cubic inches
or 1 millilitre		

Imperial		**Metric equivalent**
1 cubic yard	9 cubic feet	0.7646 cubic metres
1 cubic foot	1728 cubic inches	28.317 litres
	6.2288 gallons	
	7.4805 US gallons	
1 cubic inch		16.387 cubic centimetres
1 gallon	8 pints	4.5461 litres
1 pint		0.5683 litres

US		
1 barrel	42 gallons	158.99 litres
1 gallon	8 pints	3.7854 litres
1 pint		0.4732 litres

WEIGHT (MASS)

Metric		**Imperial equivalent**
1 tonne	1000 kilograms	0.9842 tons
		1.1023 US tons
		2204.6 pounds
1 kilogram	1000 grams	2.2046 pounds
		35.274 ounces
1 gram		0.0353 ounces

Imperial		**Metric equivalent**
1 ton	20 hundredweights	1.0160 tonnes
	2240 pounds	1016.0 kilograms
1 hundredweight	112 pounds	50.802 kilograms
1 pound	16 ounces	0.4536 kilograms
		453.59 grams
1 ounce		28.350 grams

US		
1 ton	20 hundredweights	0.9072 tonnes
	2000 pounds	907.18 kilograms
1 hundredweight	100 pounds	45.359 kilograms

FORCE

Metric		**Imperial equivalent**
1 kilonewton	1000 newtons	0.1004 tons force
		0.1124 US tons force
1 newton		0.2248 pounds force

Imperial		**Metric equivalent**
1 ton force	2240 pounds force	9.9640 kilonewtons
1 pound force		4.4482 newtons

US		
1 ton force	2000 pounds force	8.8964 kilonewtons

PRESSURE

Metric	**Imperial equivalent**
1 newton per square millimetre	145.04 pounds force per square inch
1 kilonewton per square metre	20.885 pounds force per square foot

Imperial	**Metric equivalent**
1 pound force per square inch	6.8948 kilonewtons per square metre
	0.0069 newtons per square millimetre
1 ton force per square inch	107.25 kilonewtons per square metre
	0.1073 newtons per square millimetre

US	
1 ton force per square foot	95.761 kilonewtons per square metre
	0.9576 newtons per square millimetre

Davis Langdon & Seah International

Practice Profile

Davis Langdon & Seah International (DLSI) is a worldwide organization which provides professional quantity surveying, cost engineering and construction cost consultancy services, project management and quality management consultancy and training. DLSI operates throughout the Asia Pacific region, Australia, the Middle East, the UK and mainland Europe and has associations with firms in Canada, Africa, New Zealand and Japan. The DLSI group employs some 1,700 staff managed by over 100 partners or directors in 52 offices located in 19 countries around the world.

Offices in the Asia Pacific region and Australia:

- Singapore   : Davis Langdon & Seah Singapore Pte Ltd
- Hong Kong   : Davis Langdon & Seah Hong Kong Ltd
- Malaysia   : Davis Langdon & Seah Malaysia
                    Juru Ukur Bahan Malaysia
                    JUBM Sdn Bhd
                    DLS Management (M) Sdn Bhd
- Brunei   : Davis Langdon & Seah
                    Petrokon Utama Sdn Bhd
- Indonesia   : Davis Langdon & Seah Indonesia PT
- Philippines   : Davis Langdon & Seah Philippines Inc
- Thailand   : Davis Langdon & Seah (Thailand) Ltd
- China   : Davis Langdon & Seah China Ltd
- Vietnam   : Davis Langdon & Seah
- Australia   : Davis Langdon & Beattie
                    Davis Langdon & Silver
                    Davis Langdon Management
                    DLIQ Quality System Certification Services
                    Davis Langdon Quality Management Pty Ltd

Offices in Europe:

- United Kingdom   : Davis Langdon & Everest
                       Davis Langdon Consultancy
                       Davis Langdon Management
- Germany   : Davis Langdon & Weiss
- Spain   : Davis Langdon Edetco
- France   : Davis Langdon Economistes
- The Czech Republic : Davis Langdon Cesko*Slovensko

Offices in the Middle East:

- Bahrain   : Davis Langdon Arabian Gulf
- Qatar   : Davis Langdon Arabian Gulf
- United Arab Emirates   : Davis Langdon Arabian Gulf
- Lebanon   : Davis Langdon Lebanon

In addition to the financial management of construction projects, DLSI, through Davis Langdon Consultancy, also undertakes varied construction industry research and consultancy assignments worldwide, ensuring a broadly based and truly international information service to their clients.

The value of the organization's international experience, research and information is distilled into the strategic advice and services offered to DLSI's individual clients and also provides data for publications, such as this current Asia Pacific Construction Costs Handbook.

Professional Services

DLSI specializes in the financial management of construction projects, from inception to completion. Their range of services includes:

- Feasibility Studies
- Construction Cost Management
- Cost Planning
- International Procurement
- Tender and Contract Documentation
- Project Management

- Claims Negotiation
- Development Economics and Appraisals
- Risk Analysis and Management
- Value Analysis and Management
- Construction Litigation Services
- Construction Insolvency Services
- Quality Management Consultancy and Training
- Research and Consultancy

The organization's experience covers a wide range of construction projects, such as:

- Airports and Airport Buildings
- Arts and Cultural Buildings
- Business Park Developments
- Civic Buildings
- Civil Engineering and Infrastructure Works
- Educational Buildings
- Health and Hospital Buildings
- Historic and Gazetted Buildings
- Hotels
- Industrial/Warehouse Developments
- Leisure Projects
- Office Buildings and Fit-out Works
- Petro-chemical Projects
- Power Generation Projects
- Public Buildings
- Residential Developments
- Retail Developments
- Sports Centres
- Transportation
- Water and Waste Projects

Practice Statement

Davis Langdon & Seah International is committed to giving the best possible professional service in meeting the needs of each client - whether large or small, local, multi-national or international.

The strategic and integrated management of cost, time and quality - the client's 'risk' areas of a contract - are essential functions, which are necessary to ensure the satisfactory planning, procurement, execution and operation of construction projects.

DLSI specializes in the financial management of construction projects and their risk areas, from project inception to completion.

The organization employs highly qualified and skilled professional staff, with specialist experience in all sectors of the construction industry, including international cost variables, procurement options and management structures.

It operates a sophisticated information support system, based on the latest computer technology, enabling large-scale capture and retrieval of cost and relevant market data.

The highest operational standards are observed to ensure quality of product and are quality assured in respect of the services in those countries where formal registration is available.

DLSI draws upon their international network of offices but works in manageable teams under direct partner or director leadership, and maintains personal client contact at all stages of a project.

The organization concentrates on:

- being positive and creative in their advice, rather than simply reactive;
- providing value for money via efficient management, rather than by superficial cost monitoring;
- giving advice that is matched to the client's specific requirements, rather than imposing standard or traditional solutions;
- paying attention to the life-cycle costs of constructing and occupying a building, rather than to the initial capital cost only.

The overall objective is to control cost, limit risk and add value for its clients.

EVERYTHING YOU WANTED TO KNOW ABOUT
QUANTITY SURVEYORS
BUT WERE TOO AFRAID TO ASK

What exactly do
Quantity Surveyors do?

- They manage client risk, control costs, add value

What areas of client risk?

- Those risks associated with financial assessment and investment

On what?

- All types of construction projects

When do these risks arise?

- At all stages of projects from inception to completion

How do they deal with
these risks?

- By effective advice, cost planning and management

What is achieved as a result?

- Risk limitation, cost control and added-value for clients

Who are the clients?

- Anyone contemplating, planning or carrying out a construction project

Does the client come first
and is confidentiality ensured?

- Yes

How can we be sure?

- Ask one of our clients.

Do quantity surveyors
charge much?

- Much less than you would think

IF YOU HAVE ANY MORE QUESTIONS - ASK DLSI

DAVIS LANGDON & SEAH INTERNATIONAL

ASIA PACIFIC

BRUNEI

DAVIS LANGDON & SEAH
No 1, First Floor, Block H
Abdul Razak Complex Gadong
P O Box 313
Bandar Seri Begawan 1903
Brunei Darussalam
Tel : (673-2) 446888
Fax : (673-2) 445555

CHINA

**DAVIS LANGDON & SEAH
CHINA LTD**
Shanghai Representative Office
Room 2409, 24/F
Shartex Plaza
88 Zhun Yi Nan Road
Shanghai 200335
China
Tel : (86-21) 62191107
Fax : (86-21) 62193680

Beijing Representative Office
Suite 101, Level 1 North Tower
Rainbow Plaza
14 Dong San Huan Bei Road
Chao Yang District
Beijing 100026
China
Tel : (86-1) 5954923
Fax : (86-1) 5954927

Guangzhou Representative Office
Unit 04, 11/F New Century Plaza
2-6 Hong De Road
Guangzhou 510235
China
Tel : (86-20) 4328565
Fax : (86-20) 4528567

HONG KONG

**DAVIS LANGDON & SEAH
HONG KONG LTD**
21st Floor, Leighton Centre
77 Leighton Road
Causeway Bay
Hong Kong
Tel : (852) 28303500
Fax : (852) 25760416

INDONESIA

**DAVIS LANGDON & SEAH
INDONESIA PT**
Wisma Metropolitan 1, Level 13
Jalan Jendral Sudirman Kav. 29
PO Box 3139/Jkt
Jakarta 10001, Indonesia
Tel : (62-21) 5254745
Fax : (62-21) 5254764

Wisma Bumi Bapindo
4th Floor Jalan Jendral Basuki
Rachmat 129-137
Surabaya 60271 , Indonesia
Tel : (62-31) 520691/2

MALAYSIA

**DAVIS LANGDON & SEAH
MALAYSIA**
124 Jalan Kasah
Damansara Heights
50490 Kuala Lumpur
Malaysia
Tel : (60-3) 2543411
Fax : (60-3) 2559660

Suite 8A, Wisma Pendidikan
Jalan Padang
PO Box 1598
88817 Kota Kinabalu
Malaysia
Tel : (60-88) 223369
Fax : (60-88) 216537

2nd Floor, Lot 142
Bangunan WSK, Jalan Abell
93100 Kuching
Sarawak
Malaysia
Tel : (60-82) 417357
Fax : (60-82) 426416

9 Jalan Padang Victoria
10400 Penang
Malaysia
Tel : (60-4) 2287630
Fax : (60-4) 2298031

49-01 Jalan Tun Abdul Razak
Susur 1/1 Medan Cahaya
80000 Johor Bahru
Malaysia
Tel : (60-7) 2236229
Fax : (60-7) 2235975

PHILIPPINES

**DAVIS LANGDON & SEAH
PHILIPPINES INC**
4/F Kings Court I
2129 Pasong Tamo
Makati City, Philippines
Tel : (63-2) 8112971
Fax : (63-2) 8112071

SINGAPORE

**DAVIS LANGDON & SEAH
SINGAPORE PTE LTD**
135 Cecil Street #12-00
LKN Building
Singapore 069536
Tel : (65) 2223888
Fax : (65) 2247089

THAILAND

**DAVIS LANGDON & SEAH
(THAILAND) LTD**
8th Floor, Kian Gwan Building
140 Wireless Road
Bangkok 10330 , Thailand
Tel : (66-2) 2537390
Fax : (66-2) 2534977

VIETNAM

DAVIS LANGDON & SEAH
83A Ly Thuong Kiet Street
5th Level
Hoan Kiem
Hanoi, Vietnam
Tel : (84-4) 8240395
Fax : (84-4) 8240394

1B Ngo Van Nam Street
District 1, Ho Chi Minh City
Vietnam
Tel : (84-8) 8295959

DAVIS LANGDON & SEAH INTERNATIONAL

AUSTRALIA

**DAVIS LANGDON &
BEATTIE**
1st Floor, 79-81 Franklin Street
Melbourne
Victoria 3000
Australia
Tel : (61-3) 9663 1277
Fax : (61-3) 9663 8039

1st Floor
146 Arthur Street
North Sydney
New South Wales 2060
Australia
Tel : (61-2) 9956 8822
Fax : (61-2) 9956 8848

19th Floor
141 Queen Street
Brisbane
Queensland 4000
Australia
Tel : (61-7) 32211788
Fax : (61-7) 32213417

53 Salamanca Place
Hobart
Tasmania 7000
Australia
Tel : (61-2) 348788
Fax : (61-2) 311429

**DAVIS LANGDON
QUALITY MANAGEMENT
PTY LTD**
1st Floor, 79-81 Franklin Street
Melbourne
Victoria 3000
Australia
Tel : (61-3) 9663 4925
Fax : (61-3) 9663 8039

**DAVIS LANGDON &
SILVER**
255 Beaufort Street
Perth
Western Australia 6000
Australia
Tel : (61-9) 2271477
Fax : (61-9) 2271737

MIDDLE EAST

**DAVIS LANGDON
ARABIAN GULF**
PO Box 640
Manama, State of Bahrain
Arabian Gulf
Tel : (973) 251755
Fax : (973) 232291

PO Box 7856
Deira, Dubai
United Arab Emirates
Arabian Gulf
Tel : (971-4) 227424
Fax : (971-4) 220069

PO Box 3206
Doha, State of Qatar
Arabian Gulf
Tel : (974) 328440
Fax : (974) 437349

**DAVIS LANGDON
LEBANON**
PO Box 135422-Shouran
Australia Street, Chatila Building
Beirut, Lebanon
Tel : (9611) 603104/809045
Fax : (9611) 603104

EUROPE

SPAIN
DAVIS LANGDON EDETCO
Av. Sant Narcis 28 pral 2⁰
17005 - Girona
Spain
Tel : (34-72) 221878
Fax : (34-72) 223545

C/Ferrer del Rio, 14
28028 - Madrid
Spain
Tel : (34-1) 611805
Fax : (34-1) 612951

C/Avinyó, 52, pral.
08002 - Barcelona
Spain
Tel : (34-3) 23108
Fax : (34-3) 22664

FRANCE

**DAVIS LANGDON
ECONOMISTES**
16, Rue Albert Einstein
Champs sur Marne
77436 Marne la Valle
Cedex 2
France
Tel : (33-1) 64620724
Fax : (33-1) 64119087

GERMANY

**DAVIS LANGDON &
WEISS**
Böblinger Strasse 63
70199 Stuttgart - 1
Germany
Tel : (49-711) 602225
Fax : (49-711) 609812

Altkönigstrasse 124
61440 Oberursel
Nr Frankfurt
Germany
Tel : (49-69) 7126213
Fax : (49-69) 7124928

Gotlandstrasse 16
010439 Berlin
Germany
Tel : (49-30) 4175710
Fax : (49-30) 4175715

CZECH REPUBLIC

**DAVIS LANGDON
CESKO*SLOVENSKO**
Sokolovská 22
180 00 Prague 8
The Czech Republic
Tel : (42) 2360876
Fax : (42) 2360878

DAVIS LANGDON & SEAH INTERNATIONAL
UNITED KINGDOM

DAVIS LANGDON & EVEREST
DAVIS LANGDON MANAGEMENT
DAVIS LANGDON CONSULTANCY

LONDON
Princes House
39 Kingsway
London
WC2B 6TP
Tel : (44-171) 4979000
Fax : (44-171) 4978858

BRISTOL
St Lawrence House
29/31 Broad House
Bristol
BS1 2HF
Tel : (44-117) 277832
Fax : (44-117) 251350

CAMBRIDGE
36 Storey's Way
Cambridge
CB3 ODT
Tel : (44-223) 351258
Fax : (44-223) 321002 .

CARDIFF
3 Raleigh Walk
Brigantine Place
Atlantic Wharf
Cardiff
CF1 5LN
Tel : (44-1222) 471306
Fax : (44-1222) 471465

CHESTER
Ford Lane Farm
Lower Lane
Aldford
Chester
CH3 6HP
Tel : (44-244) 620222
Fax : (44-244) 620303

EDINBURGH
74 Great King Street
Edinburgh
EH3 6QU
Tel : (44-131) 575306
Fax : (44-131) 575704

GATESHEAD
11 Regent Terrace
Gateshead
Tyne and Wear
NE8 1LU
Tel : (44-914) 77 3844
Fax : (44-914) 90 1742

GLASGOW
Cumbrae House
15 Carlton Court
Glasgow
G5 9JP
Tel : (44-141) 296677
Fax : (44-141) 292255

IPSWICH
17 St Helens Street
Ipswich
IP4 1HE
Tel : (44-473) 253405
Fax : (44-473) 231215

LEEDS
Duncan House
14 Duncan Street
Leeds
LS1 6DL
Tel : (44-113) 432481
Fax : (44-113) 424601

LIVERPOOL
Cunard Building
Water Street
Liverpool
L3 1JR
Tel : (44-151) 361992
Fax : (44-151) 275401

MANCHESTER
Boulton House
Chorlton Street
Manchester
M1 3HY
Tel : (44-161) 282011
Fax : (44-161) 286371

MILTON KEYNES
6 Bassett Court
Newport Pagnell
Buckinghamshire MK16 OJN
Tel : (44-908) 613777
Fax : (44-908) 210642

NEWPORT
34 Godfrey Road
Newport
Gwent NP9 4PE
Tel : (44-633) 259712
Fax : (44-633) 215694

NORWICH
63A Thorpe Road
Norwich NR1 1UD
Tel : (44-603) 628194
Fax : (44-603) 615928

OXFORD
Avalon House
Marcham Road
Abingdon
Oxford OX14 1TZ
Tel : (44-235) 555025
Fax : (44-235) 554909

PLYMOUTH
Barclays Bank Chambers
Princess Street
Plymouth PL1 2HA
Tel : (44-752) 668372
Fax : (44-752) 221219

PORTSMOUTH
Kings House, 4 Kings Road
Portsmouth
Hampshire P05 3BQ
Tel : (44-705) 815218
Fax : (44-705) 827156

SOUTHAMPTON
Clifford House, New Road
Southampton SO2 OAB
Tel : (44-1703) 333438
Fax : (44-1703) 226099

PART ONE
REGIONAL OVERVIEW

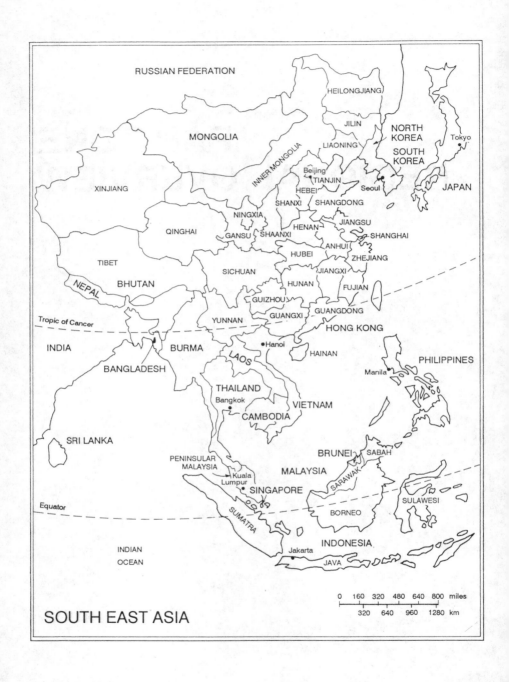

SOUTH EAST ASIA

1. The construction industry in the Asia Pacific region

INTRODUCTION

This book covers sixteen major countries bordering the Pacific Ocean. It also includes the UK for comparative purposes. The region includes the two major industrialized powers - the USA and Japan, thirteen Asian countries varying from the vast area of China to tiny Hong Kong and Singapore as well as Australia and New Zealand. The levels of development range from some of the poorest countries of the world to the very richest and from long established market economies to centrally planned and transition economies.

Included in this book are the countries known as the `Asian Tigers` - Hong Kong, South Korea, Singapore and Taiwan. It is these countries, as well as the newly industrializing economies of Indonesia, Malaysia and Thailand and the rapidly developing transition economies of China and Vietnam that have positioned East Asia as the region of the fastest, sustained economic growth in the world.

This introduction describes the international groupings of the countries, their key characteristics and various measures of their standard of living. The section on Construction Output and the Economy relates value of construction output to Gross Domestic Product (GDP) and to levels of investment for each country. It includes some data on housing stock. Finally there is a section on the Organization of the Construction Sector.

The main active regional grouping is the Association of Southeast Asian Nations (ASEAN) established in 1967 with the aims of accelerating economic growth, social progress and cultural development, the promotion of collaboration and mutual assistance in matters of common interest and the continuing stability of the region.

The selection of the countries to be included in this book is in part based on their importance and in part on the availability of data both published and unpublished. Table A lists the countries, indicating their membership of international groupings and whether they have formal Davis Langdon & Seah International (DLSI) offices or are represented by a firm associated with the DLSI Group.

Table A: MEMBERSHIP OF INTERGOVERNMENTAL ORGANIZATIONS
AND DLSI REPRESENTATION

Country	ASEAN	OECD	DLSI offices (X) or associates (*)
Australia		X	X
Brunei	X		X
China			X
Hong Kong		X	X
Indonesia	X		X
Japan		X	*
Malaysia	X		X
New Zealand		X	*
Philippines	X		X
Singapore	X		X
South Korea			
Sri Lanka			
Taiwan			
Thailand	X		X
UK		X	X
USA		X	*
Vietnam	X		X

Sources : OECD, Organization for Economic Co-operation and Development
  ASEAN, Association of Southeast Asian Nations

Table B, in summarizing the key characteristics of the countries included in this volume, highlights their diversity. Populations range from 300,000 in Brunei to nearly 1.2 billion in China. The smallest country in terms of area is Singapore and the largest, China - just a fraction larger than the USA and 24% larger than Australia. Density of population is high in the smallest countries but only two persons per square kilometre in Australia, 27 persons in the USA and 123 in China. The table is arranged in order of GNP per capita, with Vietnam indicated as even poorer than China, and Singapore and Hong Kong with a standard of living approaching that of the richest countries. Definitions of the statistical terms in Table B and others used in this book are discussed in Part Two section 2. Of the countries in this book two have been planned economies: China and Vietnam, but both are already moving towards a market economy.

Because of the need to use monetary values and exchange rates for conversion to a common currency, GDP and GNP are not always the best indicators of standard of living. Table C compares the money value of GNP per capita with estimates of GNP per capita on a purchasing power parity (PPP) basis, that is an approximation to what the GNP per capita will actually buy in the respective countries. In Table C, overleaf, the countries are arranged as in Table B but in fact it is clear that on a PPP basis the order changes noticeably. Sri Lanka moves up from third to fourth place. At the top end the USA is the highest while Hong Kong overtakes the UK, Singapore and even Japan.

Table B : KEY CHARACTERISTICS OF COUNTRIES

Country	Population mn	Land area km²	Population per km²	GDP US$bn 1993	GNP per capita US$ 1993
Low Income Economies					
Vietnam	71.3	332,000	215	12.8	170
China	1,178.4	9,561,000	123	425.6	490
Sri Lanka	17.9	66,000	271	9.4	600
Middle Income Economies					
Indonesia	187.2	1,905,000	98	144.7	740
Philippines	64.8	300,000	216	54.1	850
Thailand	58.1	513,000	113	124.9	2,110
Malaysia	19.0	330,000	58	64.5	3,140
South Korea	44.1	99,000	445	330.8	7,660
High Income Economies					
Taiwan	21.1	36,000	586	218.5	10,350
New Zealand	3.5	271,000	13	43.7	12,600
Brunei	0.3	5,765	52	4.0	13,450
Australia	17.6	7,713,000	2	289.4	17,500
Hong Kong	5.8	1,076	5,390	90.0	18,060
United Kingdom	57.9	245,000	236	819.0	18,060
Singapore	2.8	639	4,382	55.2	19,850
USA	258.3	9,373,000	27	6,259.9	24,740
Japan	124.8	378,000	330	4,214.2	31,490

Sources: World Development Report 1995, World Bank except that GNP for Taiwan and Brunei are from Economist Intelligence Unit Country Reports
GNP figure for Hong Kong is for GDP not GNP. The figures of GNP/GDP for China are preliminary estimates

Table C : GNP PER CAPITA ON A PPP AND MONEY BASIS, 1993

Country	GNP per capita on PPP basis US$	Index USA=100	Rank order	GNP per capita US$
Low Income Economies				
Vietnam	*1,300	5.5	1	170
China	2,300	9.4	2	490
Sri Lanka	3,000	12.1	4	600
Middle Income Economies				
Indonesia	3,100	12.7	5	740
Philippines	2,700	10.8	3	850
Thailand	6,300	25.3	6	2,110
Malaysia	7,900	32.1	7	3,140
South Korea	9,600	38.9	8	7,660
High Income Economies				
Taiwan	*11,600	50.2	9	10,350
New Zealand	16,000	64.8	11	12,600
Brunei	*14,400	62.4	10	13,450
Australia	17,900	72.4	13	17,500
Hong Kong	21,500	87.1	16	18,060
United Kingdom	17,200	69.6	12	18,060
Singapore	19,500	78.9	14	19,850
USA	24,700	100.0	17	24,740
Japan	20,900	84.3	15	31,490

Sources :   World Development Report 1995, World Bank. Figures of GNP on a PPP basis with
*asterisk * from Asia Week 23.11.94. Other GNP figures from Table B*

Other factors are also relevant in assessing the standard of living and quality of life. Table D, overleaf, shows some non-monetary indicators of development. Here there are some interesting surprises particularly for Sri Lanka whose infant mortality rates are lower than most middle income economies and whose secondary school enrolment is higher than in most middle income economies. Secondary school enrolment in South Korea is higher than New Zealand, Australia and the UK. Brunei is low on telephone provision.

Table D : SELECTED NON-MONETARY INDICATORS OF DEVELOPMENT

Country	% of population with access to safe water 1991	Telephone lines per 1000 persons 1992	Infant mortality rate * 1993	Secondary school enrolment # 1992
Low Income Economies				
Vietnam	50	2	41	**33
China	71	10	30	**51
Sri Lanka	60	8	17	**74
Middle Income Economies				
Indonesia	42	8	56	38
Philippines	81	10	42	**74
Thailand	**72	**31	36	33
Malaysia	78	112	13	58
South Korea	78	357	11	90
High Income Economies				
Taiwan	n.a.	n.a.	n.a.	n.a.
New Zealand	97	449	9	84
Brunei	n.a.	**154.	n.a.	n.a.
Australia	100	471	7	82
Hong Kong	100	485	7	n.a.
United Kingdom	100	473	7	**86
Singapore	100	415	6	n.a.
USA	100	565	9	n.a.
Japan	n.a.	464	4	n.a.

Sources :   World Development Report 1995, World Bank and other sources

 # Children engaged in secondary school as a percentage of population of secondary
school age, usually 12 to 17 years

* Per 1,000 live births

** Figures are for years other than those specified

n.a. = not available

None of these factors shows the financial viability of the economies. Foreign aid and borrowings are pointers to this. Table E, overleaf, shows Official Development Assistance and net present value of external debt, both as a percentage of GNP, for the countries for which information is available. Vietnam has a heavy load of external debt which will be a burden in future years and makes it imperative to increase GNP as fast as it intends. Aid as a proportion of GNP is highest in Sri Lanka and high but less so in the Philippines and Vietnam. It must be borne in mind that the percentage of aid of GNP is an annual figure but the external debt is accumulated over several years. Although the receipt of aid or external loans by a country indicates a degree of dependence, if it is for capital projects it should eventually strengthen the economy. The level of investment is clearly of great importance and is included for the countries listed in Table E. Investment is very high in China which has very low dependence on external sources and also in Thailand. However, in Vietnam, Sri Lanka, Indonesia and the Philippines, where dependence on foreign sources is highest, the level of investment though high by developed country standards, is not outstanding.

Table E : AID, FOREIGN DEBT AND INVESTMENT

Country	Official development assistance + % of GNP 1993	Net present value of external debt as % of GNP 1993	Gross domestic investment as a % of GDP 1993
Low Income Economies			
Vietnam	2.5	161.8	21
China	0.8	18.0	41
Sri Lanka	5.3	41.9	25
Middle Income Economies			
Indonesia	1.4	58.5	28
Philippines	2.8	59.8	24
Thailand	0.5	36.5	40
Malaysia	0.2	37.0	33
South Korea	0.3	13.9	34

Sources :   World Bank Development Report 1995, World Bank
        + Net disbursement of official development assistance from all sources

CONSTRUCTION OUTPUT AND THE ECONOMY

Table F, overleaf, shows the relationship of investment, gross construction output and net construction output to GDP and to each other. Gross output is the total value of construction produced. Net output is the gross output minus the inputs from other industries (see Statistical Notes in section 2). These inputs are mainly materials but also plant and equipment and other goods and services. Thus net output consists mainly of labour, management costs and profits. The gross and net output consists mainly of labour, management costs and profits. The gross and net output figures are those contained in the country sections.

Table F : INVESTMENT AND CONSTRUCTION OUTPUT RELATED TO GDP

Country	Net output as a % of GDP	Gross output as a % of GDP	Net output as a % of gross ouput	Gross domestic investment as a % of GDP
Low Income Economies				
Vietnam	7.4	*15	49	21
China	6.7	23.4	29	41
Sri Lanka	7.3	*17	43	25
Simple average	7	19	40	29
Middle Income Economies				
Indonesia	*6	*15	40	28
Philippines	5.4	*13	41	24
Thailand	6.9	*18	38	40
Malaysia	*7	*15	46	33
South Korea	*8	*19	42	34
Simple average	7	16	41	32
High Income Economies				
Taiwan	5.6	*13	43	-
New Zealand	4.0	*9	44	21
Brunei	5.2	*10	57	-
Australia	6.7	*13	52	20
Hong Kong	4.6	8.7	53	27
United Kingdom	5.3	7.4	72	15
Singapore	7.4	*19	39	44
USA	3.7	8.7	43	16
Japan	10.3	17.8	58	30
Simple average	6	12	51	25

Sources : Official country statistics, Economic Intelligence Unit Country Report; World Bank Development Report, 1995; DTI, Construction Industry Development Board Singapore and authors' estimates

* Figures of net output and gross output as a percentage of GDP are given to one decimal point except where estimated by the authors

For some countries a considerable amount of estimation is involved. Generally the national accounts contain estimates of the contribution of construction to GDP which is net output. It is often difficult to obtain estimates of gross construction output for developing countries. Because of the difficulty in gathering data on construction, any figures of gross and net output are subject to considerable margins of error. These are a result of large numbers of small projects particularly in renovation and repair and maintenance; the wide geographical dispersion of construction activity; the fact that the price of a construction project is not always determined in one operation and changes may not be recorded; and the large number of construction clients and construction firms.

It is possible however to make estimates of gross output especially if data for net output and investment are available. The relationship between gross construction output and net construction output depends on:

- the work mix. Some work is more labour intensive than other, for example repair and maintenance in the UK probably involves about three times more labour input than new civil engineering work
- the sophistication of construction including the extent of use of capital equipment
- wage rates and productivity

Thus a country which has low wage rates and high productivity would be expected to have low net output in relation to gross output but in fact low wage rates are usually combined with low productivity so that the effects to some extent cancel each other out. A country with a sophisticated construction product probably uses a high level of equipment and expensive materials so that the tendency would be for net output to be a low proportion of gross output. Such a country however probably also has high wage rates and high productivity thus compensating to some extent for the high input costs. In general the proportion of net output of gross output is around 50%.

Another factor to be taken into account is the relationship between construction new work output and total investment. In most countries construction accounts for about half of all investment and is likely to be higher in less developed countries than in developed ones because the construction industry provides much of the very basic infrastructure.

Where the authors have estimated gross output they have generally done so by estimating the percentage which it is likely to take of GDP bearing in mind the proportion accounted for by net output and by total investment.

Considering the individual countries in Table F the preceding general statements may be seen reflected in the figures. In the case of Japan, the USA and the UK both gross and net output were available, but for other countries gross output has been estimated.

The UK has a very high proportion of net output of gross output. The explanation probably lies in the high proportion of non-new work in the table output mix. All repair and maintenance, refurbishment and rehabilitation account for over 60% of total UK output. This is very labour intensive work with new materials being a relatively small proportion of the total value of the work. However, this may not be sufficient to explain the very high figure of 72%. It is noteworthy that the data on gross output and net output come from different sources and use different methods. There may well be a need to review the official statistics. The collection of construction industry data in the UK has been arguably the best in the world. If the UK figures are peculiar, the caution to be adopted in accepting other countries' official statistics is clear and this is one of the reasons for the estimates having been used in some cases in preference to official statistics.

In general the table shows that high income economies have a higher percentage of net output of gross output. However, it also shows that they have a lower percentage of gross output of GDP than less rich countries and also invest a lower proportion of GDP than poorer countries.

An important component of output in any construction industry is housing. Unfortunately both the stock of housing and the number of dwellings completed is poorly documented by international organizations. The latest edition (at the end of 1995) of the *UN Construction Statistics Yearbook* is the 1988 edition giving 1985 data. There are some data stock of housing produced by the *Economist* in 1990 giving the latest available data in the period 1980-88. These are still of relevance because, unless the rate of construction is very high, e.g. in Singapore where in some years completions have been over 10% of stock, the relative position of the countries will change only slowly. The figures are shown in Table G.

Population per dwelling generally decreases with increases in income. It would appear that the Singaporean authorities were determined to tackle the housing problem and it may well have halved the population per dwelling sometime in the 1990s. Japan regards its supply of dwellings and particularly space standards as unsatisfactory and is trying to remedy the situation. However, the life span of housing in Japan is low so that the stock in terms of number of dwellings will not increase very rapidly even if their average size increases.

Table G : HOUSING STOCK (LATEST AVAILABLE YEAR IN 1980s)

Country	Dwelling stock 000s	Population per dwelling
Low Income Economies		
Vietnam	12,456	5.1
China	290,456	3.6
Sri Lanka	3,050	5.3
Middle Income Economies		
Indonesia	40,920	4.1
Philippines	8,972	5.6
Thailand	9,200	5.1
Malaysia	2,850	3.4
South Korea	n.a.	n.a.
High Income Economies		
Taiwan	4,500	4.3
New Zealand	1,250	2.6
Brunei	n.a.	n.a.
Australia	5,690	2.8
Hong Kong	1,348	4.1
United Kingdom	23,055	2.6
Singapore	552	5.7
USA	88,073	2.7
Japan	40,125	3.0

Sources : The Economist, Vital World Statistics

THE ORGANIZATION OF THE CONSTRUCTION SECTOR

In market economies throughout the world the contracting sector in each country typically consists of a large number of small firms and a few larger ones. In the UK for example the top 100 firms out of some 200,000 firms carry out only about 20% of the work. The average number of persons per establishment in Australia, Hong Kong and Japan as well as the UK and USA is small - under five in the UK, USA and Australia and under 15 in Hong Kong and Japan. This is due to the large amount of subcontracting but is also a function of the large number of small jobs especially in repair and maintenance and in many countries the wide geographical dispersion of work coupled with high transport costs. Malaysia, of the market economies described here, has a greater prevalence of large firms.

By contrast, in planned economies, most work is undertaken by giant organizations. In China, the average employment in over 4,000 state owned enterprises approaches 1,500 and even in rural construction teams is over 100. In Vietnam, the contracting industry is dominated by a few giant organizations, though there are now some smaller private firms. The large size of firms mirrors the tendency for large projects with very little repair and maintenance but also reflects the strong central control in such economies.

Many of the large construction companies have some part to play in exporting to other parts of the world. The international role of companies in various countries is reported in Table H.

Table H : NUMBER OF CONSTRUCTION COMPANIES IN
        TOP 225 INTERNATIONAL COMPANIES, 1994

Country	Number in top 100 companies	Number in top 225 companies
Australia	1	2
China	4	23
Hong Kong	-	1
Japan	19	26
Malaysia	-	1
South Korea	6	9
Taiwan	-	2
UK	9	12
USA	19	52
All	58	128

Source: Engineering News Record, 28.8.95

It can be seen that the USA, Japan and China have a large number of construction companies that operate internationally. In the section on China in this book, the increasing importance of Chinese contractors in earning revenue from international contracts is discussed.

PART TWO
INDIVIDUAL COUNTRIES

2. Introductory notes to country sections

INTRODUCTION

In this part of the book, seventeen countries are arranged alphabetically, and each country is presented as far as possible in a similar format, under five main headings - Key data, The construction industry, Construction cost data, Exchange rates and inflation, and Useful addresses. These notes introduce the five main sets of information presented on the individual countries and provide, in one place, general notes, definitions and explanations, in order to keep the individual country sections as succinct as possible. A final heading, Statistical notes, discusses and explains the statistical definitions and concepts adopted in the book.

KEY DATA

The key data sheet at the start of each country lists main population, geographic, economic and construction indicators and thus provides a brief statistical overview of that country. In many cases data produced by national statistical offices have been used; in other cases, UN or World Bank sources have been relied on. Some estimates are included for construction data especially for gross construction output. The methods are discussed in Part One - The Construction Industry in the Asia Pacific Region. In Part Three, Comparative Data, international agency data has been used throughout in order to ensure consistency. Further notes on economic indicators are provided below in the Statistical notes.

THE CONSTRUCTION INDUSTRY

The main topics covered in this section are the contribution of the industry to the economy; the structure of the industry; the availability of and constraints on construction labour and materials; tendering and contract procedures and standards.

Although construction is often fragmented and tends to be labour intensive with low capital investment, it is invariably the single largest industry in a country. In most countries the net output of construction contributes between 5% and 15% to Gross Domestic Product (GDP) and a similar percentage to direct construction employment (indirect employment - in the construction materials industries and other related activities - can more than double the contribution). Gross construction output including materials and plant and equipment is normally around twice net output but the range is quite wide and the reasons are discussed in Part One - The Construction Industry in the Asia Pacific Region.

CONSTRUCTION COST DATA

This section includes both construction costs incurred by contractors and the costs they charge their clients. The costs of labour and materials are input costs of construction, i.e. the costs incurred by contractors.

Unit costs, measured rates for construction work and approximate estimating costs per square metre are output costs, i.e. the costs contractors charge their clients. Problems of definition make meaningful and consistent presentation of unit rates extremely difficult. For unit rates to be useful it is essential to be clear what is included and what excluded. Notes are provided in each country section, for example, on the treatment of preliminary items and on the methods of measurement adopted for approximate estimating rates per square metre.

Cost of labour and materials

Typical costs for construction labour and materials are given in most country sections. Two figures are generally given for each grade of labour. The wage rate is the basis of an employee's income - his basic weekly wage will be the number of hours worked multiplied by his wage rate. The cost of labour, on the other hand, is the cost to the employer of employing that employee; it is also based on the wage rate but includes (where applicable) allowances for:

- incentive payments
- travelling time and fares
- lodging and subsistence
- public and annual holidays with pay
- training levies
- employer's liability and third party insurances
- health insurance
- payroll taxes
- other mandatory and voluntary payments.

The costs of main construction materials are given as delivered to site in quantities appropriate to a reasonably substantial building project. It is presumed that there are no particular difficulties of access etc. which would significantly affect costs. Generally tax, and particularly any value added tax, is excluded from material costs mainly because the rate of tax to be levied may depend on the type of work in which the material is to be incorporated.

Unit rates

Rates for a variety of commonly occurring construction items are provided for most countries. They are usually based on a major, if not the capital, city and the relevant date is always third quarter of 1995. Rates generally include all necessary labour, materials, plant and equipment and, where appropriate, allowances for contractors' overheads and profit, preliminary and general items associated with site set-up, etc. and contractors' profit and attendance on specialist trades. Where the basis of rates is different from this, notes are provided in the text in each country section. Value added tax and other taxes are excluded. The rates are appropriate to a reasonably substantial building project.

In the country sections abbreviated descriptions are given for each work item; a full description of each work item is presented in section 4.

Approximate estimating

Approximate estimating costs per unit area (square metres and square feet) are given for most countries for a variety of building types. Notes on the method of measurement and what is or is not included in unit rates are provided in each country section. Areas generally are measured on all floors inside external walls and with no deduction for internal walls, columns, etc. Where this is not the case it is noted. Generally tax, and particularly value added tax, is excluded in approximate estimating costs.

When making comparisons of construction costs between countries it is important to be clear about what is being compared. There are two main methods of comparison: first the comparison of identical buildings in each country and, second, the comparison of functionally similar buildings in each country. In the country sections, the approximate estimating rates given are for the standard of building of each type normally built in that country. Rates are therefore closer to the 'functionally similar' approach. The rate per square metre given for an office building, for example, or a warehouse in any particular country refers to the normal type of office building or warehouse built in that country. In country sections they are presented in national currencies. A selection of approximate estimating costs are also presented in pound sterling, US dollar and 100 Japanese yen equivalents in Part Three thus enabling comparisons on a common currency basis to be made.

EXCHANGE RATES AND INFLATION

Exchange rates

Currency exchange rates are important when comparing costs between one country and another. While it is most useful to consider costs within a country in that country's currency, it is necessary, from time to time, to use a common currency in order to compare one country's costs with another. But exchange rates can fluctuate dramatically and few currencies (even those considered strong) can be considered really stable. It can be risky to think in terms, for example, of one country being consistently a set percentage more or less expensive than another.

Different rates of internal inflation affect the relative values of currencies and, therefore, the rates of exchange between them. However, the reasons behind exchange rate fluctuations are complex and often political as much as economic; they include such factors as interest rates, balance of payments, trade figures and, of course, government intervention in the foreign exchange markets, and, for that matter, other government actions.

Graphs of exchange rates since 1980 against the US dollar, the pound sterling and the Japanese yen are included for most countries. They have been calculated by averaging the published weekly values in each quarter. The values given are therefore smoothed - the most dramatic peaks and troughs have been ironed out. They are, however, useful for indicating long term trends. As far as possible, the form of the graph is kept the same, hence the vertical scale is adjusted to accommodate different currencies. It should always be checked whether marked movement in a graph is a result of erratic exchange rates or merely the selected vertical scale.

If a line moves up from left to right (for example, the Philippines peso against the pound sterling to 1991 - see below) it indicates that the subject currency (the peso) is declining in value against the currency of the line (the pound sterling). The higher the line is, the more subject currency is required to purchase the line currency. If, on the other hand, a line moves down from left to right (for example, the Japanese yen against the pound sterling) it indicates the subject currency is strengthening against

the line currency. Where there is virtually no movement at all, that is
the line is horizontal, this usually indicates a currency effectively 'tied'
or 'pegged' to the line currency.

EXCHANGE RATE GRAPH

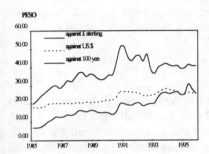
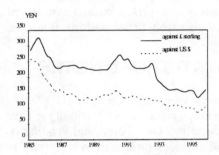

Inflation

General inflation has been measured using consumer or retail price indices.
These reflect price changes in a basket of goods and services weighted
according to the spending patterns of a typical family. Weights are changed
periodically, and new items inserted. General inflation indices usually rise
and, in so doing erode the purchasing power of a given currency unit.
Other measures of inflation tend to be related to specific items. The two
most commonly prepared for the construction industry are discussed below.

Cost and tender price indices measure different types of inflation which
occur within the construction industry. Building costs are the costs actually
incurred by a contractor in the course of his business, the major ones being
labour and materials; tender prices are the prices for which a contractor
offers to erect a building. Tender prices include building costs but also
take into account the prevailing market situation. When there is plenty of
construction work tender prices may increase at a greater rate than building
costs while, when work is scarce, tender prices may actually fall even if
building costs are rising.

Most countries have building cost indices - the method of compilation
is generally relatively simple, basically comprising a weighted basket of
the main inputs to construction. Rather fewer countries have tender price
indices - their method of compilation is more complex usually involving

a detailed analysis of accepted tenders for construction work and comparing these with a common base schedule of prices. When construction indices are described as price indices it is not always clear what these are.

USEFUL ADDRESSES

At the end of each country section, a list of addresses is given. This usually comprises main government, contracting, professional, standards and research organizations involved in the construction industry.

STATISTICAL NOTES

Gross Domestic Product (GDP) is the total value of all the goods and services produced in a country. Thus it shows the wealth generated within a country. Gross National Product (GNP) is the total value of all the goods and services produced in a country plus or minus net income from outside. Thus it represents the total amount of income available to the population. Reasons why GNP can be greater than GDP include that nationals abroad send back money, that the country receives aid or that the country has an income from investment abroad. Debt repayment and payment of interest can make GNP less than GDP.

It is appropriate to use GNP as a measure of wealth when income is being considered, e.g. in allocation for various purposes. GDP is more appropriate where productive capacity is being considered. Because a primary focus of this book is on the productive capacity of the construction industry in the key data sheets for each country the emphasis is on GDP, although there are a few countries where only statistics of GNP are available.

In considering expenditure the data for private and public consumption and investment are expressed as a proportion of GDP. This is partly because the main source for this expresses it this way and use of this one source gives a consistent picture. Because expenditure is made out of GNP the three percentages do not always total to 100, e.g. Philippines receives remittances from abroad which make its GNP greater than GDP and hence it is able to spend more than its own production on consumption and investment. Central government expenditure is, however, expressed as a percentage of GNP as in the World Development Report published by the World Bank.

Data on construction output for most countries are available in the form of net output or value added, that is, broadly, gross value of construction output minus the value of the material input, and the cost of plant and equipment. However, the method of arriving at this data and gross value of construction output varies from country to country and is sometimes so indirect that it is of dubious reliability/quality. Both gross and net construction output are given where possible. The authors have made estimates based on relationships to other indicators and past data of gross output where reliable data are not available and have for some countries also estimated net output.

The exchange rates given in the key data are those which are appropriate for use with the cost data. For conversion of figures for a year, e.g. GDP in 1993, the mid-year exchange rate has been used. Because a single yen has a small value compared to the US dollar or the pound sterling, a rate for 100 yen is given in each case. Purchasing power parity (PPP) is the exchange rate which would be appropriate to express an income in one country in terms of its purchasing power in another country.

All the statistics are subject to considerable margins of error but particularly so for the less developed countries. As soon as they are converted from national currencies to US$ in order to permit comparison, the difficulty arises that the exchange rate may not reflect the purchasing power parity (PPP). In using exchange rates to convert value of construction output the difficulty is greater because of the greater specificity of production. In one case - that of China - a comment has been made in the text that the statistics do not reflect the real situation, but the problems exist in a greater or lesser degree for all countries. Indeed even taking authoritative sources, variations of a factor of eight are possible. Table C in section 1 shows a comparison of money and purchasing power parity GNP or GDP. The statistics in this volume are those considered by the editors to be as accurate and as representative of the real situation as possible.

DAVIS LANGDON & BEATTIE
DAVIS LANGDON & SILVER
DAVIS LANGDON MANAGEMENT
DAVIS LANGDON QUALITY MANAGEMENT PTY LTD
DLIQ QUALITY SYSTEM CERTIFICATION SERVICES

The strategic and integrated management of cost, time and quality - the client "risk" areas of a contract - are essential functions, which are necessary to ensure the satisfactory planning, procurement, execution and operation of construction projects.

We specialise in the financial management of construction projects and their risk areas, from project inception to completion and we concentrate on:

- being positive and creative in our advice, rather than simply reactive;

- providing value for money via efficient management, rather than on superficial cost monitoring;

- giving advice that is matched to the client's requirements, rather than imposing standard or traditional solutions;

- paying attention to the life-cycle costs of constructing and occupying a building, rather than to the initial capital cost only.

Our aim is to provide our clients with risk assurance, cost control and value for money, via effective advice, cost planning and management.

Melbourne, Brisbane, Sydney, Hobart, Perth

DAVIS LANGDON & SEAH INTERNATIONAL

3. Individual countries

Australia

KEY DATA

Population

Population	17.6mn
Urban population	85%
Population under 15 (1991)	22%
Population 65 and over (1991)	11%
Average annual growth rate (1990 to 1993)	1.5%

Geography

Land area	7,713,000 km²
Agricultural area	63%
Capital city	Canberra
Population of capital city (1990)	0.28mn
Largest city	Sydney
Population of largest city (1991)	3.5mn

Economy

Monetary unit	Australian dollars (A$)
Exchange rate (average third quarter of 1995) to:	
the pound sterling	A$ 2.16
the US dollar	A$ 1.36
the yen x 100	A$ 1.48
Average annual inflation (1980 to 1993)	6.1%
Inflation rate (1994)	1.9%
Gross Domestic Product (GDP) at market prices	A$ 414.8bn
GDP per capita	A$ 23,568
Average annual real change in GDP (1980 to 1993)	3.1%
Private consumption as a proportion of GDP	63%
General government consumption as a proportion of GDP	18%
Gross domestic investment as a proportion of GDP	20%
Central government expenditure as a proportion of Gross National Product	28%

Construction

Gross value of construction output *+	A$ 55.0bn
Net value of construction output +	A$ 28.6bn
Net value of construction output as a proportion of GDP	6.7%

All data relate to 1993 unless otherwise indicated
+For year June 1993 to June 1994
*Authors' estimate

THE CONSTRUCTION INDUSTRY

Construction output

Gross construction output is estimated to be A$55 billion for the year 1993-94, equivalent to US$37 billion, or 13% of GDP (1993-94). The net value of construction output for the year 1993-94 was A$28.6 billion, equivalent to US$19 billion, or 6.7% of GDP (1993-94).

Construction output is divided into three broad sectors: residential building, non-residential building and engineering construction. Table below shows the level of output in each sector in 1989-90 prices.

CONSTRUCTION ACTIVITY BY SECTOR
AND TYPE OF WORK, 1992-93 (Value at 1989-90 prices)

Type of Work	A$ billion	%
Private		
Residential building	14.3	40
Non-residential building	6.2	18
Engineering construction	2.8	8
Total private	23.2	66
Public		
Residential building	0.8	2
Non-residential building	3.1	9
Engineering construction	7.9	22
Total public	11.9	33
Total	35.1	100

Source: Yearbook Australia

It will be seen that the public sector is largely involved in engineering construction presumably for infrastructure. The public sector plays a small role in housing construction but provides a third of non-residential building. The private sector is the dominant client for construction especially for residential building.

More up to date information is available for building. The table below shows a breakdown for 1994-95.

VALUE OF BUILDING WORK DONE, 1994-1995 (current prices)

Type of building	Value A$ million	Percentage of total building work (%)
New residential	15,920	56
Alterations and additions to residential buildings	2,597	9
Non-residential building		
hotels	479	2
shops	1,916	7
factories	873	3
offices/business premises	2,900	10
educational	1,128	4
health	861	3
entertainment/recreational	892	3
other	624	3
Total non-residential building	9,673	35
Total building	28,190	100
of which,		
Private building	24,638	87
Public building	3,552	13

Source: Australian Bureau of Statistics, Building Activity Australia, June Quarter 1995

Information on the breakdown of civil engineering work is more difficult to obtain. The latest is for 1992-93 as shown in the table below.

CIVIL ENGINEERING WORK, 1992-93

Type of work	%
Roads, highways and other transport	42
Water storage and supply, sewerage and drainage	12
Electricity generation, transmission and distribution	17
Telecommunications	16
Heavy industry	12
Other	4

Source: Engineering Construction Activity, Australia

It can be seen that roads are the most important element of this sector, with telecommunications and heavy industry (heavy industrial and electrical plant and equipment) also significant. Due to the high level of public-sector spending on non-building construction, this sector was not as severely hit by the economic downturn as the other two sectors described above. Engineering construction expanded by 0.6% in the year to 1990/91, followed by a fall of 6% in 1991/92 and 1% in 1992/93. In 1993/94, however, with a recovery in the economy as a whole, there was a demand for more infrastructure and engineering construction rose by more than 8%.

The table below shows the distribution of work by type in Australia as a whole and in the five states with the largest building programs - 93% of the total. It will be seen that new dwellings account for between 43% and 69% of the building total.

BUILDING COMMENCEMENT BY TYPE AND STATE, AUSTRALIA, 1994 (1989/90 PRICES)

	Australia A$m	%	New South Wales % of total	Victoria % of total	Queensland % of total	South Australia % of total	Western Australia % of total
Residential							
New dwellings	15,000	56	50	43	67	61	69
Alterations and							
additions	2,400	9	12	10	3	9	5
Total	17,400	65	62	53	70	71	74
Other buildings							
Offices	1,600	6	8	5	3	6	4
Shops	1,700	6	6	9	8	3	8
Hotels	460	2	1	4	3	1	1
Other business							
premises	1,400	5	6	7	6	3	4
Factories	760	3	3	4	2	2	2
Education and							
health	2,100	8	10	8	5	12	6
Other social	1,550	5	3	10	3	2	1
Total	9,570	35	38	47	30	29	26
Grand Total	26,970	100	100	100	100	100	100

Characteristics and structure of the industry

There are a number of large contractors in terms of turnover but because subcontracting is so prevalent in the building industry, the largest has personnel of less than 2,000. In total there are about 20 contractors who operate all over Australia out of a total of some 100,000 firms. Average employment is four persons. Some subcontractors, especially in the mechanical and electrical services, are large. On an average contract for a high rise office building, the number of subcontracts may be 100 to 150 while on very large projects it may be 250. There is some labour-only subcontracting, for example in bricklaying.

Two Australian contractors are included in the *Engineering News Record's* list of top international contractors.

MAJOR AUSTRALIAN INTERNATIONAL CONTRACTORS, 1994

Contractor	Place in ENR list	Total	1994 revenue international
Leighton Holdings New South Wales	68	US$1,208m	US$320m
ABB EPT Construction, New South Wales	179	US$173m	US$37m

Source: Engineering News Record, 28/8/95

Architects usually undertake a complete design service. On large projects they are seldom responsible for supervision of work on site.

Civil engineers are the dominant profession for civil works. Quantity surveyors are slowly moving away from work on bills of quantities towards cost control and advice to clients. Quantity surveyors are regulated by the Australian Institute of Quantity Surveyors which approves the course content of various educational institutions as a qualification and carries out assessment of professional competence.

Clients and finance

In 1992-93 in Australia 97% of dwellings commenced were for private clients, only 3% being for government bodies; 70% - 80% of other buildings is privately funded but in civil engineering work 94% is publicly funded. There will be an increase in private funding because of the privatization of some public sector organizations.

Selection of design consultants

There is generally uniformity across Australia in the way consultants are appointed. In the states of New South Wales, Victoria and Queensland the architect is always appointed directly by the client but in Victoria this is usually after some form of competition whereas there is a mixture of direct and competitive selection in New South Wales and Queensland. Other consultants may be appointed by the client or by a main consultant and, again in Victoria, some competition is likely to be held. Price is most important in New South Wales and Victoria but contacts and recommendations are more critical in Queensland. Track record is taken into account everywhere and, together with contacts, is more important in the private sector than in the public sector where price is significant save that in Tasmania competition is rare and price least important in selection.

Some states have more formal systems than others. In Tasmania the State Government keeps a register of consultants and has standard conditions of engagement and there are *State Government Purchasing Guidelines* for Queensland.

Professional bodies all publish fee scales but they are not mandatory and are not usually used except in Tasmania.

Contractual arrangements

Contractual arrangements are influenced both by State and by Federal Governments and there are some 20 contract types in use.

Government departments regularly publish invitations for construction companies to join approved lists for various categories of work. Evidence of financial stability, experience in similar work and extent of turnover are usually the type of information required. In Federal Government work and for the majority of State contracts there is some prequalification and companies have to satisfy the client on their training record, meeting of contract obligations etc.

After preselection, competitive lump sum tender is the most common form of contractor selection. Construction management and cost plus fee arrangements are used occasionally.

A Bank Guarantee and retention of 5% of contract value may be withheld until the maintenance period has expired. This is retained at the rate of 10% until the level of 5% of the contract sum has been reached.

Liability and insurance

Several insurances are required by contract.

Development control and standards

The planning system is based on a fairly detailed land usage designation for many areas in the country. This might specify, for example, single family housing or industrial development for the chemical industry. If proposed development conforms to this land usage, planning permission is not necessary.

For building in an area where there is no land usage designation or where the proposed project does not conform to it then planning permission is necessary. If the proposed development does not present problems approval would be given within six months and most problems would be resolved within a year. However, there are cases which receive publicity where it may take years to agree, with proposals and counter proposals going to and fro.

Building design standards are set by the Building Code of Australia administered by local municipal councils. Building approval is necessary for all projects.

CONSTRUCTION COST DATA

Cost of labour

The figures below are typical of labour costs in Melbourne as at the third quarter of 1995. The wage rate is the basis of an employee's income, while the cost of labour indicates the cost to a contractor of employing that employee. The difference between the two covers a variety of mandatory and voluntary contributions - a list of items which could be included is given in section 2.

	Wage rate (per week) AU$	Cost of labour (per hour) AU$	Number of hours worked per year
Site operatives			
Mason/bricklayer	475	27	1,656
Carpenter	480	27	1,656
Plumber	513	29	1,656

	Wage rate (per week) AU$	Cost of labour (per hour) AU$	Number of hours worked per year
Electrician	523	29	1,656
Structural steel erector	480	27	1,656
HVAC installer	490	28	1,656
Semi-skilled worker	443	26	1,656
Unskilled labourer	402	24	1,656
Equipment operator	440	26	1,656
Watchman/security	435	26	1,656

Site supervision

General foreman	-	53	1,656
Trades foreman	-	38	1,656

	(per year)	(per hour)	
Contractors' personnel			
Project manager	110,000	83	1,656
Site manager	80,000	60	1,656
Contract administrator/QS	65,000	49	1,656
Junior co-ordinator	45,000	34	1,654
Junior administrator	45,000	34	1,654
Planner	70,000	53	1,654
Consultants' personnel			
Senior architect	60,000	82.50	1,760
Senior engineer	80,000	110	1,760
Senior surveyor	55,000	75	1,760
Qualified architect	42,000	65	1,654
Qualified engineer	42,000	50	1,654
Qualified surveyor	38,000	60	1,654

Cost of materials

The figures that follow are the costs of main construction materials, delivered to site in the Melbourne area, as incurred by contractors in the third quarter of 1995. These assume that the materials would be in quantities as required for a medium sized construction project and that the location of the works would be neither constrained nor remote.

	Unit	*Cost AU$*
Concrete		
Ready mixed concrete (Grade 40MPa)	m^3	132.00
Ready mixed concrete (Grade 10MPa)	m^3	113.00
Steel		
Mild steel reinforcement	tonne	1,000.00
Structural steel sections	tonne	1,200.00
Bricks and blocks		
Common bricks (230 x 110 x 76mm)	1000	380.00
Good quality facing bricks (230 x 110 x 76mm)	1000	485.00
Hollow concrete blocks (400 x 200 x 100mm)	1000	132.00
Solid concrete blocks (400 x 200 x 100mm)	1000	152.00
Precast concrete cladding units with exposed aggregate finish	m^2	280.00
Timber and insulation		
Softwood sections for carpentry - scantlings	m^3	600.00
Softwood for joinery - dressed	m^3	1,200.00
Hardwood for joinery - dressed	m^3	725.00
Exterior quality plywood (6mm)	m^2	26.00
Plywood for interior joinery (6mm)	m^2	23.00
Softwood strip flooring (17mm)	m^2	23.00
Chipboard sheet flooring (19mm)	m^2	23.00
100mm thick quilt insulation	m^2	9.00
Softwood internal door complete with frames and ironmongery	each	285.00
Glass and ceramics		
Float glass (6mm)	m^2	32.00
Plaster and paint		
Good quality ceramic wall tiles (150 x 150mm)	m^2	30.00
Plaster in 25 kg bags	tonne	392.00
Plasterboard (13mm thick)	m^2	4.60
Acrylic paint in 4 litre tins	litre	8.28
Gloss oil paint in 4 litre tins	litre	11.95
Tiles and paviors		
Quarry floor tiles (150 x 150mm)	m^2	24.00
Sheet vinyl 2mm thick	m^2	17.75

	Unit	Cost AU$
Precast concrete paving slabs (400 x 400 x 25mm)	m²	40.00
Terracotta roof tiles	m²	14.00
Precast concrete roof tiles	m²	10.00

Drainage

	Unit	Cost AU$
WC suite complete	each	500.00
Lavatory basin complete	each	300.00
100mm diameter clay drain pipes	m	11.46
150mm diameter cast iron drain pipes	m	20.00

Unit rates

The descriptions below are generally shortened versions of standard descriptions listed in full in section 4. Where an item has a two digit reference number (e.g. 05 or 33), this relates to the full description against that number in section 4. Where an item has an alphabetic suffix (e.g. 12A or 34B) this indicates that the standard description has been modified. Where a modification is major the complete modified description is included here and the standard description should be ignored; where a modification is minor (e.g. the insertion of a named hardwood) the shortened description has been modified here but, in general, the full description in section 4 prevails.

The unit rates below are for main work items on a typical construction project in the Melbourne area in the third quarter of 1995. The rates include all necessary labour, materials, equipment and contractors' overheads and profit. An allowance has been added to cover preliminary and general items.

		Unit	Rate AU$
Excavation			
01	Mechanical excavation of foundation trenches	m³	43.00
02	Hardcore filling making up levels	m³	88.00
03	Earthwork support	m²	5.50
Concrete work			
04	Plain insitu concrete in strip foundations in trenches	m³	151.00
05	Reinforced insitu concrete in beds	m³	138.00
06	Reinforced insitu concrete in walls	m³	174.00

		Unit	Rate AU$
07	Reinforced insitu concrete in suspended floors or roof slabs	m³	157.00
08	Reinforced insitu concrete in columns	m³	186.00
09	Reinforced insitu concrete in isolated beams	m³	157.00
10	Precast concrete slab	m³	616.00

Formwork

11	Metal formwork to concrete walls	m²	66.00
12	Metal formwork to concrete columns	m²	77.00
13	Metal formwork to horizontal soffits of slabs	m²	50.00

Reinforcement

14	Reinforcement in concrete walls	tonne	1,595.00
15	Reinforcement in suspended concrete slabs	tonne	1,595.00
16	Fabric reinforcement in concrete beds	m²	9.40

Steelwork

17	Fabricate, supply and erect steel framed structure	tonne	2,640.00
18	Framed structural steelwork in universal joist sections	tonne	2,640.00
19	Structural steelwork lattice roof trusses	tonne	3,300.00

Brickwork and blockwork

20	Precast lightweight aggregate hollow concrete block walls	m²	39.00
21A	Solid (perforated) concrete blocks	m²	61.00
22	Sand lime bricks	m²	66.00
23	Facing bricks	m²	72.00

Roofing

24	Concrete interlocking roof tiles 430 x 380mm	m²	28.00
25A	Terracotta roof tiles 260 x 160mm	m²	38.00
26	Fibre cement roof slates 600 x 300mm	m²	61.00
27	Sawn softwood roof boarding	m²	33.00
28	Particle board roof coverings	m²	30.00
29	3 layers glass-fibre based bitumen felt roof covering	m²	66.00
30	Bitumen based mastic asphalt roof covering	m²	68.00
31A	Glass-fibre mat roof insulation 100mm thick	m²	11.00
33	Troughed galvanised steel roof cladding	m²	26.00

		Unit	Rate AU$

Woodwork and metalwork

34	Preservative treated sawn softwood 50 x 100mm	m	8.30
35	Preservative treated sawn softwood 50 x 150mm	m	11.60
36	Single glazed casement window in local hardwood	m²	330.00
37A	Two panel glazed door in local hardwood, size		
	820 x 2040mm with frame and hardware	each	880.00
38	Solid core half hour fire resisting hardwood internal flush		
	doors, size 820 x 2040mm with frame and hardware	each	704.00
39	Aluminium double glazed window	m²	440.00
40A	Aluminium single glazed door, size 850 x 2100mm	each	1,980.00
41	Hardwood skirtings	m	11.00

Plumbing

42A	Steel quadrant eaves gutter	m	18.20
43	UPVC rainwater pipes	m	19.00
44A	Light gauge copper cold water tubing 20mm diameter	m	21.00
45	High pressure plastic pipes for cold water supply	m	15.40
46	Low pressure plastic pipes for cold water distribution	m	13.20
47A	UPVC soil and vent pipes 50mm diameter	m	22.00
48	White vitreous china WC suite	each	440.00
49	White vitreous china lavatory basin	each	407.00
50A	Porcelain enamelled shower tray	each	253.00
51	Stainless steel single bowl sink and double drainer	each	930.00

Electrical work

52	PVC insulated and copper sheathed cable	m	3.30
53A	10 amp power point	each	17.60
54	Flush mounted, 1 way light switch	each	17.60

Finishings

55	2 coats gypsum based plaster on brick walls	m²	33.00
56	White glazed tiles on plaster walls	m²	71.50
57	Red clay quarry tiles on concrete floors	m²	77.00
58	Cement and sand screed to concrete floors	m²	33.00
59	Thermoplastic floor tiles on screed	m²	38.50
60	Mineral fibre tiles on concealed suspension system	m²	46.20

Glazing

61A	Glazing to wood 6mm	m²	91.30

	Unit	Rate AU$
Painting		
62A Acrylic on plaster walls	m²	7.15
63 Oil paint on timber	m²	11.00

Approximate estimating

The building costs per unit area given below are averages incurred by building clients for typical buildings in the Melbourne area as at the third quarter of 1995. They are based upon the total floor area of all storeys, measured between external walls and without deduction for internal walls.

Approximate estimating costs generally include mechanical and electrical installations but exclude furniture, loose or special equipment, and external works; they also exclude fees for professional services. The costs shown are for specifications and standards appropriate to Australia and this should be borne in mind when attempting comparisons with similarly described building types in other countries. A discussion of this issue is included in section 2. Comparative data for countries covered in this publication, including construction cost data, are presented in Part Three.

Approximate estimating costs must be treated with caution; they cannot provide more than a rough guide to the probable cost of building.

	Cost m² AU$	Cost ft² AU$
Industrial buildings		
Factories for letting	385	36
Factories for owner occupation (light industrial use)	470	44
Factories for owner occupation (heavy industrial use)	540	50
Factory/office (high-tech) for letting (ground floor shell, first floor offices)	800	74
Factory/office (high tech) for owner occupation (controlled environment, fully finished)	1,000	93
High tech laboratory workshop centres (air conditioned)	1,750	163
Warehouses, low bay (6 to 8m high) for letting	350	33
Warehouses, low bay for owner occupation (no heating)	400	37
Warehouses, high bay for owner occupation (no heating)	440	41
Administrative and commercial buildings		
Civic offices, fully air conditioned	1,400	130
Offices for letting, 5 to 10 storeys, air conditioned	1,150	107

	Cost m² AU$	Cost ft² AU$
Offices for letting, high rise, air conditioned	1,500	140
Offices for owner occupation, high rise, air conditioned	1,900	177
Prestige/headquarters office, 5 to 10 storeys, air conditioned	1,700	158
Prestige/headquarters office, high rise, air conditioned	2,100	195

Health and education buildings

General hospitals (150 beds)	1,750	163
Teaching hospitals (200 beds)	2,300	214
Private hospitals (100 beds)	1,500	139
Health centres	1,000	93
Nursery school	750	70
Primary/junior schools	800	74
Secondary/middle schools	1,000	93
University (arts) buildings	1,400	130
University (science) buildings	1,820	169
Management training centres	1,600	149

Recreation and arts buildings

Theatres (over 500 seats) including seating and stage equipment	2,100	195
Theatres (less than 500 seats) including seating and stage equipment	2,300	214
Sports halls including changing and social facilities	1,000	93
Swimming pools (international standard) excluding changing and social facilities	each	600,000
Swimming pools (schools standard) excluding changing facilities	each	370,000
National museums including full air conditioning and standby generator	2,700	251
Local museums including air conditioning	1,800	167
Branch/local libraries	1,400	130

Residential buildings

Social/economic single family housing (multiple units)	500	47
Private/mass market single family housing 2 storey detached/semidetached (multiple units)	600	56
Purpose designed single family housing 2 storey detached (single unit)	1,000	93

	Cost m² AU$	Cost ft² AU$
Social/economic apartment housing, low rise (no lifts)	850	79
Social/economic apartment housing, high rise (with lifts)	1,000	93
Private sector apartment building (standard specification)	1,100	102
Private sector apartment buildings (luxury)	1,600	149
Student/nurses halls of residence	1,300	121
Homes for the elderly (shared accommodation)	800	74
Homes for the elderly (self contained with shared communal facilities)	1,050	98
Hotel, 5 star, city centre	2,200	205
Hotel, 3 star, city/provincial	1,800	167
Motel	1,200	112

Regional variations

The approximate estimating costs are based on projects in Melbourne. For other parts of Australia, adjust these costs by the following factors:

Sydney	:	+ 1%
Brisbane	:	- 5%
Perth	:	+ 4%
Adelaide	:	- 2%
Hobart	:	+ 4%
Canberra	:	+12%
Darwin	:	+ 20%

EXCHANGE RATES AND INFLATION

The combined effect of exchange rates and inflation on prices within a country and price comparisons between countries is discussed in section 2.

Exchange rates

The graph below plots the movement of the Australian dollar against sterling, the US dollar and 100 Japanese yen since 1985. The values used for the graph are quarterly and the method of calculating these is described and general guidance on the interpretation of the graph provided in section 2. The average exchange rate in the third quarter of 1995 was A$2.16 to the pound sterling, A$1.36 to the US dollar and A$1.48 to 100 Japanese yen.

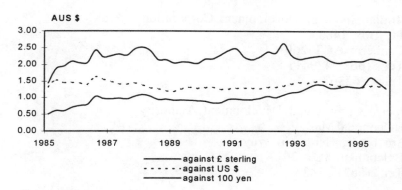

Price inflation

The table below represents general price and building materials and price inflation in Australia since 1985. Building prices have increased consistently with general prices after showing a decline since 1990.

CONSUMER PRICE AND BUILDING COST AND PRICE INFLATION

Year	Consumer price inflation average index	Building materials average index	Building price average index
1985-1986	73.5	72.4	80
1986-1987	80.3	78.0	88
1987-1988	86.3	84.8	95
1988-1989	92.6	92.7	105
1989-1990	100.0	100.0	113
1990-1991	105.3	105.1	114
1991-1992	107.3	105.7	110
1992-1993	108.4	106.0	106
1993-1994	110.3	107.5	107

USEFUL ADDRESSES

Public organizations

Australian Bureau of Statistics
   Cameron Offices
   Chandler Street
   Belconnen ACT 2616

Australian Industry Development Corporation - AIDC
   PO Box 1483
   Canberra ACT 2601
   Tel: (062) 479411
   Telex: 62307

Canberra Commercial Development Authority
   Belconnen Mall
   3rd Floor, Benjamin Way
   Belconnen ACT 2617
   Tel: (062) 51433

Department of Employment and Industrial Relations
   1 Farrell Place
   Canberra ACT 2601
   Tel: (062) 437333
   Fax: (062) 437598
   Telex: 62210

Trade and professional associations

ACT Civil Engineering Contractors Association
   PO Box 364
   Canberra City
   ACT 2601

Association of Consulting Engineers
   PO Box 1002
   North Stanet
   NSW 2060

Australian Chamber of Commerce (ACC)
    Commerce House
    Brisbane Avenue,
    Barton
    ACT 2600

Australian Federation of Construction Contractors
    PO Box 320
    St Leonards
    NSW 2065

Australian Institute of Building
    PO Box 1467
    Canberra City
    ACT 2601

Australian Institute of Quantity Surveyors
    National Surveyors House
    27-29 Napier Close
    Deakin
    ACT 2600

Confederation of Australian Industry (CAI)
    Industry House
    National Circuit
    Barton
    Canberra ACT 2600

Housing Industry Association
    79 Constitution Avenue
    Campbell
    ACT 2601

Royal Australian Institute of Architects (RAIA)
    PO Box 373
    Manuka
    ACT 2603

Royal Australian Planning Institute Inc (RAPI)
    PO Box 263
    Canberra ACT 2601

DAVIS LANGDON & SEAH
PETROKON UTAMA SDN BHD

The strategic and integrated management of cost, time and quality - the client "risk" areas of a contract - are essential functions, which are necessary to ensure the satisfactory planning, procurement, execution and operation of construction projects.

We specialise in the financial management of construction projects and their risk areas, from project inception to completion and we concentrate on:

- being positive and creative in our advice, rather than simply reactive;

- providing value for money via efficient management, rather than on superficial cost monitoring;

- giving advice that is matched to the client's requirements, rather than imposing standard or traditional solutions;

- paying attention to the life-cycle costs of constructing and occupying a building, rather than to the initial capital cost only.

Our aim is to provide our clients with risk assurance, cost control and value for money, via effective advice, cost planning and management.

DAVIS LANGDON & SEAH
No. 1, First Floor, Block H
Abdul Razak Complex Gadong
P O Box 313
Bandar Seri Begawan 1903
Brunei Darussalam
Tel : (673) 2-446888
Fax : (673) 2-445555

PETROKON UTAMA SDN BHD
No. 3, First Floor, Block H
Adbul Razak Complex Gadong
P O Box 1188
Bandar Seri Begawan 1911
Brunei Darussalam
Tel : (673) 2-441384
Fax : (673) 2-441382

DAVIS LANGDON & SEAH INTERNATIONAL

Brunei Darussalam

KEY DATA

Population
Population	276,000

Geography
Land area	5,765 km²
Agricultural area	2%
Capital city	Bandan Seri Begawan
Population of capital city (1991)	46,230

Economy
Monetary unit	Brunei dollar (B$)
Exchange rate (average third quarter 1995) to:	
the pound sterling	B$2.23
the US dollar	B$1.41
the yen x 100	B$1.53
Average annual inflation (1980 to 1993)	-5.1%
Inflation rate (1994)	3%
Gross Domestic Product (GDP) at market price	B$6.5bn
GDP per capita	B$23,460

Construction
Gross value of construction output*	B$0.6bn
Net value of construction output	B$0.34bn
Net value of construction output as a proportion of GNP	5.2%

All data relate to 1993 unless otherwise indicated

* Author's estimate

THE CONSTRUCTION INDUSTRY

Construction output

The value of the gross output of the construction industry in 1993 is estimated to be B$0.6 billion, equivalent to US$0.4 billion, or 10% of GDP. This compares with a net output in 1993 of B$0.34 billion, equivalent to US$0.21 billion, or 5.2% of GDP.

Brunei is heavily reliant on its oil and gas industry and its GNP has fallen since the late 1970s in conjunction with falling oil prices. The non-oil sector of the economy represents an increasingly high proportion of GDP, having grown from 26% in 1983 to 63% in 1993.

Although the contribution of construction to GDP is small in relation to Brunei's other sectors - oil and gas at 37.5%, community, social and personal services at 30.9% - the absolute level of construction output is significant and the construction industry is an important sector of the economy. In 1992, the construction industry employed more than 40% of the private sector work force.

Statistics of GNP and construction output at current prices are shown below. They illustrate the increasing importance of construction in GNP.

GROSS NATIONAL PRODUCT AND NET VALUE OF CONSTRUCTION OUTPUT, 1983 TO 1993, CURRENT PRICES

Year	Gross national product B$ million	Construction B$ million	%
1983	8,123	266	3.3
1984	8,069	207	2.6
1985	7,752	159	2.1
1986	5,136	170	3.3
1987	5,801	183	3.2
1988	5,415	195	3.6
1989	5,845	255	4.4
1990	6,509	277	4.3
1991	6,604	291	4.4
1992	6,372	312	4.9
1993	6,475	341	5.3

Source : Statistic Division of Economic Planning Unit, Ministry of Finance

The decrease in GNP at current prices is not a real fall because price levels have fallen substantially in Brunei.

The Ministry of Finance prepares statistics for sectors including oil and gas, transport and communication, real estate, electricity, gas and water distribution. It should be noted that the figures may include construction and engineering expenditure directly associated with these sectors and, for this reason, the figures given for the construction industry may be underestimating its contribution to GNP.

The level of construction activity is heavily dependent on government development projects. Under the *1991-1995 Sixth National Development Plan*, B$5,509 million of funding was allocated and the main items of proposed expenditure are shown in the table below.

PROPOSED EXPENDITURE UNDER SIXTH DEVELOPMENT PLAN, 1991-1995

Proposed items of expenditure	Funding allocation B$ million
Upgrading public utilities (electricity, sanitation, water supply and drainage)	1,102
New public buildings and facilities	799
Government and national housing	783
Roads	490
New educational facilities	384
Telecommunications	393
Improvement of medical services	103

However, under the previous plan, the *Fifth Development Plan*, only 55% of the funds allocated were actually expended. It is expected that the level will have been much higher for the *Sixth Development Plan*.

Private housebuilding and commercial developments are the main types of private works.

Characteristics and structure of the industry

The majority of projects are undertaken by a main contractor through single stage competitive tendering, on the basis of drawings and measured bills of quantities, resulting in a traditional fixed price contract. Variations from this contractual route are not widespread, though there is some design and build.

The number of larger locally based contractors capable of undertaking multi-million dollar contracts is small. Architectural firms maintain a fairly high profile, with a handful of locally owned practices undertaking the majority of public sector work. Engineers and surveyors are in a similar position to architects. There is generally a sufficient number of both consultants and contractors already based in Brunei to cater to the local needs on all but very large and technically complicated projects.

Over previous years the general construction workers in Brunei comprises mainly Filipinos and Thai workers, with the more skilled workers being obtained from Malaysia. However, recently a number workers are being obtained from the Indian sub-continent.

The sponsoring ministry for the construction industry is the Ministry of Development set up in 1984, with a number of functional departments (public works, electrical services, housing development, land, survey, town and country planning, and construction planning and research).

- The Public Works Department (PWD) is responsible for the design and construction of various government projects such as bridges, roads, water and sewerage. It also promotes *Bumiputra* (local) contractors and keeps a register of consultants and contractors.

- The Electrical Services Department is in charge of electricity provision and registering electrical contractors.

- The Housing Development Department is charged with implementing the government's objective for every citizen to own a house. The department builds between 500 and 600 houses each year under its housing programme.

- The Land Department is responsible for registration of privately owned land.

- The Survey Department is responsible for surveys throughout the country.

- The Town and Country Planning Department is responsible for land use planning and control, covering both structure and local development plans, as well as setting and monitoring minimum environmental standards. The department is showing increasing concern for the conservation and protection of the natural environment.

Clients and finance

The industry is very dependent on public sector projects. Government expenditure plans are set out in *National Development Plans* usually covering five years. Most construction and civil engineering work from the public sector is administered by the Ministry of Development.

Of private sector clients, however, the most prominent is Brunei Shell Petroleum Company and a few local property developers who concentrate on providing residential, retail and commercial space. These developers are mainly self-financed or receive assistance from local banks. There are a lot of small construction projects providing private housing where finance is often obtained from local commercial banks through personal loans.

CONSTRUCTION COST DATA

Cost of labour

The figures below are typical of labour costs in Bandar Seri Begawan as at the third quarter of 1995. The wage rate is the basis of an employee's income, while the cost of labour indicates the cost to a contractor of employing that employee. The difference between the two covers a variety of mandatory and voluntary contributions - a list of items which could be included is given in section 2.

	Wage rate (per day) B$	Cost of labour (per day) B$	Number of hours worked per year
Site operatives			
Mason/bricklayer	40	-	2,625
Carpenter	45	-	2,625
Plumber	40	-	2,625
Electrician	50	-	2,625
Structural steel erector	60	-	2,625
Semi-skilled worker	30	-	2,625
Unskilled labourer	20	-	2,625
Equipment operator	60	-	2,625
Watchman/security	40	-	2,625
	(Month B$)	*(Month B$)*	
Site supervision			
General foreman	3,000	3,500	2,040
Trades foreman	2,300	2,800	2,040
Clerk of works	2,500	3,500	2,040

	Wage rate (per month) B$	Cost of labour (per month) B$	Number of hours worked per year
Contractors' personnel			
Site manager	4,500	6,000	2,040
Resident engineer	4,000	5,500	2,040
Resident surveyor	3,500	5,000	2,040
Junior engineer	2,500	4,000	2,040
Junior surveyor	2,500	4,000	2,040
Planner	3,500	5,000	2,040
Consultants' personnel			
Senior architect	5,000	7,000	2,040
Senior engineer	5,000	7,000	2,040
Senior surveyor	4,500	6,500	2,040
Qualified architect	3,500	5,500	2,040
Qualified engineer	3,500	5,500	2,040
Qualified surveyor	3,500	5,500	2,040

Cost of materials

The figures that follow are the costs of main construction materials, delivered to site in the Bandar Seri Begawan area, as incurred by contractors in the third quarter of 1995. These assume that the materials would be in quantities as required for a medium sized construction project and that the location of the works would be neither constrained nor remote.

	Unit	Cost B$
Cement and aggregate		
Ordinary portland cement in 50kg bags	tonne	190.00
Coarse aggregates for concrete	m³	40.00
Fine aggregates for concrete	m³	16.00
Ready mixed concrete (1:1.5:3)	m³	185.00
Ready mixed concrete (1:2:4)	m³	165.00
Steel		
Mild steel reinforcement	tonne	600.00
High tensile steel reinforcement	tonne	600.00
Structural steel sections	tonne	1,000.00

	Unit	Cost B$
Bricks and blocks		
Common bricks (4" x 9" x 3")	1,000	170.00
Good quality facing bricks (4" x 9" x 3")	1,000	600.00
Hollow concrete blocks (6" x 9" x 4")	1,000	450.00
Solid concrete blocks (4" x 9" x 3")	1,000	200.00
Timber and insulation		
Softwood for joinery	m³	2,350.00
Hardwood for joinery	m³	735.00
Exterior quality plywood (12mm)	m²	12.00
Plywood for interior joinery (6mm)	m²	7.00
Softwood strip flooring (12mm)	m²	75.00
Chipboard sheet flooring (12mm)	m²	32.00
100mm thick quilt insulation	m²	7.00
Softwood internal door complete with frames and ironmongery	each	740.00
Glass and ceramics		
Float glass (6mm)	m²	35.00
Sealed double glazing units (50mm)	m²	400.00
Plaster and paint		
Good quality ceramic wall tiles (8" x 8")	m²	40.00
Plasterboard (12mm thick)	m²	7.00
Emulsion paint in 5 litre tins	litre	9.00
Gloss oil paint in 5 litre tins	litre	11.00
Tiles and paviors		
Clay floor tiles (8" x 4" x 0.5")	m²	35.00
Vinyl floor tiles (12" x 12" x 0.125")	m²	16.00
Precast concrete paving slabs (12" x 12" x 3")	m²	35.00
Clay roof tiles	1,000	3,000.00
Precast concrete roof tiles	1,000	1,500.00
Drainage		
WC suite complete	each	210.00
Lavatory basin complete	each	160.00
100mm diameter clay drain pipes	m	15.00
150mm diameter cast iron drain pipes	m	35.00

Unit rates

The descriptions below are generally shortened versions of standard descriptions listed in full in section 4. Where an item has a two digit reference number (e.g. 05 or 33), this relates to the full description against that number in section 4. Where an item has an alphabetic suffix (e.g. 12A or 34B) this indicates that the standard description has been modified. Where a modification is major the complete modified description is included here and the standard description should be ignored; where a modification is minor (e.g. the insertion of a named hardwood) the shortened description has been modified here but, in general, the full description in section 4 prevails.

The unit rates below are for main work items on a typical construction project in the Bandar Seri Begawan area in the third quarter of 1995. The rates include all necessary labour, materials and equipment. Allowances to cover preliminary and general items and contractors' overheads and profit have been added to the rates.

		Unit	Rate B$
Excavation			
01	Mechanical excavation of foundation trenches	m³	11.00
02	Hardcore filling making up levels	m²	8.40
03	Earthwork support	m²	14.40
Concrete work			
04	Plain insitu concrete in strip foundations in trenches	m³	216.00
05	Reinforced insitu concrete in beds	m³	216.00
06	Reinforced insitu concrete in walls	m³	216.00
07	Reinforced insitu concrete in suspended floors or roof slabs	m³	216.00
08	Reinforced insitu concrete in columns	m³	216.00
09	Reinforced insitu concrete in isolated beams	m³	216.00
10	Precast concrete slab	m²	120.00
Formwork			
11	Softwood or metal formwork to concrete walls	m²	24.00
12	Softwood or metal formwork to concrete columns	m²	24.00
13	Softwood or metal formwork to horizontal soffits of slabs	m²	24.00
Reinforcement			
14	Reinforcement in concrete walls	tonne	1,440.00

		Unit	Rate B$
15	Reinforcement in suspended concrete slabs	tonne	1,440.00
16	Fabric reinforcement in concrete beds	m^2	6.60

Steelwork

17	Fabricate, supply and erect steel framed structure	tonne	4,440.00
18	Framed structural steelwork in universal joist sections	tonne	3,840.00
19	Structural steelwork lattice roof trusses	tonne	4,800.00

Brickwork and blockwork

21A	Solid (perforated) concrete blocks	m^2	36.00
22	Sand lime bricks	m^2	30.00
23	Facing bricks	m^2	66.00

Roofing

24	Concrete interlocking roof tiles 430 x 380mm	m^2	60.00
25	Plain clay roof tiles 260 x 160mm	m^2	80.40
26	Fibre cement roof slates 600 x 300mm	m^2	66.00
27	Sawn softwood roof boarding	m^2	30.00
29	3 layers glass-fibre based bitumen felt roof covering	m^2	63.60
30	Bitumen based mastic asphalt roof covering	m^2	60.00
33	Troughed galvanised steel roof cladding	m^2	36.00

Woodwork and metalwork

34	Preservative treated sawn softwood 50 x 100mm	m	7.20
35	Preservative treated sawn softwood 50 x 150mm	m	9.60
36	Single glazed casement window in Nyatoh hardwood, size 650 x 900mm	each	336.00
37	Two panel glazed door in Nyatoh hardwood, size 850 x 2000mm	each	1,140.00
38	Solid core half hour fire resisting hardwood internal flush doors, size 800 x 2000mm	each	1,140.00
39	Aluminium double glazed window, size 1200 x 1200mm	each	756.00
40	Aluminium double glazed door, size 850 x 2100mm	each	552.00
41	Hardwood skirtings	m	10.80

Plumbing

42	UPVC half round eaves gutter	m	36.00
43	UPVC rainwater pipes	m	24.00
44	Light gauge copper cold water tubing	m	24.00
45	High pressure plastic pipes for cold water supply	m	12.00
46	Low pressure plastic pipes for cold water distribution	m	14.40

	Unit	Rate B$
47 UPVC soil and vent pipes	m	26.40
48 White vitreous china WC suite	each	480.00
49 White vitreous china lavatory basin	each	360.00
50 Glazed fireclay shower tray	each	360.00
51 Stainless steel single bowl sink and double drainer	each	720.00

Electrical work

52 PVC insulated and copper sheathed cable	m	3.60
53 13 amp unswitched socket outlet	each	87.60
54 Flush mounted 20 amp, 1 way light switch	each	218.40

Finishings

55 2 coats gypsum based plaster on brick walls	m²	18.00
56 White glazed tiles on plaster walls	m²	51.60
57 Red clay quarry tiles on concrete floors	m²	72.00
58 Cement and sand screed to concrete floors	m²	12.00
59 Thermoplastic floor tiles on screed	m²	44.40
60 Mineral fibre tiles on concealed suspension system	m²	36.00

Glazing

61 Glazing to wood	m²	57.60

Painting

62 Emulsion on plaster walls	m²	7.20
63 Oil paint on timber	m²	13.20

Approximate estimating

The building costs per unit area given opposite are averages incurred by building clients for typical buildings in the Bandar Seri Begawan area as at the third quarter of 1995. They are based upon the total floor area of all storeys, measured between external walls and without deduction for internal walls.

Approximate estimating costs generally include mechanical and electrical installations but exclude furniture, loose or special equipment, and external works; they also exclude fees for professional services. The costs shown are for specifications and standards appropriate to Brunei and this should be borne in mind when attempting comparisons with similarly described building types in other countries. A discussion of this issue is included in section 2. Comparative data for countries covered in this publication, including construction cost data, is presented in Part Three.

Approximate estimating costs must be treated with caution; they cannot provide more than a rough guide to the probable cost of building.

	Cost m² B$	Cost ft² B$
Industrial buildings		
Factories for letting	550	51
Factories for owner occupation (light industrial use)	720	67
Factories for owner occupation (heavy industrial use)	855	80
Factory/office (high-tech) for letting (shell and core only)	655	61
Factory/office (high-tech) for letting (ground floor shell, first floor offices)	750	70
Factory/office (high tech) for owner occupation (controlled environment, fully finished)	1,200	112
High tech laboratory workshop centres (air conditioned)	1,420	132
Warehouses, low bay (6 to 8m high) for letting (no heating)	690	64
Cold stores/refrigerated stores	1,320	123
Administrative and commercial buildings		
Civic offices, non air conditioned	655	61
Civic offices, fully air conditioned	790	73
Offices for letting, 5 to 10 storeys, non air conditioned	970	90
Offices for letting, 5 to 10 storeys, air conditioned	1,150	107
Offices for owner occupation 5 to 10 storeys, non air conditioned	1,100	102
Offices for owner occupation 5 to 10 storeys, air conditioned	1,230	114
Prestige/headquarters office, 5 to 10 storeys, air conditioned	1,570	146
Health and education buildings		
General hospitals (500 beds)	1,730	161
Teaching hospitals (100 beds)	1,470	137
Private hospitals (100 beds)	1,580	147
Health centres	1,260	117
Nursery schools	740	69
Primary/junior schools	790	73
Secondary/middle schools	1,160	108
Management training centres	1,160	108

	Cost m² B$	Cost ft² B$
Recreation and arts buildings		
Theatres (over 500 seats) including seating and stage equipment	3,520	327
Theatres (less than 500 seats) including seating and stage equipment	3,300	307
Concert halls including seating and stage equipment	2,100	195
Sports halls including changing and social facilities	1,780	165
Swimming pools (schools standard) including changing facilities	each	650,000
National museums including full air conditioning and standby generator	2,940	273
City centre/central libraries	2,100	195
Branch/local libraries	1,420	132
Residential buildings		
Social/economic single family housing (multiple units)	790	73
Private/mass market single family housing 2 storey detached/semidetached (multiple units)	950	88
Purpose designed single family housing 2 storey detached (single unit)	1,160	108
Social/economic apartment housing, low rise (no lifts)	760	71
Social/economic apartment housing, high rise (with lifts)	880	82
Private sector apartment building (standard specification)	1,100	102
Private sector apartment buildings (luxury)	1,260	117
Student/nurses halls of residence	910	84
Hotel, 5 star, city centre	3,420	318
Hotel, 3 star, city/provincial	2,760	257
Motel	1,990	185

Regional variations

The approximate estimating costs are based on projects in the Bandar Seri Begawan area. For other parts of Brunei, adjust these costs by the following factors:

Kuala Belait	+ 5%
Temburong	+ 7.5%

EXCHANGE RATES

The graph below plots the movement of the Brunei dollar against sterling, US dollar and 100 Japanese yen since 1985. The values used for the graph are quarterly and the method of calculating these is described and general guidance on the interpretation of the graph provided in section 2. The average exchange rate in the third quarter of 1995 was B$2.23 to the pound sterling, B$1.41 to US dollar and B$1.53 to 100 Japanese yen.

THE BRUNEI DOLLAR AGAINST STERLING, US DOLLAR AND JAPANESE YEN

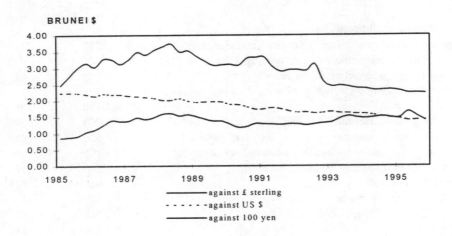

USEFUL ADDRESSES

Public organizations

Construction Planning and Research Unit
    Ministry of Development
    Bandar Seri Begawan 1190
    Negara Brunei Darussalam
    Tel: 02 241911
    (Comprising Departments of Town and Country Planning,
    Survey, Land, Housing Development, Public Works and Electrical
    Services)

Economic Planning Unit
    Ministry of Finance
    PO Box 2222
    Bandar Seri Begawan 1922
    Negara Brunei Darussalam
    Tel : 02 241991

Industry Unit
    Ministry of Industry and Primary Resources
    Bandar Seri Begawan 1220
    Negara Brunei Darussalam
    Tel : 02 244822

Trade and professional associations

Association of Surveyors, Engineers and Architects
    Pertubuhan Ukur Jurutera dan Arkitek (PUJA)
    PO Box 1069
    Bandar Seri Begawan 1910
    Negara Brunei Darussalam
    Tel : 02 424261

The Brunei Darussalam International Chamber of Commerce and Industry
    PO Box 2246
    Bandar Seri Begawan 1922
    Negara Brunei Darussalam
    Tel : 02 236601

DAVIS LANGDON & SEAH CHINA LTD

The strategic and integrated management of cost, time and quality - the client "risk" areas of a contract - are essential functions, which are necessary to ensure the satisfactory planning, procurement, execution and operation of construction projects.

We specialise in the financial management of construction projects and their risk areas, from project inception to completion and we concentrate on:

- being positive and creative in our advice, rather than simply reactive;

- providing value for money via efficient management, rather than on superficial cost monitoring;

- giving advice that is matched to the client's requirements, rather than imposing standard or traditional solutions;

- paying attention to the life-cycle costs of constructing and occupying a building, rather than to the initial capital cost only.

Our aim is to provide our clients with risk assurance, cost control and value for money, via effective advice, cost planning and management.

Hong Kong Head Office
21st Floor, Leighton Centre
77 Leighton Road
Causeway Bay
Hong Kong
Tel : (852) 28303500
Fax : (852) 25760416

Beijing Representative Office
Suite 101, Level 1 North Tower
Rainbow Plaza
14 Dong San Huan Bei Road
Chao Yang District
Beijing 100026, China
Tel : (8610) 5954923
Fax : (8610) 5954927

Shanghai Representative Office
Room 2409, 24/F Shartex Plaza
88 Zhun Yi Nan Road
Shanghai 200335 China
Tel : (8621) 62191107
Fax : (8621) 62193680

Guangzhou Representative Office
Unit 04, 11/F New Century Plaza
2-6 Hong De Road
Guangzhou 510235, China
Tel : (8620) 4328565
Fax : (8620) 4328567

DAVIS LANGDON & SEAH INTERNATIONAL

China

KEY DATA

Population
Population	1,178mn
Urban population	29%
Population under 15 (1991)	27%
Population 65 and over (1991)	7%
Average annual growth rate (1980 to 1993)	1.4%

Geography
Land area	9,561,000 km²
Agricultural area	42%
Capital city	Beijing
Population of capital city (1990)	10.9mn

Economy
Monetary unit	renminbi (Rmb) (or yuan)
Exchange rate (average third quarter 1995) to:	
the pound sterling	Rmb 13.17
the US dollar	Rmb 8.31
the yen x 100	Rmb 9.06
Average annual inflation (1980 to 1993)	7.0%
Inflation rate (1994)	24.1%
Gross Domestic Product (GDP) at market prices	Rmb 3,138bn
GDP per capita	Rmb 2,663
Average annual real change in GDP (1980 to 1993)	9.6%
Private consumption as a proportion of GDP	51%
General government consumption as a proportion of GDP	9%
Gross domestic investment as a proportion of GDP	41%
Central government expenditure as a proportion of Gross National Product	9%*

Construction
Gross value of construction output	Rmb 733.5bn
Net value of construction output	Rmb 210.5bn
Net value of construction output as a proportion of GDP	6.7%

All data relate to 1993 unless otherwise indicated

* *Data for budgetary accounts only*

THE CONSTRUCTION INDUSTRY

Construction output

The value of the gross output of the construction industry in 1993 was Rmb 733.5 billion, equivalent to US$130 billion, or 23.4% of GDP. The net value of construction output in 1993 was 6.7% of GDP or Rmb 210.5 billion, equivalent to US$3.7 billion.

Rapid changes in China have brought about an accelerated pace of growth in construction. The role of the construction industry is seen as vital to economic and social development and has become one of the five major industries in the national economy. It is estimated that China's GNP will increase at the rate of 8%-9% per annum in the next few years and demand in the building industry at the rate of 12% per annum between 1993 and 2000.

Special economic zones, in which trading and customs privileges prevail, have been the focus of building work. Shanghai and Beijing, have been transformed by such activity. The Pudong New Zone in Shanghai is an area that is currently the focus of development. This new zone of 518 km^2 is attracting investment of the order of Rmb 100 billion. Construction work is expected to continue into the early part of the next century supporting Shanghai's transformation into a major international economic, trade and financial centre. The Yangpu Economic Zone in Hainan Province is the first large free harbour area in China and is also the largest project to be developed with foreign funds.

The regions of greatest construction activity are Guangdong, Liaoning, Beijing, Sichuan and Jiangsu, as shown in the table overleaf.

REGIONAL DISTRIBUTION OF CONSTRUCTION OUTPUT COMPARED TO POPULATION, 1993

Region	% of population	% of construction output	Rank by population	Rank by construction output
Beijing	1.0	6.5	25	3
Tianjin	0.8	1.9	26	21
Hebei	5.4	4.9	7	6
Shanxi	2.5	2.7	19	14
Inner Mongolia	1.9	2.2	22	18
Liaoning	3.5	9.8	12	2
Jilin	2.2	3.3	20	11
Heilongjiang	3.1	4.7	15	7
Shanghai	1.2	3.1	24	12
Jiangsu	5.9	6.0	4	5
Zhejiang	3.6	3.9	10	9
Anhui	5.0	1.8	8	22
Fujian	2.7	2.6	18	15
Jiangxi	3.4	1.5	13	23
Shandong	7.3	4.3	3	8
Henan	7.6	3.1	2	12
Hebei	4.8	3.7	9	10
Hunan	5.3	2.5	6	16
Guangdong	5.6	14.0	5	1
Guangxi	3.7	2.1	11	19
Hainan	0.6	0.4	27	28
Sichuan	9.4	6.3	1	4
Guizhou	2.9	1.2	16	25
Yunnan	3.3	1.1	13	26
Tibet	0.2	0.1	30	30
Shaanxi	2.9	2.3	16	17
Gansu	2.0	1.3	21	24
Qinghai	0.4	0.4	28	28
Ningxia	0.4	0.5	28	27
Xinjiang	1.4	2.0	23	20

Source: Statistical Yearbook of China, 1994

Construction work is classified according to the following categories:
(i)   Civil engineering construction, including building, construction of
        housing, railways, highways, bridges, dams, harbours, power stations,
        airports, etc.,
(ii)   Building surveying and design,
(iii)   Decorating and finishing,
(iv)   Building repair and maintenance,
(v)   Line and equipment installation,
(vi)   Building products and building equipment manufacturing -
        manufacturing of non-standard equipment (specifically for
        construction projects).

Of these, item (ii) and much of items (v) and (vi) would be classified
as construction output in most market economies. However, the gross output
in 1993 of state-owned and urban collective-owned construction enterprises
(excluding affiliated construction units) comprised 88% construction, 10%
installation, 1% repair and maintenance and 1% non-standard equipment
manufacture. Repair and maintenance is remarkably low but presumably
some is undertaken by other types of enterprise.

GROSS CONSTRUCTION OUTPUT OF CONSTRUCTION ENTERPRISES,
NATIONALLY AND IN PRINCIPAL REGIONS, 1993 (*Rmb billion*)

Type of work	National	Beijing	Guangdong	Sichuan	Liaoning
Building	213	15	30	15	21
Mines	5	-	-	-	1
Railways and tunnels, highways and bridges	37	2	3	2	2
Equipment installation	31	3	2	1	4
Decorating	10	1	7	-	1
Total	296	21	42	18	29

Source: Statistical Yearbook of China, 1994

Investment in construction from 1995 until 2000 is to be directed towards
transport, energy resources, water resources, telecommunications and
industrial projects.

Currently, China has a number of long-term infrastructure projects in
hand, such as the Three Gorges Dam project, which is due for completion
in 2013 and estimated to cost up to US$77 billion. China intends to invest
US$500 billion over the next decade to upgrade its infrastructure and alleviate
bottlenecks threatening to stall economic growth. In the run-up to the year
2000, China will account for the bulk of Asian infrastructure spending with
the demand for electricity and transport rising sharply as a result of robust
economic growth.

It is expected that the need for housing will increase in line with the rapid economic growth. With an estimated additional 1.6 billion m² of housing required in towns and cities and an additional 650 billion m² required in rural areas. At present levels, investment in housing accounts for about 40% of total investment in urban infrastructure. The state is running a programme to develop housing for low and medium income families and plans to invest Rmb 40 billion.

The table below shows contractors whose primary activity is general building, as placed in *Engineering News Record's* list of top international contractors. The last four contractors in the table were not placed in last year's ranking but have reached positions in the top 150 international contractors in the course of one year.

INTERNATIONAL CONTRACTORS PRIMARILY INVOLVED IN BUILDING, 1994 AND 1995*

	ENR rank (1995)	ENR rank (1994)	total	Revenue 1994 (US$ million) international
China State Construction Engineering Corp., Beijing	42	43	2728	670
China Civil Engineering Construction, Beijing	96	146	216	166
China Metallurgical Construction Corp., Beijing	101	119	401	150
Beijing Chang Cheng Construction Corp., Beijing	123	+++	527	104
China Liaoning Int. Corp of Eco. & Tech. Coop, Shenyang	131	+++	85	86
China Wu Yi Corp., Fuijian	132	+++	101	84
China Fuijian Corp. for Int. Techno-Economic Coop., Fuijian	133	+++	108	80

Source: Engineering News Record, 28 August 1995.

* *International contractors that are listed in Engineering News Record as primarily involved in general building according to 1995 ranking (based on 1994 revenue) and 1994 ranking (based on 1993 revenue)*

+++ *Not previously ranked in the top 225 international contractors*

The Chinese economy is based on three types of enterprise : state, collective (or co-operative) and individual private. State-owned enterprises have traditionally been located in urban areas while collective enterprises were mainly in rural areas. The individual or private element is largely involved in service trades, both in rural and urban areas.

Of the 94,000 enterprises in the construction industry, approximately 6,000 are state-owned (with an additional 3,000 affiliated construction units), 14,000 collectively-owned in towns or cities and 70,000 recorded as rural construction teams. Rural construction teams are generally small groups of unskilled workers building housing and other small projects for the local community. The larger construction enterprises tend to work on the major construction projects.

The table below shows the main types of construction enterprises and their employment in 1993.

CONSTRUCTION ENTERPRISES AND EMPLOYMENT

Type of construction enterprise	Enterprise numbers	Employment thousands	Average employment number
State-owned	9,966	7,742	776
Urban collective-owned	14,130	4,557	322
Rural construction teams	70,486	9,268	131
Total	94,582	21,567	228

Source: China Statistical Yearbook

Characteristics and structure of the industry

State-owned enterprises consist of local units (effectively construction companies) spread throughout the country and account for 43% of the work done by the state: the Ministry of Affiliated Units undertakes the remaining 57%. The most important ministries for construction output (which may include plant and machinery) are the Ministry of Energy Resources and the Ministry of Railways (which together account for 63% of the work), plus the Ministries of Metallurgical Industry and Communications, and the China State Construction Engineering Corporation. State enterprises also do some geotechnical investigation, surveying and design both in the local Units and in the Ministries. Government departments act both as developers and contractors.

The China State Construction Engineering Corporation (CSCEC) is the only contractor to operate directly under the Ministry of People's Construction, the others normally being under municipal or provincial government or under other ministries e.g. Railway, Waterworks, Army, etc. It is organized into eight construction companies and undertakes overseas commitments (as well as those in China). It has been involved in 400 projects in 50 countries and as a result it is accustomed to western types of contract and work arrangement. Other leading Chinese contracting organizations are the China Metallurgical Construction Group (with a turnover of over US$1 billion but only US$212 million abroad), the China Road and Bridge Corporation and the China International Water and Electrical Corp.

Within the state enterprises three main parties are involved in the construction industry: the Development Unit, the Design Unit and the Construction Unit. The Development Unit is the project developer, and is responsible for initiating a project, organizing the team members and making sure that the project is satisfactorily completed. Recently it has become a requirement that a Construction Management Unit be employed whose role is primarily concerned with the quality of the works. The Construction Unit carries out the construction work with, usually, separate construction units for specialist work such as mechanical and electrical installations. It is similar to a main contractor, though the contracts between the various parties are usually simple, setting out the benefits, duties and obligations of the various units.

Contractors are licensed and classified into four categories on the basis of fixed assets, expertise and previous experience. Apart from the national contractors, they normally work locally in their region and must obtain permission to go outside that region. All contractors have to register with their Local Construction Commission. Only the state authorities can give permission to work abroad.

Joint ventures

Increasingly, projects are carried out as joint ventures with foreigners, in particular firms from Hong Kong. The law on joint ventures was introduced in 1979 when China had an open door policy towards foreign investment and gave preference to foreign investors.

Expatriate construction and professional personnel operate in China under the general laws that govern foreign investment.

Although there is no shortage of labour in China, the domestic construction industry is hampered by a lack of modern know-how and engineering ability and is therefore anxious to acquire skills from abroad. It is this deficiency that has created a niche for international contractors and specialist subcontractors in China. Foreign construction involvement, however, tends to be limited to the provision of the design and construction management techniques required for complex projects plus technology transfer connected with the installation of sophisticated plant and machinery. The construction work itself is invariably carried out by domestic contractors. The state is involved in all contracts, though this can be at a variety of levels, depending upon the nature of the project. It is only construction works undertaken by ministry level units that can employ foreign contractors directly. Projects are assessed and approved by the Ministry of Foreign Economic Relations and Trade (MOFERT). However, the majority of foreign investment in China is carried out using co-operative joint ventures. Essentially, these consist of agreements between State bodies - professional units, tourist corporations, etc., whereby the Chinese party usually provides resources such as land and labour whilst the foreign party provides capital, advanced technology and key equipment. The joint venture parties agree to co-operate for a period of years after which the whole of the enterprise will come under Chinese ownership.

Overseas contractors may become involved in joint venture projects in one of two ways, either as the foreign party to the joint venture or as a subcontractor employed by the joint venture to construct the project. The first involves a long-term commitment that goes beyond simple contracting. The second is the most common, and the contractor is likely to find that his negotiations are largely with the foreign party to the joint venture as it is often that party's obligation to provide the management contractor and the finance to pay him. However, the final contract will have to be approved and registered with the State. The *China Investment Guide (5th edition, 1995)* gives comprehensive information on joint ventures.

In January 1995, Bechtel of the USA became the first overseas construction company to obtain a construction licence allowing it to tender for projects without the requirement of a local partner. It is possible that other such licences will be issued in the near future.

Basic building materials are available in China but many finishing materials and engineering and mechanical systems have to be imported. Material production has not always kept up with the increase in demand and shortages have occurred. To meet demand, even some basic materials have sometimes to be imported. China is a vast country and delays in the delivery of building materials due to transport difficulties are common. The State no longer controls the supply of materials by stockpiling them in each region; instead they are sent direct to the construction unit that contracts for a project.

Clients and finance

Of the 1993 capital investment in construction, 9.6% is funded from state budgets, 43.1% is self-financed, 24.2% is from bank loans, 9.9% from foreign capital and the remaining 13.2% from other sources.

In 1993, 17% of total government capital spending was on construction. The market for constructing by joint ventures was Rmb 25 billion (US$3 billion) in 1993. In the mid 1980s the boom in non-government work led to a shortage of building materials and to higher prices.

Restrictions on extra-budgetary projects were introduced and access to loans limited.

However, joint venture companies comprising a partner from China and one or more foreign partners are now responsible for a large proportion of development in China.

The Construction Bank of China is responsible for providing funds to the various construction departments or units. The State allocates a total sum to the Bank which will in turn issue it to the departments or units as required. Savings achieved as a result of better efficiency or shorter construction periods may be retained by the construction department while any extra cost due to delays must be repaid.

Funds for extra-budgetary projects must now be placed with the People's Construction Bank for six months before they can be used.

Non-productive (e.g. housing and social) projects outside the State Plan are subject to a special 30% tax and in practice it is difficult to get approval of funds. Priority is given to key construction projects. In spite of these and other moves to control projects there is still a major increase in investment.

Selection of design consultants

It is compulsory for a foreign design consultant to work together with a local design institute because only the latter is authorized to submit drawings to the local authority for approval. In addition to this, the local knowledge of their staff is invaluable. A joint venture company, therefore, can have its design completed by one of the following arrangements:

● the employment of a local China design institute

● the employment of a foreign design consultant working with a local design institute or vice versa

● the employment of a joint venture design consultant

The selection of a foreign design consultant is based on the same criteria as in other parts of the world. Similar criteria are used when selecting a local design institute. There is a wide variation in the size, scope and abilities of design institutes. Most of them are involved mainly in local projects and have no experience of working with foreigners.

According to the *Standards of Qualification Grouping of Design Institutes for Building and Civil Engineering Works* promulgated in 1986, design institutes are divided into integrated or specialized institutes. Integrated ones cover all aspects of design including structural, mechanical and electrical engineering. Specialized units only undertake one or a limited number of aspects.

Design institutes are allocated to one of four classifications (see table on later page), Class A being the highest of these. Institutes belonging to this class are authorized to work on any China project, no matter how complex that project might be, whereas class B institutes are able to work not only in their own region but outside of it. The smaller design institutes belong to classes C and D. Strict minimum qualifications and numbers of staff are laid down for each category. Class A for example must have at least five lead architects, five structural engineers and three other specialized designers of university or college standard with at least five years experience on major projects. Fifty per cent of their designers must be university or college trained with a minimum of five years experience. They will be working with sophisticated equipment. For Class B there must be at least three lead architects and the qualifications and experience can be slightly less. Only 40% of the staff of Class B must have university or college education and five years experience. Classes C and D may be at a lower level of qualification and experience. The table given on a later page shows which projects each of the four classes are authorized to undertake. Some institutes are permitted to work on both building and civil engineering projects, whereas others are limited to one or the other.

Local institutes in the China have a good knowledge of structural design and civil engineering, but benefit from guidance in technological advances in the industry and the use of imported materials. In recent years they have started to make advances in these fields.

Many foreign firms have forged good working relationships with particular institutes, but should a developer need a suitable local connection, advice may be required on which one is most suitable for his needs.

Contractual arrangements

In 1984, the Sixth National People's Congress in Beijing called for shorter construction durations, and improved quality. In order to encourage competition and to prevent monopolies, open tendering was introduced. Construction and design units from all over China can now bid for projects previously not available to them. The result is reported to be a reduction in construction costs. Now, open tendering is being practised in most areas of China. Administrative procedures and regulations in China regarding tendering have been set. Negotiation occurs very frequently during the tendering period.

The involvement of American, European and Japanese companies, banks, architects and contractors has led to a great diversity in the way construction contracts are structured. In response to this a more comprehensive version of a Chinese Form of Contract has now been issued by the Ministry of Construction although other international forms, often amended, are still in use. All contracts have to be translated into Chinese and are generally expressed as subject to Chinese law though both versions are considered to be equally authentic for legal purposes. Usually the Chinese party prefers to sign a contract document in Chinese.

Before tendering can be carried out, the tender documents and the estimated pre tender price would have to be submitted to and approved by the local Tender Board. They would then establish the "floor price". This practice was introduced to ensure fair tender prices and to avoid local contractors, who were not accustomed to open tendering, from submitting below cost tender prices.

There are various government building regulations and specifications and the various provinces and cities have their own schedules of rates used for estimating and for valuing construction work. However, these rates might not be applicable directly to a joint-venture development depending on its type and location.

PROJECTS PERMITTED FOR GRADES OF DESIGN INSTITUTES

Public buildings	Residential buildings	Industrial buildings and warehouses	Other
Class A			
All types	All types	All types	All types
Class B			
High rise max height 50m grade 2 fireproofing	Max storeys 18	Single storey max span 30m max crane capacity 30 tons	Chimneys, water towers and tanks, etc.
Single storey max span 30m		Multi storey max span 12m max storeys 6	
Class C			
Single storey max span 24m		High rise max height 24m	Medium chimneys, water towers, tanks, etc.
		Single storey max span 24m max crane capacity 10 tons	
		Multi storey max span 9m max storeys 4	
Class D			
No basements	No basements	No basements	No basements
Framed buildings max span 7.5m max storeys 3	Houses, dormitories brick walls reinforced concrete floor max storeys 6	Single storey max span 15m max single beam crane capacity 5 tons	Medium and small chimneys, water towers, tanks, etc. with standardized drawings
Single storey max span 15m		Light buildings max span 75m max storeys 3	

max: maximum
min: minimum

Development control and standards

Under Chinese law, all property is owned by the State. Individuals and companies are permitted to lease land under the concept of land use rights granted for a specific period which is very similar to a leasehold estate from the Crown in Hong Kong. Subject to payment of annual land use fees and observation of covenants in the grant contract, a holder of land use rights may exercise practically all the rights of an owner during the term of grant.

Under the *Provisional Regulations* of the People's Republic of China concerning the *Grant and Assignment of the Right to Use State Land in Urban Areas* (*Urban Land Regulations*) promulgated in May 1990, the State may grant land use rights for a definite period of time and against payment of a grant premium. The grant of land use rights may be pursuant to a negotiated agreement, through the submission of tenders or by auction. Local governments at or above the county level may grant land. Their scope of authority varies in accordance with their position in the administrative hierarchy. However, the regulations set forth the maximum period of grant for different uses of land ranging from 40 years for commercial development and 50 years for industrial building and public facilities and mixed use to 70 years for residential development.

Under the *Urban Land Regulations*, land use rights which have been lawfully acquired will enjoy legal protection and the State generally may not resume possession prior to expiration of the term of grant. In the event that the public interest requires the resumption of possession by the State, compensation must be paid.

While the grant of land use rights for a premium implements the official policy of economic use of land, it is the ability of grantees to transfer land use rights through sale, exchange or gift which breathes real economic life into the system. The *Urban Land Regulations* require the registration of all transfers and the imposition of a certain degree of administrative market control. The government maintains the right to purchase if the transfer price is obviously below market price and the right to intervene if the market price rises unreasonably.

Assignment of land use rights from, or joint development with, current owners of land use rights are becoming more frequent. The *Urban Land Regulations* state that assignment or mortgage of allocated land in urban areas is subject to the approval of the relevant land and real estate departments. The relevant procedures are set forth in the *Provisional Measures on the Management of Allocated Land Use Rights*, promulgated on March 8 1992.

China has a system of registration of title which is slowly recovering from chronic mismanagement. Most localities in China still have two separate registration systems administered by separate departments, viz. one for land and one for buildings. Certificates issued following registration serve as legal evidence of ownership and other rights. However, it appears that their validity is not absolute. There have been cases where certificates have been successfully challenged in court and where certificates have been invalidated owing to corrupt practices or other irregularities at the time of issue.

Subject to the approval of the relevant real estate department, the sale of uncompleted buildings, known as pre-sale, is permitted. Standard pre-sale contracts and other documents must be submitted for approval.

A number of taxes and fees may be levied during the course of real estate development and on income derived from real estate development in China. These include land use tax, turnover tax, income tax, real property tax, contract tax, stamp duty, transfer appreciation fee, registration fee, transaction fee and notarization fee.

CONSTRUCTION COST DATA

Cost of labour

The figures below are typical of labour costs in Guangdong Province as at the third quarter of 1995. The wage rate is the basis of an employee's income, while the cost of labour indicates the cost to a foreign contractor of employing that employee. The difference between the two covers a variety of mandatory and voluntary contributions - a list of items which could be included is given in section 2.

	Wage rate (per month) Rmb	Cost of labour (per month) Rmb	Number of hours worked per year
Site operatives			
Mason/bricklayer	1,000 - 1,500	2,000	2,450
Carpenter	1,000 - 1,500	2,000	2,450
Plumber	1,000 - 1,500	2,000	2,450
Electrician	1,000 - 1,500	2,000	2,450
Structural steel erector	1,000 - 1,500	2,000	2,450
HVAC installer	1,500 - 1,800	2,200	2,450
Semi-skilled worker	800 - 1,000	1,300	2,450
Unskilled labourer	500 - 600	800	2,450
Equipment operator	1,000 - 1,500	2,000	2,450
Watchman/security	300 - 600	800	2,450

	Wage rate (per month) Rmb	Number of hours worked per year
Site supervision		
General foreman	3,000 - 4,000	2,450
Trades foreman	2,000 - 3,000	2,450
Clerk of works	3,000 - 4,000	2,450
Contractors' personnel		
Site manager	5,000 - 6,000	2,450
Resident engineer	2,500 - 3,500	2,450
Resident surveyor	2,000 - 3,000	2,450
Junior engineer	1,500 - 2,500	2,450
Junior surveyor	1,500 - 2,500	2,450
Planner	1,500 - 2,500	2,450
Consultants' personnel		
Senior architect	5,000 - 6,000	2,200
Senior engineer	5,000 - 6,000	2,200
Senior surveyor	5,000 - 6,000	2,200
Qualified architect	2,500 - 3,500	2,200
Qualified engineer	2,500 - 3,500	2,200
Qualified surveyor	2,500 - 3,500	2,200

Labour costs (for expatriates from Hong Kong, for example) incurred by joint venture developers are as follows.

	Wage rate (per day) HK$	Cost of labour (per day) HK$	Number of hours worked per year
Site operatives			
Mason/bricklayer	600 - 700	900 - 1,000	2,450
Carpenter	600 - 700	900 - 1,000	2,450
Plumber	600 - 700	900 - 1,000	2,450
Electrician	500 - 600	800 - 900	2,450
Structural steel erector	600 - 700	900 - 1,000	2,450
HVAC installer	550 - 650	900 - 950	2,450
Semi-skilled worker	400 - 500	650 - 750	2,450

	Wage rate (per month) HK$	Number of hours worked per year
Site supervision		
General foreman	28,000 - 35,000	2,450
Trades foreman	17,000 - 20,000	2,450
Clerk of works	28,000 - 35,000	2,450
Contractors' personnel		
Site manager	35,000 - 42,000	2,450
Resident engineer	35,000 - 42,000	2,450
Resident surveyor	35,000 - 42,000	2,450
Junior engineer	15,000 - 42,000	2,450
Junior surveyor	15,000 - 20,000	2,450
Consultants' personnel		
Senior architect	55,000 - 66,000	2,200
Senior engineer	55,000 - 66,000	2,200
Senior surveyor	55,000 - 66,000	2,200
Qualified architect	28,000 - 35,000	2,200
Qualified engineer	28,000 - 35,000	2,200
Qualified surveyor	28,000 - 35,000	2,200

Labour cost is inclusive of overseas allowance, accommodation allowance, travelling expenses to and from Guangdong and profit and overheads (15%).

Cost of materials

The figures that follow are the costs of main construction materials, delivered to site in Guangdong Province, as incurred by contractors in the third quarter of 1995. These assume that the materials would be in quantities as required for a medium sized construction project and that the location of the works would be neither constrained nor remote. All the costs in this section exclude tax (see below).

	Unit	Cost Rmb
Cement and aggregate		
Ordinary portland cement in 50kg bags	tonne	500
Coarse aggregates for concrete	tonne	65
Fine aggregates for concrete	tonne	75

	Unit	Cost Rmb
Steel		
Mild steel reinforcement	tonne	3,100
High tensile steel reinforcement	tonne	3,300
Bricks and blocks		
Common bricks (240 x 115 x 53mm)	1,000	265
Good quality facing bricks (240 x 115 x 53mm)	1,000	350
Hollow concrete blocks	1,000	2,000
Precast concrete cladding units with exposed aggregate finish	m²	550
Timber and insulation		
Softwood sections for carpentry	m³	1,200
Softwood for joinery	m³	1,600
Hardwood for joinery	m³	2,100
Exterior quality plywood (18mm thick)	m²	85
Plywood for interior joinery (12mm thick)	m²	55
Hardwood strip flooring	m²	132
100mm thick quilt insulation	m²	50
Hardwood internal door complete with frames and ironmongery	each	1,500
Glass and ceramics		
Float glass (4mm)	m²	36
Sealed double glazing units	m²	300
Plaster and paint		
Good quality ceramic wall tiles (152 x 152mm)	m²	35
Plaster in 50kg bags	tonne	230
Plasterboard (12mm thick)	m²	18
Emulsion paint in 5 litre tins	kg	5
Gloss oil paint in 5 litre tins	kg	9
Tiles and paviors		
Clay floor tiles (200 x 200 x 8mm)	m²	35
Non-slip vinyl floor tiles (305 x 305 x 1.5mm)	m²	30
Precast concrete paving slabs (490 x 490 x 40mm)	m²	40
Clay roof tiles (200 x 500mm)	1,000	220
Precast concrete roof tiles (390 x 390 x 40mm)	1,000	2,500

	Unit	Cost Rmb
Drainage		
WC suite complete	each	500
Lavatory basin complete	each	300
100mm diameter clay drain pipes (2500mm long)	m	30
150mm diameter cast iron drain pipes (1830mm long)	m	75

Unit rates

The descriptions below are generally shortened versions of standard descriptions listed in full in section 4. Where an item has a two digit reference number (e.g. 05 or 33), this relates to the full description against that number in section 4. Where an item has an alphabetic suffix (e.g. 12A or 34B) this indicates that the standard description has been modified. Where a modification is major the complete modified description is included here and the standard description should be ignored; where a modification is minor (e.g. the insertion of a named hardwood) the shortened description has been modified here but, in general, the full description in section 4 prevails.

The unit rates below are for main work items on a typical construction project in the Guangdong Province in the third quarter of 1995. The rates include all necessary labour, materials, equipment and an allowance to cover preliminary and general items. Five per cent should be added to the rates to cover contractors' overheads and profit. All the rates in this section exclude tax (see below).

		Unit	Rate Rmb
Excavation			
01	Mechanical excavation of foundation trenches	m³	35
02	Hardcore filling making up levels (150mm)	m²	33
Concrete work			
04A	Plain insitu concrete in strip foundations in trenches (C30)*	m³	600
05A	Reinforced insitu concrete in beds (C40)*	m³	650
06A	Reinforced insitu concrete in walls (200mm thick) (C40)*	m³	650
07A	Reinforced insitu concrete in suspended floors or roof slabs (C40)*	m³	650
08A	Reinforced insitu concrete in columns (C40)*	m³	650
09A	Reinforced insitu concrete in isolated beams (C40)*	m³	650
10	Precast concrete slab	m²	650

		Unit	Rate Rmb

Formwork

11	Softwood formwork to concrete walls	m^2	35
12	Softwood or metal formwork to concrete columns	m^2	40
13	Softwood or metal formwork to horizontal soffits of slabs	m^2	48

* Note : Concrete strength grades are based on PRC standard

Reinforcement

| 14 | Reinforcement in concrete walls | tonne | 5,500 |
| 15 | Reinforcement in suspended concrete slabs | tonne | 5,500 |

Steelwork

| 17 | Fabricate, supply and erect steel framed structure | tonne | 13,000 |

Brickwork and blockwork

| 23A | Red brick wall (half brick thick) | m^2 | 40 |
| 23B | Red brick wall (one brick thick) | m^2 | 65 |

Roofing

| 24A | Concrete interlocking roof tiles 490 x 490mm | m^2 | 100 |
| 29A | Felt roof covering | m^2 | 55 |

Woodwork and metalwork

34	Preservative treated sawn softwood 50 x 100mm	m	15
35	Preservative treated sawn softwood 50 x 150mm	m	20
37	Two panel glazed door in hardwood, size 850 x 2000mm	each	3,000
38	Solid core half hour fire resisting hardwood internal flush door, size 800 x 2000mm	each	2,000
41	Hardwood skirtings	m	14

Plumbing

| 44 | Light gauge copper cold water tubing (20mm diameter) | m | 100 |

Sanitary Ware

| 48 | White vitreous china WC suite | each | 600 |
| 49 | White vitreous china lavatory basin | each | 400 |

Electrical work

52A	PVC insulated and copper sheathed cable ($4mm^2$)	m	10
53	13 amp unswitched socket outlet (excluding power point)	each	45
54	Flush mounted 20 amp, 1 way light switch (excluding power point)	each	30

	Unit	Rate Rmb
Finishings		
55 2 coats gypsum based plaster on brick walls	m²	20
56 White glazed tiles on plaster walls (P.C Rmb 80/m2)	m²	140
57 Red clay quarry tiles on concrete floors (Ditto)	m²	160
59 Thermoplastic floor tiles on screed	m²	80
60 Mineral fibre tiles on concealed suspension system	m²	160
Glazing		
61 Glazing to wood	m²	100
Painting		
62 Emulsion on plaster walls	m²	15
63 Oil paint on timber	m²	20

Approximate estimating

The building costs per unit area given below are expressed in US$ and are averages incurred by building clients for typical buildings in the Guangdong Province as at the third quarter of 1995. They are based upon the total floor area of all storeys, measured between external walls and without deduction for internal walls.

Approximate estimating costs generally include mechanical and electrical installations but exclude furniture, loose or special equipment, and external works; they also exclude fees for professional services. The costs shown are for specifications and standards appropriate to China and this should be borne in mind when attempting comparisons with similarly described building types in other countries. A discussion of this issue is included in section 2. Comparative data for countries covered in this publication, including construction cost data, is presented in Part Three.

Approximate estimating costs must be treated with caution; they cannot provide more than a rough guide to the probable cost of building. All the rates in this section exclude tax (see below).

	Cost m² US$	Cost ft² US$
Residential buiidings		
Detached houses and bungalows	470	44
High rise apartment, no air conditioning	480	45
High rise, luxury, air conditioned	700	65

	Cost m² US$	Cost ft² US$
Commercial		
Average standard office high rise	850	79
Prestige office high rise	1,100	10
Industrial		
Light duty factories	425	40
Single storey conventional factory of structural steelwork	600	56
Hotels		
Hotel, 5 star, city centre	1,730	160
Hotel, 3 star, city/provincial	1,100	102
Others		
Carpark above ground	330	31
Retail/Department store (without finishes)	900	84

Regional variations

The approximate estimating costs are based on projects in the Guangdong Province. For other parts of China, adjust these costs by the following factors:

Beijing   +8%
Shanghai   +12%

Tax

The tax authorities in China, at the end of 1994, introduced some new tax rules such as VAT and land appreciation tax and changed some existing tax rules such as individual income tax. It is recommended that a tax consultant's advice be sought on the new tax rules.

Building materials and equipment imported to China must pay import duty except in the case of joint venture companies' own factories and offices, i.e. all works built for sale or rent must pay import duty for the import of building materials and equipment used in the construction.

EXCHANGE RATES AND INFLATION

The combined effect of exchange rates and inflation on prices within a country and price comparisons between countries is discussed in section 2.

Exchange rates

The graph below plots the movement of the Chinese Renminbi against sterling, US dollar and 100 Japanese yen since 1985. The values used for the graph are quarterly and the method of calculating these is described and general guidance on the interpretation of the graph provided in section 2. The average exchange rate in the third quarter of 1995 was Rmb 13.17 to pound sterling, Rmb 8.31 to US dollar and Rmb 9.06 to 100 Japanese yen.

THE CHINESE RENMINBI AGAINST STERLING, US DOLLAR AND JAPANESE YEN

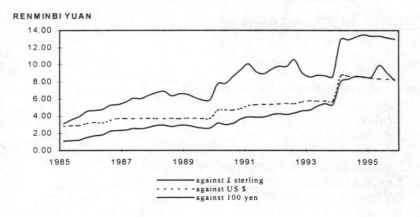

Consumer price inflation

The table below presents consumer price inflation in China since 1983.

CONSUMER PRICE INFLATION

Year	Consumer price inflation	
	average index	average change %
1983	100	-
1984	103	3
1985	112	8.7
1986	119	6.2
1987	127	6.7
1988	151	18.9
1989	178	17.8
1990	181	2.1
1991	186	2.9
1992	196	5.4
1993	222	13.2

USEFUL ADDRESSES

Public organizations

Beijing Urban Construction Design Institute
    Chegongzhuang
    Beijing
    Tel : 861-8318887

China National Democratic Construction Association
    Jing Xin Building
    2A Dong Sanhuan Beilu
    Beijing
    Tel : 861-4663366

Chinese Academy of Science
    Fuwai Sanlihe
    Beijing
    Tel: 861-8527969

Chinese Information Centre of Standardization
    Bucheng Road
    Beijing
    Tel: 861-8352236

Chinese Institute of Architectural Sciences
    Xiaohuangzhuang
    Beijing
    Tel: 861-4211133

Chinese Institute of Urban and Rural Construction and Economy
    Baiwanzhuang
    Beijing
    Tel: 861-8311336

Chinese Urban Planning Design Institute
    Baiwanzhuang,
    Beijing
    Tel: 861-8329944

Ministry of Construction
    Baiwanzhuang Avenue
    Beijing
    Tel: 861-8394114

Ministry of Foreign Trade & Economic Cooperation
    Dong Chang'an Jie
    Beijing
    Tel: 861-5198114

Shanghai Glass Fibre Reinforced Plastic Institute
    Jiyang Lu
    Shanghai
    Tel : 8621-8836700

Standardization Industry (Min CI)
    Heping Jie Beikou
    Beijing
    Tel : 861-4214818

State Bureau of Building Materials Industry
    Baiwanzhuang
    Beijing
    Tel: 861-8311144

State Bureau of Land Administration
    Daliushubeicun
    Beijing
    Tel : 861-8350561

State Bureau of Prices
    Yuetan Beixiaojie
    Beijing
    Tel : 861-8350651

State Bureau of Standardization
    Zhichun Lu
    Beijing
    Tel: 861-2022288

State Bureau of Statistics
    38 Yuetan Nanjie
    Beijing
    Tel: 861-8033618

State Planning Commission
    Yuetan S. Street
    Beijing
    Tel: 861-8502114

Trade and professional associations

China Civil Engineering Society
    Baiwanzhuang
    Beijing
    Tel: 861-8311313

Chinese Architectural Mechanization Association
    Baiwanzhuang
    Beijing
    Tel: 861-8327620

Chinese Society of Mechanical Engineering
        Fuxingmenwai Sanlike
        Beijing
        Tel: 861-8595316

State Bureau of Land Administration
        Daliushubeicun
        Beijing
        Tel: 861-8350561

The Architectural Society of China
        Xijiao Baiwanzhuang
        Beijing
        Tel: 861-8393284

DAVIS LANGDON & SEAH HONG KONG LTD

The strategic and integrated management of cost, time and quality - the client "risk" areas of a contract - are essential functions, which are necessary to ensure the satisfactory planning, procurement, execution and operation of construction projects.

We specialise in the financial management of construction projects and their risk areas, from project inception to completion and we concentrate on:

- being positive and creative in our advice, rather than simply reactive;

- providing value for money via efficient management, rather than on superficial cost monitoring;

- giving advice that is matched to the client's requirements, rather than imposing standard or traditional solutions;

- paying attention to the life-cycle costs of constructing and occupying a building, rather than to the initial capital cost only.

Our aim is to provide our clients with risk assurance, cost control and value for money, via effective advice, cost planning and management.

DAVIS LANGDON & SEAH HONG KONG LTD
21st Floor, Leighton Centre
77 Leighton Road
Causeway Bay
Hong Kong
Tel : (852) 28303500
Fax : (852) 25760416

DAVIS LANGDON & SEAH INTERNATIONAL

Hong Kong

KEY DATA

Population

Population	5.8mn
Urban population	95%
Population under 15	19%
Population 65 and over	9%
Average annual growth rate (1980 to 1993)	1.1%

Geography

Land area	1,076 km²
Agricultural area	8%
Capital city	Victoria

Economy

Monetary unit	Hong Kong dollar (HK$)
Exchange rate (average third quarter 1995) to	
the pound sterling	HK$12.27
the US dollar	HK$7.74
the yen x 100	HK$8.44
Average annual inflation (1980 to 1993)	7.9%
Inflation rate (1994)	8.1%
Gross Domestic Product (GDP) at market price	HK$900.2bn
GDP per capita	HK$155,200
Average annual real change in GDP (1980 to 1993)	6.5%
Private consumption as a proportion of GDP	60%
General government consumption as a proportion of GDP	9%
Gross domestic investment as a proportion of GDP	27%

Construction

Gross value of construction output	HK$78.5bn
Net value of construction output	HK$41.5bn
Net value of construction output as a proportion of GDP	4.6%

All data relate to 1993 unless otherwise indicated

THE CONSTRUCTION INDUSTRY

Construction output

The value of gross construction output in 1993 was HK$78 billion, equivalent to US$10 billion, or 8.7% of GDP. The net value of construction output for 1993 was HK$41.5 billion, equivalent to US$6 billion, or 4.6% of GDP. Of this, building including housing accounted for 58% of the total, and civil engineering, 42%. The Housing Authority is committed to a planned maintenance expenditure in 1994 exceeding HK$2.25 billion.

In recent years the most significant impact on the Hong Kong construction industry has come from the Port and Airport Strategy Project 1991-2000 which is valued at US$20 billion. The strategy outlines plans for a new airport development, roads, rail links, land reclamation and container terminals. There is to be a third cross harbour tunnel, waste treatment and other environmental projects. The progressive implementation of these major infrastructural programmes has resulted in an intensive period of construction activity with work on the airport core programme reaching its peak in 1996, US$8.4 billion of contracts having been awarded by the end of 1994. Private sector development has also received a boost as land and development sites come on stream as a result of the airport programme and related works. Major mixed use developments are planned at each of the new stations along the new airport rail link.

The residential market continues to grow, if slowly. In 1994 a total of 56,444 housing units were completed of which 21,692 were public housing. The forecast for 1995 is 63,843 residential units and in 1996, 66,295 units - a slow upward trend being evident from the figures. The government however, has plans to increase the overall public housing stock by about 340,000 residential units by the turn of the century. This is deemed necessary in order to meet the current and anticipated demand.

In general terms overall expenditure on building and construction in 1994 had a growth of 15% (following an increase of 9% in 1993) and a figure of 15% has been forecast for 1995. The majority of this growth may be attributed to the increase in infrastructure works.

The table below shows the types of public work construction.

DISTRIBUTION OF PUBLIC WORKS - BASED ON ESTIMATES OF TENDER
VALUES (1993)

Types of work	%
Buildings	31
Port works	2
Site formation	8
Roads and drainage	31
Waterworks	12
Public utilities	6
Landscaping	1
Other	9

Source : Work Digest, Hong Kong Government

Characteristics and structure of the industry

There are around 3,700 registered contractors and approved suppliers of materials in Hong Kong. The Hong Kong Government maintains lists of approved contractors for public works. Once registered, a company is designated by group with relation to any or all of five possible categories: buildings, port works, roads and drainage, site formation and waterworks. As at June 1995 there were 65 contractors approved for building contracts of unlimited value (Group C), 38 contractors approved for contracts up to HK$50 million and 37 contractors approved for contracts up to HK$20 million. In addition there were 29 international contractors approved for contracts of unlimited value. In practice, private sector projects also usually employ contractors who only appear on the *Government List of Approved Contractors.*

For most projects a main contractor is chosen who is responsible for completing the project and employing approved subcontractors for major sections of works such as curtain walling or windows and building services. These latter elements are tendered separately. Main contractors tend to carry out very little construction work themselves, apart from possibly the concrete structure, and prefer to employ small subcontractors and labour-only gangs.

Design-and-build or turnkey contracts are gathering favour but their use is not yet widespread.

During 1980s, the number of foreign contractors in the market increased. In 1982, for example, their market share in public housing projects was 9% but by 1986, 25% and most were from mainland China and Korea. This figure reduced following a tightening of government regulations. However, with the onset of the airport and ports programme this number has again increased although often in joint venture with a local contractor. Of the airport core programme projects tendered by the end of 1994, Japan had won the largest share by value with 25% of the total, followed by Hong Kong (21%), the United Kingdom (13%), the Netherlands (8%), France (8%), PRC (7%), Belgium (4%), Australia (3.2%), Spain (3%), USA (2.2%) and the remainder split between a further five countries. Firms winning consultancies have come from the UK, USA, Japan, the Netherlands, Australia, France, New Zealand, Germany and Hong Kong.

The majority of construction workers are engaged on a daily basis with only a very small percentage being employed by the month. There is no unionization in construction. If over four hours overtime is worked, an extra day's pay is usually due. Restrictions on foreign labour, especially supervisory staff, arise from immigration controls which apply to all contracts and the hiring of immigrants has to be justified and approved.

It should be noted that to meet worker requirements for the new airport scheme the government has raised the ceiling of the importation of labour from 5,500 to 17,000. UK nationals are not subject to restrictions. Labour ordinance regulates the employment and termination of labour and the observance of statutory holidays.

The Construction Industry Training Authority runs a training centre providing basic courses for craftsmen and technicians. On completion of these, trainees are apprenticed to building contractors for a period of two or three years. The Authority is funded by a special levy on newly completed construction works. Currently the rate paid by contractors is 0.25% of the value of work exceeding HK$1 million.

The construction industry depends heavily on imported materials. Local quarries and plants can supply only a small portion of the aggregates and cement consumed each year. Similarly the production of rolling mills in Hong Kong is too small to meet demand for iron and steel. There is a wide variety of sources and qualities of materials available with correspondingly wide price variation. Hong Kong is a free port and has no exchange controls and few import restrictions. Import licences are generally not required. No sales or purchase taxes apply to construction materials or equipment. Because of the dependence of Hong Kong on imports, the prices of materials are heavily influenced by exchange rates.

Hong Kong has a large number of well-established firms of architects, both of overseas and local origin and some foreign architects, mainly from Britain and America, are employed by them. Small interior design and minor work practices proliferate on the back of the never-ending fitting out of offices, shops, flats, etc. All public work, such as hospitals, schools, museums and council chambers fall under the ambit of the Architectural Services Department. The Housing Authority is responsible for government initiated housing in Hong Kong and is supplemented by the Housing Society (see under Clients and finance).

The main professional bodies in the construction industry are the Hong Kong Institute of Architects with approximately 1,590 members, the Hong Kong Institute of Engineers with approximately 4,000 members. On many large schemes a project manager has replaced the architect as the project co-ordinator, but in most cases the project manager himself will be a member of one of the above institutes.

The profession of the quantity surveyor is recognized in Hong Kong but there is no compulsory registration scheme. The government set up a Hong Kong Institute of Surveyors in 1984 but there are no restrictions on membership. Anyone can set up as a quantity surveyor cost consultant by obtaining a Business Registration Certificate. There are as yet no Hong Kong surveying qualifications; the territory relies on RICS qualifications. However, the Hong Kong Institute of Surveyors does run an Assessment of Professional Competence (APC) exercise.

Clients and finance

The private sector accounts for about 60% of all new works in Hong Kong and the public sector about 40%.

PUBLIC AND PRIVATE SECTOR OUTPUT, HONG KONG

Type of work	Private %	Public %	Mixed (1) %	Total %
Building	84.1	15.9	-	100
of which housing(1)	48.8	40.7	10.5	100
other construction	23.4	76.6	-	100
Total	58.6	41.4	-	100

(1) Mixed are the Home Ownership Schemes built under the Private Sector Participation Schemes and the Middle Income Housing

The Housing Authority is a statutory body established in April 1973 under the Housing Ordinance. At first it was responsible for co-ordinating public housing but since April 1988 it has been responsible for nearly all public housing in Hong Kong including policy formulation. The Housing Authority is required to be self-financing on its current account which amounted to HK\$6,791 million in 1993-1994. Over 45% of housing stock is in the Authority's control. The construction branch includes architectural, engineering, planning and redevelopment, construction and maintenance divisions. The construction division has a quantity surveying and a building services section.

Most dwellings constructed by the Housing Authority are for public rental (78% of stock) but 22% of the stock are in the Home Ownership Scheme (HOS) under which flats were built by the government for purchase by families in the middle income bracket and the Private Sector Participation Scheme (PSPS), under which sites are offered for sale to real estate developers on condition that flats produced are sold at a fixed price to purchasers nominated by the government. Finance for new public housing comes from the Housing Authority's own funds, from revenue account surplus, from rents generated from the commercial elements in the developments, and from sale of HOS flats and land for PSPS. The remainder comes from permanent capital injected by the government.

Private building work is financed by property developers and by big businesses such as Hutchinson Whampoa in the communications and property businesses, the Swire Group (which controls Cathay Pacific Airlines and has shipping, insurance and property interests), and Jardines (which controls the Hong Kong Land Company, a large property group which in turn controls the land in the central business district).

Another major source of funds for development is the Royal Hong Kong Jockey Club. Of the very large sums of money which accrue to the Club from racing and lotteries the majority is of course returned to the punters. However, 19% is retained, 13% going to government as betting tax and 6% to the Club. This latter sum is used for charities and financing community development projects. This is at the discretion of the Stewards. For example, the University of Science and Technology, Kowloon Park, the Centre for the Performing Arts and the Ocean Park Oceanarium have all been partially or wholly funded by this body.

Selection of design consultants

No guidelines are published for selection of consultants and even the government will not comment on their selection criteria. However, the

Provisional Airport Authority (PAA) requires its consultants, as well as contractors, to operate a Quality Assurance System to ISO 9000. Certain other public bodies have a similiar requirement. The comments below are based on observations by local participants in the construction process.

Architects are usually appointed directly by the client without formal competition though competitions may be held in some cases. In the private sector track record is the most important criterion; personal contacts and recommendations play a part but price is less important. In the public sector architects are given jobs in rotation.

In the private sector engineers are sometimes appointed directly by the client and sometimes by the architect taking into account equally track record, recommendations and price. In the public sector selection is again on a rotation basis.

Surveying and cost consultants are mostly appointed by the client with some form of competition. Price is the dominant criterion in the private sector, usually a lump sum fee - with track record and recommendations important. In the public sector for surveyors, too, selection is on a rotation basis.

Other specialist consultants are appointed less formally usually on the basis of personal contact or recommendation.

All the main professional bodies publish non-mandatory fee scales and they are sometimes used for public work and for private work. However, it is not known how often they are used nor what discounts are negotiated. Fees generally are being driven down by competition. Until now the lowest fee usually secured the appointment, at least of quantity surveyors, but it is now becoming common to be advised of the lowest fee and asked to match it. Some clients are becoming aware that low fees are reducing the levels of service provided and a few discard the lowest bid if a better quality firm quotes a reasonably competitive fee. Recently, the government has been investigating the introduction of competitive fees for all consultants and negotiations on the basis for this are ongoing with the respective institutes.

Contractual arrangements

The majority of contracts are awarded on a lump sum basis as a result of competitive tenders received from a short list of firms that have been selected by the clients and his consultant. The Government has *Standard Conditions of Tender* which outline the procedures to be adopted for tendering. Generally prices are based upon measured bills of quantities though other methods may sometimes be used.

The most common form of contract used in Hong Kong for private clients is the *Agreement and Schedule of Conditions of Building Contract for use in Hong Kong, Private Edition, Second Edition 1976 (May 1979 Revision)*. There are two versions available; one is the 'with quantities' form which assumes the use of measured bills of quantities that are normally prepared by the quantity surveyor; the other is the 'without quantities' version. Both contracts are issued under the sanction of the Hong Kong Institute of Architects, the Royal Institution of Chartered Surveyors (HK Branch) and the Society of Builders. The RICS (HK Branch) also issue standard forms which are identical in all respects to those described above, with the exception of a slightly different presentation format.

It is normal for these contracts to be modified by a series of special conditions, introduced by the client or his advisors which serve to supplement the general conditions of contract to suit particular requirements of individual projects.

The Hong Kong Government issued in 1985 three separate forms of contract for use in the construction industry, these are:

- General Conditions of Contract for Building Works

- General Conditions of Contract for Civil Engineering Works

- General Conditions of Contract for Electrical and Mechanical Engineering Works

Piling and basement contracts sometimes may be let under FIDIC *(Federation Internationale des Ingenieurs-Conseils)* conditions. These Conditions provide for the contractor to design part of the permanent works if expressly stated. Sectional possession and phased completion are also possible with these conditions.

Contracts are generally let on a firm price basis, the client being keen to eliminate the cost uncertainty associated with fluctuations. For some public clients, such as the Architectural Services Department or the Housing Authority, fluctuation price tenders may be called for if the duration of the contract period exceeds a certain stipulated length of time. Fluctuations can be applied to either labour and materials, dependent upon the instructions of the clients and the conditions of contract in use. Other alternative contractual arrangements are available such as management contracting, design and build and construction management. However, none of these alternatives have found much popularity in Hong Kong with the perference still being for more traditional forms of contract.

Liability and insurance

Any departure by either party from the strict terms of the agreement is at least a technical breach of contract and therefore actionable at law with the remedy of damages. The courts, however, would in most cases seek to ensure that settlement procedures built into the agreement itself have been tried or were inapplicable to the circumstances which have arisen. For a contract executed under hand, claims for breach of contract may only be made within six years from the date of the breach. Where a contract is executed under seal, that period is extended to twelve years.

The contractor also has liability in common law to use proper skill and care in his operations. Such liability can arise between two parties who have no direct contractual connection. It is sufficient to demonstrate that one party owes a duty of care to the other party.

The consultants have a contractual relationship only with their Employer (the client) via their contract of service. Breach of their contract of service which affects the contractor may only be remedied by the contractor suing the Employer and the Employer in turn taking action against the consultants. It is common for consultants to carry professional indemnity insurance which offers the Employer protection. Consultants and contractors may also be subject to criminal sanctions or claims for breach of statutory duties if the parties fail to comply with the local legislative framework. A typical example would be a breach of *Health & Safety Statutes.*

All nominated subcontractors are required to be subjected to broadly the same terms as the main contractor and to indemnify the contractor against the same liabilities as the contractor himself bears. In the *Standard Hong Kong Form of Contract* there is no contractual relationship between the Employer and the nominated subcontractor. In response to this it is common for the Employer to enter into a collateral agreement with the nominated subcontractor in order to create a contractual link.

Insurances covering the construction works themselves, people/employees engaged in the works, and third party/public liability are addressed in the *Standard Forms of Contract.*

Development control and standards

The government owns all land and allocates its use in accordance with outline zoning plans. Planning laws are not too onerous but are currently being tightened. Planning and control of development is the responsibilty of the Town Planning Board and the Town Planning Office. The use of a site is designated by means of outline *Zoning Plans* and a plot ratio and height limit are set and then leases are auctioned. The shortage of land in Hong Kong means that typically more than 70% of the cost of a city centre development is land. Land auctions are an important source of revenue for the exchequer. Applications to modify the zoning of a particular site may be made to the Town Planning Board. If approved the case will be passed to the Land Department who will determine the conversion premium. The conversion premium is a payment made to the government calculated on the increased market value of a site based on its new designated use, often the premium can be significant.

Planning applications are made to the Building Ordinance Office and decisions are normally given within three months of submission. Typically there will be some negotiation with the Planners and a resubmission may be necessary. All projects must comply with the government regulations of which the main one is the *Building Ordinance (Cap 123 of the Laws of Hong Kong)*. Building control is exercised through the appropriate department of the Building Ordinance Office which approves development and building plans ensuring they comply with the relevant regulations. During construction the Architect is directly responsible to the Building Ordinance Office and "spot" site inspections are carried out.

Geotechnical conditions in Hong Kong are a major factor in any development. Piling or other major foundation work together with slope stabilization is the "norm". Calculations and construction details for these items are submitted to the *Geotechnical Control Office* for approval. An advisory service is also provided by the Geotechnical Information Unit.

There is also a move to raise building standards which is being supported by new Building Regulations. Typical of this was the introduction of *Energy Efficiency Regulations* in July 1995. This is seen as the first step in developing a comprehensive building energy code.

CONSTRUCTION COST DATA

Cost of labour

The figures opposite are typical of labour costs in Hong Kong as at the third quarter of 1995. The wage rate is the basis of an employee's income, while the cost of labour indicates the cost to a contractor of employing that employee. The difference between the two covers a variety of mandatory and voluntary contributions - a list of items which could be included is given in section 2.

	Wage rate (per day) HK$	Cost of labour (per day) HK$	Number of hours worked per year
Site operatives			
Bricklayer	690	759	2,400
Mason	675	743	2,400
Carpenter	678	746	2,400
Plumber	645	710	2,400
Electrician	542	596	2,400
Structural steel erector	727	800	2,400
Semi-skilled worker	571	628	2,400
Unskilled labourer	452	497	2,400
Equipment operator	542	596	2,400
	(per month)	*(per month)*	
Watchman/security	8,000	9,600	2,400
Site supervision			
General foreman	25,000	30,000	2,400
Trades foreman	15,000	18,000	2,400
Clerk of works	15,000	18,000	2,400
Contractors' personnel			
Site manager	30,000	36,000	2,400
Resident engineer	30,000	36,000	2,400
Resident surveyor	30,000	36,000	2,400
Junior engineer	13,000	16,000	2,400
Junior surveyor	13,000	16,000	2,400
Planner	20,000	24,000	2,400
Consultants' personnel			
Senior architect	48,000	58,000	1,900
Senior engineer	48,000	58,000	1,900
Senior surveyor	48,000	58,000	1,900
Qualified architect	36,000	43,000	1,900
Qualified engineer	36,000	43,000	1,900
Qualified surveyor	36,000	43,000	1,900

The figures that follow are the costs of main construction materials, delivered to site in the Hong Kong area, as incurred by contractors in the third quarter of 1995. These assume that the materials would be in quantities as required for a medium sized construction project and that the location of the works would be neither constrained nor remote.

	Unit	Cost HK$
Cement and aggregate		
Ordinary portland cement in 50kg bags	tonne	675
Coarse aggregates for concrete	m³	85
Fine aggregates for concrete	m³	75
Ready mixed concrete (Grade 40)	m³	550
Ready mixed concrete (Grade 10)	m³	400
Steel		
Mild steel reinforcement	tonne	2,900
High tensile steel reinforcement	tonne	2,850
Structural steel sections	tonne	5,000
Bricks and blocks		
Common bricks (225 x 105 x 70mm)	1,000	870
Good quality facing bricks (225 x 105 x 70mm)	1,000	1,100
Hollow concrete blocks (300 x 150 x 75mm)	1,000	4,000
Solid concrete blocks (300 x 150 x 75mm)	1,000	5,000
Precast concrete cladding units with exposed aggregate finish	m²	700
Timber and insulation		
Softwood sections for carpentry	m³	1,600
Softwood for joinery	m³	1,700
Hardwood for joinery	m³	1,891
Exterior quality plywood (19mm)	m²	76
Plywood for interior joinery (19mm)	m²	65
Softwood strip flooring (25mm)	m²	110
Chipboard sheet flooring (19mm)	m²	60
100mm thick quilt insulation	m²	45
100mm thick rigid slab insulation	m²	65
Softwood internal door complete with frames and ironmongery	each	2,500
Glass and ceramics		
Float glass (6mm)	m²	80
Sealed double glazing units (4 x 4m)	m²	500
Plaster and paint		
Good quality ceramic wall tiles (150 x 75mm)	m²	150
Plasterboard (12mm thick)	m²	110
Emulsion paint in 5 litre tins	litre	22
Gloss oil paint in 5 litre tins	litre	30

	Unit	Cost HK$
Tiles and paviors		
Clay floor tiles (250 x 250 x 20mm)	m²	100
Vinyl floor tiles (300 x 300 x 2.3mm)	m²	45
Precast concrete paving slabs (250 x 250 x 25mm)	m²	120
Clay roof tiles	1,000	4,000
Precast concrete roof tiles (300 x 300 x 25mm)	1,000	5,000
Drainage		
WC suite complete	each	1,400
Lavatory basin complete	each	1,200
150mm diameter cast iron drain pipes	m	120

Unit rates

The descriptions below are generally shortened versions of standard descriptions listed in full in section 4. Where an item has a two digit reference number (e.g. 05 or 33), this relates to the full description against that number in section 4. Where an item has an alphabetic suffix (e.g. 12A or 34B) this indicates that the standard description has been modified. Where a modification is major the complete modified description is included here and the standard description should be ignored; where a modification is minor (e.g. the insertion of a named hardwood) the shortened description has been modified here but, in general, the full description in section 4 prevails.

The unit rates below are for main work items on a typical construction project in Hong Kong in the third quarter of 1995.The rates include all necessary labour, materials and equipment. Allowances to cover preliminary and general items and contractor's overheads and profit have been added to the rates.

		Unit	Rate HK$
	Excavation		
01	Mechanical excavation of foundation trenches	m³	140
02	Hardcore filling making up levels	m²	50
03	Earthwork support	m²	55
	Concrete work		
04	Plain insitu concrete in strip foundations in trenches	m³	700
05	Reinforced insitu concrete in beds	m³	760
06	Reinforced insitu concrete in walls	m³	760
07	Reinforced insitu concrete in suspended floors or roof slabs	m³	810
08	Reinforced insitu concrete in columns	m³	810
09	Reinforced insitu concrete in isolated beams	m³	810
10	Precast concrete slab	m²	440

	Unit	Rate HK$

Formwork

		Unit	Rate HK$
11	Softwood formwork to concrete walls	m²	106
12	Softwood formwork to concrete columns	m²	160
13	Softwood formwork to horizontal soffits of slabs	m²	120

Reinforcement

14	Reinforcement in concrete walls	tonne	5,000
15	Reinforcement in suspended concrete slabs	tonne	5,000
16	Fabric reinforcement in concrete beds	m²	50

Steelwork

17	Fabricate, supply and erect steel framed structure	tonne	19,000
18	Framed structural steelwork in universal joist sections	tonne	19,000
19	Structural steelwork lattice roof trusses	tonne	20,000

Brickwork and blockwork

20	Precast lightweight aggregate hollow concrete block walls	m²	170
21	Solid (perforated) concrete blocks	m²	170
22	Sand lime bricks	m²	151
23	Facing bricks	m²	180

Roofing

24	Concrete interlocking roof tiles 430 x 380mm	m²	450
25	Plain clay roof tiles 260 x 160mm	m²	400
27	Sawn softwood roof boarding	m²	270
28	Particle board roof coverings	m²	240
29	3 layers glass-fibre based bitumen felt roof covering	m²	195
30	Bitumen based mastic asphalt roof covering	m²	170
31	Glass-fibre mat roof insulation 160mm thick	m²	90
32	Rigid sheet loadbearing roof insulation 75mm thick	m²	130
33	Troughed galvanized steel roof cladding	m²	300

Woodwork and metalwork

34	Preservative treated sawn softwood 50 x 100mm	m	70
35	Preservative treated sawn softwood 50 x 150mm	m	85
36	Single glazed casement window in hardwood, 650 x 900mm	each	1,400
37	Two panel glazed door in hardwood, size 850 x 2000mm	each	4,300
38	Solid core half hour fire resisting hardwood internal flush door, size 800 x 2000mm	each	3,500
39	Aluminium double glazed window, size 1200 x 1200mm	each	2,600
40	Aluminium double glazed door, size 850 x 2100mm	each	5,700
41	Hardwood skirtings	m	60

		Units	*Rate HK$*
Plumbing			
42	UPVC half round eaves gutter	m	138
43	UPVC rainwater pipes	m	195
44	Light gauge copper cold water tubing	m	125
45	High pressure plastic pipes for cold water supply	m	42
46	Low pressure plastic pipes for cold water distribution	m	95
47	UPVC soil and vent pipes	m	195
48	White vitreous china WC suite	each	1,690
49	White vitreous china lavatory basin	each	1,580
50	Glazed fireclay shower tray	each	1,580
51	Stainless steel single bowl sink and double drainer	each	1,900
Electrical work			
52	PVC insulated and copper sheathed cable	m	45
53	13 amp unswitched socket outlet	each	190
54	Flush mounted 20 amp, 1 way light switch	each	320
Finishings			
55	2 coats gypsum based plaster on brick walls	m²	75
56	White glazed tiles on plaster walls	m²	150
57	Red clay quarry tiles on concrete floors	m²	270
58	Cement and sand screed to concrete floors	m²	50
59	Thermoplastic floor tiles on screed	m²	117
60	Mineral fibre tiles on concealed suspension system	m²	260
Glazing			
61	Glazing to wood	m²	130
Painting			
62	Emulsion on plaster walls	m²	25
63	Oil paint on timber	m²	50

Approximate estimating

The building costs per unit area given below are averages incurred by building clients for typical buildings in the Hong Kong area as at the third quarter of 1995. They are based upon the total floor area of all storeys, measured between external walls and without deduction for internal walls.

Approximate estimating costs generally include mechanical and electrical installations but exclude furniture, loose or special equipment, and external works; they also exclude fees for professional services. The costs shown are for specifications and standards appropriate to Hong Kong and this should be borne in mind when attempting comparisons with similarly described building types in other countries. A discussion of this issue is included in section 2. Comparative data for countries covered in this publication, including construction cost data, is presented in Part Three.

Approximate estimating costs must be treated with caution; they cannot provide more than a rough guide to the probable cost of building.

	Cost m² HK$	Cost ft² HK$
Industrial buildings		
Factories for letting	4,600	427
Factories for owner occupation (light industrial use)	5,400	502
Factories for owner occupation (heavy industrial use)	6,200	576
Factory/office (high-tech) for letting (shell and core only)	5,800	539
Factory/office (high-tech) for letting (ground floor shell, first floor offices)	6,300	585
Factory/office (high tech) for owner occupation (controlled environment, fully finished)	7,500	697
High tech laboratory workshop centres (air conditioned)	8,000	743
Warehouses, low bay (6 to 8m high) for letting (no heating)	5,000	464
Warehouses, low bay for owner occupation	5,500	511
Warehouses, high bay for owner occupation	6,000	557
Cold stores/refrigerated stores	10,000	929
Administrative and commercial buildings		
Civic offices, fully air conditioned	8,700	808
Offices for letting, 5 to 10 storeys, air conditioned	8,000	743
Offices for letting, high rise, air conditioned	8,500	790
Offices for owner occupation high rise, air conditioned	11,000	1,022
Prestige/headquarters office, 5 to 10 storeys, air conditioned	11,500	1,068
Prestige/headquarters office, high rise, air conditioned	12,500	1,161
Health and education buildings		
General hospitals (1000 beds)	11,000	1,022
Private hospitals (500 beds)	12,500	1,161
Health centres	7,500	697
Nursery schools	5,500	511
Primary/junior schools	4,600	427
Secondary/middle schools	5,000	464
University (arts) buildings	8,000	743
University (science) buildings	8,500	790
Management training centres	8,000	743

	Cost m² HK$	Cost ft² HK$
Recreation and arts buildings		
Theatres (over 500 seats) including seating and stage equipment	12,500	1,161
Theatres (less than 500 seats) including seating and stage equipment	13,500	1,254
Concert halls including seating and stage equipment	13,000	1,208
Swimming pools (international standard) including changing and social facilities (outdoor)	each	4,300,000
Swimming pools (schools standard) including changing facilities (outdoor)	each	2,000,000
National museums including full air conditioning and standby generator	15,000	1,393
Local museums including air conditioning	10,000	929
City centre/central libraries	9,800	910
Branch/local libraries	9,800	910
Residential buildings		
Private/mass market single family housing 2 storey detached/semidetached (multiple units)	7,200	669
Purpose designed single family housing 2 storey detached (single unit)	9,200	855
Social/economic apartment housing, high rise (with lifts)	4,000	372
Private sector apartment building (standard specification)	5,700	530
Private sector apartment buildings (luxury)	9,000	836
Student/nurses halls of residence	6,000	557
Homes for the elderly (shared accommodation)	7,500	697
Homes for the elderly (self contained with shared communal facilities)	8,000	743
Hotel, 5 star, city centre	13,600	1,263
Hotel, 3 star, city/provincial	11,500	1,068

EXCHANGE RATES AND INFLATION

The combined effect of exchange rates and inflation on prices within a country and price comparisons between countries is discussed in section 2.

Exchange rates

The graph below plots the movement of the Hong Kong dollar against sterling, US dollar and 100 Japanese yen since 1985. The values used for the graph are quarterly and the method of calculating these is described and general guidance on the interpretation of the graph provided in section 2. The average exchange rate in the third quarter of 1995 was HK$12.27 to the pound sterling and HK$7.74 to US dollar and HK$8.44 to 100 Japanese yen.

THE HONG KONG DOLLAR AGAINST STERLING, US DOLLAR AND JAPANESE YEN

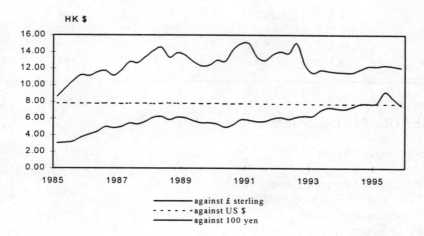

Price inflation

The table below presents consumer price, building price and tender price inflation in Hong Kong since 1985. The year on year rate of increase in the consumer price index has been easing since April 1991 and this is expected to continue largely in line with expected world trends and helped by the easing of some previous capacity constraints in the economy. Building price and tender price inflation are similar to each other and significantly higher than that for consumer prices.

CONSUMER PRICE, BUILDING PRICE AND TENDER PRICE INFLATION

Year	Consumer price inflation		Building price index		Tender price index	
------	average index	average change %	average index	average change %	average index	average change %
1985	71.6	3.6	100	-	100	2.7
1986	74.1	3.5	107	7	112	12
1987	78.4	5.8	126	18	121	8
1988	84.5	7.8	154	22	151	25
1989	93.2	10.3	177	15	162	7
1990	102.7	10.2	194	10	170	5
1991	114.2	11.2	210	8	168	-1
1992	125.2	9.6	225	7	156	-7
1993	136.2	8.8	253	12	159	2
1994	148.2	8.8	270	7	181	14

USEFUL ADDRESSES

Public organizations

Architectural Services Department
   34/F and 35/F, Queensway
   Government Offices
   66 Queensway
   Hong Kong
   Tel : 2867 3628
   Fax : 2869 0289

Buildings Department
　5/F-12/F, Murray Building
　Garden Road
　Hong Kong
　Tel : 2840 0451
　Fax : 2848 2327

Census and Statistics Department
　19/F,Wanchai Tower
　12 Harbour Road
　Wanchai
　Hong Kong
　Tel: 2582 5073
　Fax : 2802 1101

Civil Engineering Department
　101 Princess Margaret Road
　Ho Man Tin
　Kowloon
　Hong Kong
　Tel : 2762 5111
　Fax : 2714 0140

Electrical and Mechanical Services Department
　98 Caroline Hill Road
　Hong Kong
　Tel : 2882 8011
　Fax : 2890 7493

Environmental Protection Department
　28/F, Southern Centre
　130 Hennessy Road
　Wanchai
　Hong Kong
　Tel : 2835 1018
　Fax : 2838 2155

Highways Department
　5/F, Ho Man Tin Government Offices
　88 Chung Hau Street
　Ho Man Tin
　Kowloon
　Tel : 2762 3332
　Fax : 2714 5216

Hong Kong Housing Authority
  33 Fat Kwong Street
  Ho Man Tin
  Kowloon
  Hong Kong
  Tel : 2714 5119
  Fax : 2761 3649

Land Department
  4/F, Murray Building
  Garden Road
  Hong Kong
  Tel : 2848 2198
  Fax : 2868 4707

Land Development Corporation
  31/F, Great Eagle Centre
  23 Harbour Road
  Wanchai
  Hong Kong
  Tel: 2588 2222
  Fax : 2827 0175

Planning, Environment & Lands Branch
  20/F, Murray Building
  Garden Road
  Hong Kong
  Tel : 2848 2111
  Fax : 2845 3489

Planning Department
  16/F, Murray Building
  Garden Road
  Hong Kong
  Tel : 2848 2402
  Fax : 2877 0389

Provisional Airport Authority
  25/F, Central Plaza
  18 Harbour Road
  Wanchai
  Hong Kong
  Tel : 2824 7111
  Fax : 2824 0717

Territory Development Department
  13/F, Leighton Centre
  77 Leighton Road
  Hong Kong
  Tel : 2882 7170
  Fax : 2577 3562

Water Supplies Department
  1/F, Immigration Tower
  7 Gloucester Road
  Wanchai
  Hong Kong
  Tel: 2829 4500
  Fax : 2824 2455

Work Branch
  19/F, Murray Building
  Garden Road
  Hong Kong
  Tel : 2848 2111
  Fax : 2523 5327

Trade and professional associations

Chamber of Commerce
  3/F, 4 Shung Tak Street
  Tai Po
  New Territories
  Kowloon
  Hong Kong
  Tel : 2656 1288

Real Estate Developers Association of Hong Kong
  1403, World-Wide House
  19 Des Voeux Road Central
  Hong Kong
  Tel : 2826 0111
  Fax : 28452521

The Hong Kong Contractors' Association Ltd
    3/F, 182 Hennessy Road
    Wanchai
    Hong Kong
    Tel: 2572 4414
    Fax : 2572 7104

The Hong Kong Institute of Architects
    15/F, Success Commercial Building
    245-251 Hennessy Road
    Wanchai
    Hong Kong
    Tel: 2511 6323
    Fax : 2519 6011

The Hong Kong Institute of Engineers
    9/F, Island Centre
    No 1 Great George Street
    Hong Kong
    Tel: 2895 4446
    Fax : 2577 7791

The Hong Kong Institute of Surveyors
    1934 Swire House
    Chater Road Central
    Hong Kong
    Tel: 2526 3679
    Fax : 2868 4612

The Society of Builders, Hong Kong
    Room 801, On Lok Yuen Building
    25 Des Voeux Road Central
    Hong Kong
    Tel : 2523 2081
    Fax : 2845 4749

DAVIS LANGDON & SEAH INDONESIA PT

The strategic and integrated management of cost, time and quality - the client "risk" areas of a contract - are essential functions, which are necessary to ensure the satisfactory planning, procurement, execution and operation of construction projects.

We specialise in the financial management of construction projects and their risk areas, from project inception to completion and we concentrate on:

- being positive and creative in our advice, rather than simply reactive;

- providing value for money via efficient management, rather than on superficial cost monitoring;

- giving advice that is matched to the client's requirements, rather than imposing standard or traditional solutions;

- paying attention to the life-cycle costs of constructing and occupying a building, rather than to the initial capital cost only.

Our aim is to provide our clients with risk assurance, cost control and value for money, via effective advice, cost planning and management.

DAVIS LANGDON & SEAH INDONESIA PT
Wisma Metropolitan 1, Level 13
Jalan Jendral Sudirman Kav.29
PO Box 3139/Jkt
Jakarta 10001
Indonesia
Tel : (62-21) 5254745
Fax : (62-21) 5254764

DAVIS LANGDON & SEAH INTERNATIONAL

Indonesia

KEY DATA

Population
Population	187.2mn
Urban population	33%
Population under 15	35%
Population 65 and over	3%
Average annual growth rate (1980 to 1993)	1.7%

Geography
Land area	1,905,000 km²
Agricultural area	18%
Capital city	Jakarta
Population of capital city	9.2mn

Economy
Monetary unit	Indonesian Rupiah (Rp)
Exchange rate (average third quarter 1995) to:	
the pound sterling	Rp 3,556
the US dollar	Rp 2,243
the yen x 100	Rp 2,446
Average annual inflation (1980 to 1993)	8.5%
Inflation rate (1994)	9.6%
Gross Domestic Product (GDP) at market prices	Rp 329,800bn
GDP per capita	Rp 1,761,750
Average annual real change in GDP (1980 to 1993)	5.8%
Private consumption as a proportion of GDP	60%
General government consumption as a proportion of GDP	10%
Gross domestic investment as a proportion of GDP	28%
Central government expenditure as a proportion of Gross National Product	19%

Construction
Gross value of construction output *	Rp 49,470bn
Net value of construction output	Rp 19,790bn
Net value of construction output as a proportion of GDP	6.0%
Cement production (1992)	17mn tonnes

All data relate to 1993 unless otherwise indicated

* Author's estimate

THE CONSTRUCTION INDUSTRY

Construction output

The gross value of construction output in 1993 is estimated to be 15% of GDP or Rp49,470 billion, equivalent to US$23.9 billion. The net value of construction output in 1993 was Rp19,790 billion, equivalent to US$9.6 billion or 6.0% of GDP. The net value of construction output in 1994 was Rp27,550 billion, equivalent to US$12.7 billion, or 7.3% of GDP.

The breakdown of output in 1993 was approximately as shown in the table below.

CONSTRUCTION OUTPUT BY TYPE OF WORK, 1993

Type of work	Proportion of total output %
Building	42
Residential	6
Non-residential	32
Mixed type of building	<1
Specialist work related mainly to building	4
Civil Engineering	58
Water supply, gas supply and network	<1
Electrical supply and network	3
Construction or improvement of roads/bridges	33
Irrigation and drainage	12
Airports, harbours, bus stations, etc.	2
Others	6
Electrical power plant and telecommunications	<1
Total	100

Source: Government statistics

Building work accounts for 42% of total construction output, with non-residential building contributing the greatest share. Civil engineering work accounts for 58% of total construction output and the construction or improvement of roads and bridges is a significant part of it.

CONSTRUCTION OUTPUT AND POPULATION BY REGIONS, 1993

Province	Proportion of population %	Proportion of construction output %	Rank by population	Rank by construction output
D.I. Aceh	2.0	1.9	10	11
North Sumatera	5.7	3.9	4	5
West Sumatera	2.2	2.2	9	9
Riau (include Batam)	1.9	1.8	11	12
Jambi	1.2	1.6	19	15
South Sumatera	3.6	2.3	7	8
Bengkulu	0.7	0.6	26	27
Lampung	3.4	2.0	8	10
DKI Jakarta	4.7	35.1	5	1
West Java	20.0	12.5	1	2
Central Java	15.5	5.4	3	4
D.I. Yogyakarta	1.5	1.6	15	16
East Java	17.7	9.4	2	3
Bali	1.5	1.3	16	19
West Nusa Tenggara	1.9	1.0	12	24
East Nusa Tenggara	1.8	1.4	14	17
East Timor	0.4	0.9	27	25
West Kalimantan	1.8	1.3	13	18
Central Kalimantan	0.8	0.7	24	26
South Kalimantan	1.5	1.1	17	22
East Kalimantan	1.1	2.3	20	7
North Sulawesi	1.4	1.6	18	14
Central Sulawesi	1.0	1.3	22	20
South Sulawesi	3.8	3.0	6	6
South East Sulawesi	0.8	1.2	25	21
Maluku	1.1	1.1	21	23
Irian Jaya	1.0	1.6	23	13
Total	100	100	-	-

Source: Building/Construction Statistics - Central Bureau of Statistics

The capital city, Jakarta, has the greatest share of construction activity at 35% which is a substantially greater percentage than its share of the national population. West Java, Central Java and East Java, on the other hand, have construction outputs which are significantly lower than their respective shares of the national population.

The government finances a low cost housing programme through the national Urban Development Corporation, Perum Perumnas.

NUMBER OF HOUSING UNITS BUILT BY PERUM PERUMNAS

Type of unit	1989/90	1990/91	1991/92	1992/93
Basic ('core') houses	2,971	3,080	3,424	7,790
Other houses	1,526	3,508	3,741	4,588
Apartments	0	0	1,472	0
Total	4,497	6,588	8,637	12,378

Characteristics and structure of the industry

As construction activity has increased, so has the development of the domestic construction industry. It is estimated that there are now some 50,000 construction firms of all sizes. Large scale and aid-financed infrastructure projects continue to be carried out by international construction companies though usually with local participation. All government housing schemes and smaller projects are, however, undertaken by local contractors.

The construction process is managed in a number of ways. The traditional system with a main contractor is still the most usual but design and build, construction management, build, operate and transfer (BOT) and turnkey are also now important. Management contracting is not much used.

Quantity surveying practices have had a presence in Indonesia for more than seventeen years, primarily serving the private construction sector plus the oil and gas industries. There are also property and land surveying practices. All these disciplines are, however, of limited importance in the public sector. The traditional quantity surveying role is evolving into one of management, co-ordination, administration and general financial advice.

Clients and finance

The client for almost all public works is the government (central and regional), but in the last five years private companies have started to be involved to a limited extent in funding public works such as toll roads and electricity generation.

Construction work in the private sector is dominated by government backed or national contractors; it is common for large projects to involve foreign joint venture partners or consortia.

The government obtains finance from various external sources as well as the national development budget, the Asian Development Bank, the World Bank and other multilateral and bilateral aid agencies. Private sector financing is obtained through local and foreign financial institutions including state and private banks, pension funds and private investors.

Selection of design consultants

A decree of the President (No. 29 of 1984) states that a pre-qualification system should be followed in tendering for consultancy work on government projects. The procedure is set out in the decree together with a standard tender procedure in a memorandum from the Minister of Public Works.

Competition is important, especially on very large projects. In the private sector, the procedure is more flexible, but still follows the basic government rules. In-house design organizations are uncommon in Indonesia.

Housing consultancy contracts are generally awarded directly by the owner or the owner's contractor without a formal bidding process, but other building projects generally follow standard construction procedures for bidding and appointment. Most civil engineering projects originate from government and they too are usually awarded following the same standard procedures. There are no known recommended or mandatory published fee scales.

Contractual arrangements

Tenderers are selected subject to a pre-qualification process both in the public and in the private sector. In the public sector the tender is usually on a lump sum basis but in the private sector a variety of methods are used. Bills of quantities, either firm or approximate, are usually provided and contracts are based on internationally recognized forms adapted for Indonesian conditions. Bank guarantees are normally required and cash retention is usually preferred to bonds. Advance payments are sometimes made. Variations are authorized through contract instructions and change orders with consequent adjustment in the contract sum.

Liability and insurance

Insurance is compulsory for all parties. The CAR (Contractors' All Risks and Public Liability) insurance is normally taken out by the owner or the contractor in joint names for the full project value and is valid until practical completion of the project (including the maintenance period). By law, contractors must insure their workers. Insurance companies are common in Indonesia but risks are normally reinsured offshore. Insurance claims are usually settled amicably.

Development control and standards

The Directorate of Regional and City Planning produces general *Master Plans* and the regional government ensures implementation by the land user. Detailed *Master Plans* should normally be used as one of the references when seeking planning permission. If all other requirements are fulfilled, full or partial building permission takes about one month.

At the planning stage, architectural, structural and building services reviews are carried out by the appropriate authority to check that the design is in compliance with laws, rules and standing instructions relating to health and safety.

Before buildings can obtain an *Occupation Permit*, approval from the Fire Prevention Authority must be obtained.

The national standard for building materials/products is *Standard Industrial Indonesia (SII) - Indonesian Standard for Industry*. Foreign standards such as *ASTM, BS, DIN, SISIR*, and *JIS* are also used extensively.

CONSTRUCTION COST DATA

Cost of labour

The figures below are typical of labour costs in the Jakarta area as at the third quarter of 1995. The wage rate is the basis of an employee's income, while the cost of labour indicates the cost to a contractor of employing that employee. The difference between the two covers a variety of mandatory and voluntary contributions - a list of items which could be included is given in section 2.

	Wage rate (per hour) Rp	Cost of labour (per day) Rp	Number of hours worked per year
Site operatives			
Mason/bricklayer	1,125	9,000	2,208
Carpenter	1,250	10,000	2,208
Plumber	1,325	10,500	2,208

	Wage rate (per hour) Rp	Cost of labour (per day) Rp	Number of hours worked per year
Electrician	1,325	10,500	2,208
Structural steel erector	1,025	8,200	2,208
HVAC installer	1,325	10,500	2,208
Semi-skilled worker	785	6,250	2,208
Unskilled labourer	625	5,000	2,208
Equipment operator	1,000	8,000	2,208
Watchman/security	875	7,000	2,208
Site supervision			
General foreman	1,250	10,000	2,208
Trades foreman	1,185	9,500	2,208

Cost of materials

The figures that follow are the costs of main construction materials, delivered to site in the Jakarta area, as incurred by contractors in the third quarter of 1995. These assume that the materials would be in quantities as required for a medium sized construction project and that the location of the works would be neither constrained nor remote.

All the costs in this section exclude value added tax (VAT - see below).

	Unit	Cost Rp
Cement and aggregate		
Ordinary portland cement in 40kg bags	tonne	200,000
Coarse aggregates for concrete	m^3	31,500
Fine aggregates for concrete	m^3	33,500
Ready mixed concrete (K-350) slump 10	m^3	170,000
Ready mixed concrete (K-225) slump 12	m^3	145,000
Steel		
Mild steel reinforcement	tonne	835,000
High tensile steel reinforcement	tonne	875,000
Structural steel sections	tonne	1,600,000
Bricks and blocks		
Common bricks (220 x 100 x 50mm)	1,000	100,000
Hollow concrete blocks (400 x 200 x 100mm)	1,000	380,000
Solid concrete blocks (380 x 180 x 100mm)	1,000	575,000
Precast concrete cladding units with exposed aggregate finish	m^2	138,000

	Unit	Cost Rp
Timber and insulation		
Softwood sections for carpentry	m³	360,000
Softwood for joinery (Kamper)	m³	1,200,000
Hardwood for joinery (Teak)	m³	3,900,000
Exterior quality plywood (18mm)	m²	25,000
Plywood for interior joinery (18mm)	m²	23,000
100mm thick quilt insulation	m²	31,000
100mm thick rigid slab insulation	m²	24,000
Softwood internal door complete with frames and ironmongery	each	450,000
Glass and ceramics		
Float glass (8mm)	m²	42,000
Good quality ceramic wall tiles (200 x 100mm)	m²	26,000
Plaster and paint		
Plasterboard (9mm thick)	m²	14,900
Emulsion paint in 5 litre tins	litre	7,000
Gloss oil paint in 5 litre tins	litre	9,100
Tiles and paviors		
Clay floor tiles (150 x 150 x 10mm)	m²	7,500
Vinyl floor tiles (300 x 300 x 2mm)	m²	10,000
Precast concrete paving slabs (600 x 600 x 50mm)	m²	9,000
Clay roof tiles	1,000	400,000
Precast concrete roof tiles	1,000	1,500,000
Drainage		
WC suite complete	each	420,000
Lavatory basin complete	each	310,000
100mm diameter UPVC drain pipes	m	13,500

Unit rates

The descriptions on the next page are generally shortened versions of standard descriptions listed in full in section 4. Where an item has a two digit reference number (e.g. 05 or 33), this relates to the full description against that number in section 4. Where an item has an alphabetic suffix (e.g. 12A or 34B) this indicates that the standard description has been modified. Where a modification is major the complete modified description is included here and the standard description should be ignored; where a modification is minor (e.g. the insertion of a named hardwood) the shortened description has been modified here but, in general, the full description in section 4 prevails.

The unit rates below are for main work items on a typical construction project in the Jakarta area in the third quarter of 1995. The rates include all necessary labour, materials and equipment. Allowances have been included to cover contractors' overheads and profit and preliminary and general items.

All the rates in this section exclude value added tax (VAT - see below).

		Unit	Rate Rp
Excavation			
01	Mechanical excavation of foundation trenches	m³	5,286
02	Hardcore filling making up levels	m²	7,929
Concrete work			
04	Plain insitu concrete in strip foundations in trenches	m³	206,618
05	Reinforced insitu concrete in beds	m³	214,760
06	Reinforced insitu concrete in walls	m³	221,604
07	Reinforced insitu concrete in suspended floors or roof slabs	m³	218,300
08	Reinforced insitu concrete in columns	m³	219,834
09	Reinforced insitu concrete in isolated beams	m³	230,100
10	Precast concrete slabs	m³	247,210
Formwork			
11	Softwood formwork to concrete walls	m²	16,520
12	Softwood or metal formwork to concrete columns	m²	22,420
13	Softwood or metal formwork to horizontal soffits of slabs	m²	23,836
Reinforcement			
14	Reinforcement in concrete walls	tonne	1,357,000
15	Reinforcement in suspended concrete slabs	tonne	1,357,000
16	Fabric reinforcement in concrete beds	m²	17,700
Steelwork			
17	Fabricate, supply and erect steel framed structure	tonne	3,304,000
18	Framed structural steelwork in universal joist sections	tonne	3,953,000
19	Structural steelwork lattice roof trusses	tonne	3,776,000
Brickwork and blockwork			
21	Solid (perforated) concrete blocks	m²	11,800

		Unit	*Rate Rp*
Roofing			
24	Concrete interlocking roof tiles 430 x 380mm	m²	41,630
25	Plain clay roof tiles 260 x 160mm	m²	34,692
26	Fibre cement roof slates 600 x 300mm	m²	62,446
33	Troughed galvanized steel roof cladding	m²	38,905
Woodwork and metalwork			
34	Preservative treated sawn softwood 50 x 100mm	m	5,900
35	Preservative treated sawn softwood 50 x 150mm	m	6,785
36	Single glazed casement window in Kamper hardwood, size 650 x 900mm	each	141,600
37	Two panel glazed door in Kamper hardwood, size 850 x 2000mm	each	649,000
38	Solid core half hour fire resisting hardwood internal flush door, size 800 x 2000mm	each	914,500
39	Aluminium double glazed window, size 1200 x 1200mm	each	678,500
40	Aluminium double glazed door, size 850 x 2100mm	each	841,104
41	Hardwood skirtings	m	3,540
Plumbing			
42	UPVC half round eaves gutter	m	34,987
43	UPVC rainwater pipes	m	21,830
44	Light gauge copper cold water tubing	m	18,880
46	Low pressure plastic pipes for cold water distribution	m	5,900
47	UPVC soil and vent pipes	m	23,305
48	White vitreous china WC suite	each	601,800
49	White vitreous china lavatory basin	each	460,200
50	Glazed fireclay shower tray	each	472,000
51	Stainless steel single bowl sink and double drainer	each	354,000
Electrical work			
52	PVC insulated and copper sheathed cable	m	1,416
53	13 amp unswitched socket outlet	each	7,788
54	Flush mounted 20 amp, 1 way light switch	each	7,080
Finishings			
55	2 coats gypsum based plaster on brick walls	m²	4,838
56	White glazed tiles on plaster walls	m²	28,320
57	Red clay quarry tiles on concrete floors	m²	17,700
58	Cement and sand screed to concrete floors	m²	7,316
59	Thermoplastic floor tiles on screed	m²	14,160
60	Mineral fibre tiles on concealed suspension system	m²	41,890

	Unit	Rate Rp
Glazing		
61 Glazing to wood	m²	26,550
Painting		
62 Emulsion on plaster walls	m²	5,310
63 Oil paint on timber	m²	7,080

Approximate estimating

The building costs per unit area given below are expressed in US$ and are averages incurred by building clients for typical buildings in the Jakarta area as at the third quarter of 1995. They are based upon the total floor area of all storeys, measured between external walls and without deduction for internal walls.

Approximate estimating costs generally include mechanical and electrical installations but exclude furniture, loose or special equipment, and external works; they also exclude fees for professional services. The costs shown are for specifications and standards appropriate to Indonesia and this should be borne in mind when attempting comparisons with similarly described building types in other countries. A discussion of this issue is included in section 2. Comparative data for countries covered in this publication including construction cost data is presented in Part Three.

Approximate estimating costs must be treated with caution; they cannot provide more than a rough guide to the probable cost of building.

All the rates in this section exclude value added tax (VAT - see below).

	Cost m² US$	Cost ft² US$
Industrial buildings		
Factories for letting	250	23
Factories for owner occupation (light industrial use)	290	27
Factories for owner occupation (heavy industrial use)	380	35
Factory/office (high-tech) for letting (shell and core only)	280	26
Factory/office (high-tech) for letting (ground floor shell, first floor offices)	350	32
Factory/office (high tech) for owner occupation (controlled environment, fully finished)	500	46
High tech laboratory workshop centres (air conditioned)	500	46
Warehouses, low bay (6 to 8m high) for letting (no AC)	250	23
Warehouses, low bay for owner occupation (including AC)	350	32

	Cost m² US$	Cost ft² US$
Warehouses, high bay for owner occupation (including AC)	425	39
Cold stores/refrigerated stores	450	41

Administrative and commercial buildings

	Cost m² US$	Cost ft² US$
Civic offices, non air conditioned	360	33
Civic offices, fully air conditioned	450	41
Offices for letting, 5 to 10 storeys, air conditioned	600	55
Offices for letting, high rise, air conditioned	675	62
Offices for owner occupation high rise, air conditioned	450	41
Prestige/headquarters office, 5 to 10 storeys, air conditioned	675	62
Prestige/headquarters office, high rise, air conditioned	875	81

Residential buildings

	Cost m² US$	Cost ft² US$
Purpose designed single family housing 2 storey detached (single unit)	350	32
Social/economic apartment housing, low rise (no lifts)	450	41
Social/economic apartment housing, high rise (with lifts)	550	51
Private sector apartment building (standard specification)	625	58
Private sector apartment buildings (luxury)	725	67
Hotel, 5 star, city centre	1,350	129
Hotel, 3 star, city/provincial	975	90
Motel	800	74
Golf courses	350,000	per hole
Golf clubhouse	1,100	101

Regional variations

The approximate estimating costs are based on projects in Jakarta. Costs elsewhere can vary by up to plus or minus 20%.

Value added tax (VAT)

The standard rate of value added tax (VAT) is currently 10%, chargeable on general building work.

EXCHANGE RATES

The graph below plots the movement of the Indonesian rupiah against sterling, US dollar and 100 Japanese yen since 1985. The values used for the graph are quarterly and the method of calculating these is described and general guidance on the interpretation of the graph provided in section 2. The average exchange rate for the third quarter of 1995 was Rp3,556 to pound sterling, Rp2,243 to US dollar and Rp2,446 to 100 Japanese yen.

THE INDONESIAN RUPIAH AGAINST STERLING, US DOLLAR AND JAPANESE YEN

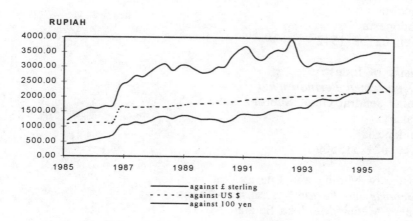

USEFUL ADDRESSES

Public organizations

Agency of Assessment and Application of Technology
  Badan Pengkajian dan Penerapan Teknologi (BPPT)
  Jalan M.H. Thamrin 8
  Jakarta
  Indonesia
  Tel: 021 3904533/3904537 - 42

Direktorat Penyelidikan Masalah Bangunan
Direcktorat Jendral Cipta Karya
Departemen Pekerjaan Umum
Directorate for Investigation into Building Problems
Directorate General Cipta Karya
Ministry of Public Works
    Jalan Tamansari 84, P.O. Box 15, Bandung
    Jawa Barat
    Indonesia
    022 81082/81083

Indonesian Institute of Science
    Lembaga Ilmu Pengetahuan Indonesia (LIPI)
    Jalan Jendral Gatot Subroto 10
    Jakarta
    Indonesia
    Tel: 021 511542

Ministry of Industry
    Departemen Perindustrian
    Jalan Jendral Gatot Subroto Kav. 52-53
    Jakarta
    Indonesia
    Tel: 021 515509

Ministry of Mining and Energy
    Departemen Pertambangan dan Energi
    Jalan Medan Merdeka Selatan No 18
    Jakarta
    Indonesia
    Tel: 021 360232

Ministry of Public Works
    Departemen Pekerjaan Umum
    Jalan Pattimura 20,
    Jakarta
    Indonesia
    Tel: 021 7395588/710311

The Ministry of Public Works is subdivided into:

- *Direktorat Binamarga*
- a directorate covering roads and bridges and construction work
- *Direktorat Cipta Karya*
- a directorate covering general building works
- *Direktorat Pengairan*
- a directorate covering hydrologic construction works
- *Direktorat Air Bersih*
- a directorate covering sanitation works

Ministry of Tourism, Post and Telecommunication
Departemen Pariwisata, Pos dan Telekomunikasi
Jalan Kebon Sirih 36
Jakarta
Indonesia
Tel: 021 366705

National Development Planning Agency
Badan Perencana Pembangunan Nasional (BAPPENAS)
Jalan Taman Suropati 2
Jakarta
Indonesia
Tel: 021 366207

National Statistic Bureau
Biro Pusat Statistik
Jalan Dr Sutomo 8
Jakarta
Indonesia
Tel: 021 3810291/3810295

Regional Goverment Construction Ministries:

- *Kantor Wilayah Pekerjaan Umum*
  Public Works; Ministry Regional Offices under coordination of
  Central Government
- *Dinas Pekerjaan Umum*
  Public Works Provincial Offices under coordination of Regional
  Government

Science and Technology Research Centre
Pusat Penelitian Ilmu Pengetahuan dan Teknologi (PUSPITEK)
Desa Setu Kecamatan Serpong, Tangerang
Jawa Barat
Indonesia
Tel: 021 7560541/7560562

State Ministry of Public Housing
Menteri Negara Perumahan Rakyat
Jalan Kebon Sirih 31
Jakarta
Indonesia
Tel: 021 323235

The Investment Coordinating Board
Badan Koordinasi Penanaman Modal (BKPM)
Jalan Jendral Gatot Subroto 44
Jakarta
Indonesia
Tel: 021 512008

Trade and professional associations

Batam Industrial Estate Development Authority
Otorita Pengembangan Daerah Industri
Pulau Batam
Jalan M.H. Thamrin 20
Jakarta
Indonesia
Tel: 021 325828

City Development Coordinator
Dinas Pengawasan Pembangunan Kota (P2K)
Kantor Gubernur D.K.I. Jakarta
Jalan Taman Jatibaru No 1
Jakarta
Indonesia
Tel: 021 352275

Indonesian Architect Association
Ikatan Arsitek Indonesia (IAI)
Jakarta Design Centre 6th Floor
Jalan Letjen S Parman 53
Jakarta
Indonesia
Tel: 021 5304711

Indonesian Contractors' Association
Asosiasi Kontraktor Indonesia
Wijaya Grand Centre Blok D No 1
Jalan Darmawangsa III
Jakarta
Indonesia
Tel: 021 7202997

Indonesian Construction Expert Association
Himpunan Ahli Konstruksi Indonesia (HAKI)
Jalan Tebet Barat Dalam X/5
Jakarta
Indonesia
Tel: 021 8298518

Indonesian Engineers Association
Persatuan Insinyur Indonesia
Jalan Teuku Umar No 23
Jakarta
Indonesia

Indonesian National Consultant Association
Ikatan Konsultan Nasional Indonesia (INKINDO)
Jakarta Design Centre 4th Floor
Jalan Letjen S Parman 53
Jakarta
Indonesia
Tel: 021 5304639

Jakarta Design Centre
Jalan Letjen S Parman 53
Jakarta
Indonesia

National Chamber of Trade and Industry
  Kamar Dagang dan Industri Nasional
  Jalan M.H. Thamrin 20
  Jakarta
  Indonesia
  Tel: 021 324064

National Contractors' Association of Indonesia
  Gabungan Pelaksana Konstruksi Nasional Indonesia (GAPENSI)
  Jalan Raya Pasar Minggu Km 17 No 11A
  Jakarta
  Indonesia
  Tel: 021 7981670

The National Centre for Research
  Science and Technology
  Jalan Raden Saleh 43
  Jakarta
  Indonesia
  Tel: 021 323209

JAPAN'S LEADING
CONSTRUCTION COST CONSULTING FIRM

Professional cost advice for your projects in Japan

Preliminary and Detailed Estimates

Value Engineering

Tender Evaluation

Pre-Contract and Post-Contract Services

FUTABA QUANTITY SURVEYORS

Odakyu Kashiwagi Building
7-7-30 Nishi Shinjuku, Shinjuku-ku
Tokyo 160, Japan
Tel.: 03-3369-1538
Fax : 03-3365-7445

Branch Offices

Osaka/Nagoya/Hiroshima/Kanazawa/Fukuoka/Nagasaki/Sapporo

Japan

KEY DATA

Population
Population	124.8mn
Urban population	77%
Population under 15 (1992)	17.2%
Population 65 and over	13.0%
Average annual growth rate (1980 to 1993)	0.5%

Geography
Land area	378,000 km²
Agricultural area	14%
Capital city	Tokyo
Population of capital city	11.9mn

Economy
Monetary unit	Japanese Yen (¥)
Exchange rate (average third quarter 1995) to:	
the pound sterling	¥ 145.39
the US dollar	¥ 91.73
Average annual inflation (1980 to 1993)	1.5%
Inflation rate (1994)	0.7%
Gross Domestic Product (GDP) at market prices	¥ 471,450bn
GDP per capita	¥ 3,786,700
Average annual real change in GDP (1980 to 1993)	2.5%
Private consumption as a proportion of GDP	57%
General government consumption as a proportion of GDP	9%
Gross domestic investment as a proportion of GDP	31%
Central government expenditure as a proportion of Gross National Product	16%

Construction
Gross value of construction	¥ 84,050bn
Net value of construction output	¥ 48,560bn
Net value of construction output as a proportion of GDP	¥10.3%
Annual cement consumption (1993)	88.3mn tonnes

All data relate to 1993 unless otherwise indicated

THE CONSTRUCTION INDUSTRY

Construction output

The value of construction works completed in 1993 was ¥84 trillion. The output was equivalent to US$782 billion or 17.8% of GDP. Net output was ¥48.6 trillion, equivalent to US$453 billion, or about 10% of GDP. Unlike other countries this output excludes most repair and maintenance.

The table below shows the type of work undertaken. The Japanese economy has slowed down and the construction industry is suffering in terms of new orders though not so much in the level of output. By 1994 housing started to rise again but construction orders generally fell further. Demand for offices and factories in the private sector fell sharply but government orders increased as normal in a period of downturn.

CONSTRUCTION COMPLETION IN 1992 AND 1993 (CURRENT PRICES)

	1992		1993	
Sector/type of work	Yen billion	% of total	Yen billion	% of total
Private				
of which:				
Residential building	24,980	29	25,600	30
Mining and manufacturing building	4,480	5	2,850	3
Commercial and services building	11,930	14	8,910	11
Other building	3,660	4	3,350	4
Total building	45,050	53	40,710	48
Civil engineering	8,690	10	8,030	10
Total private	53,740	63	48,740	58
Public				
of which:				
Residential building	1,230	1	1,330	2
Non-residential	5,080	6	5,110	6
Total building	6,310	7	6,440	8
Civil engineering	25,300	30	28,970	34
Total public	31,620	37	35,310	42
All construction	85,360	100	84,050	100

Notes: Totals do not always sum exactly due to rounding
Source: Monthly Statistics of Japan, October 1994

In 1993, 73% of the private non-residential building output was in commercial buildings and 27% in industrial buildings.

These figures include extensions and reconstruction as well as routine repair and maintenance work. Recently, the construction industry has enjoyed a boom in new building and therefore the proportion of reconstruction is currently low but its importance is expected to grow as the economy slows down. The proportion for routine repair and maintenance is also slow, perhaps less than 10% of total output. This is partly because of the type of housing constructed which are relatively new as well as the traditional Japanese 'scrap and build' approach to construction with new build clearly preferred over refurbishment.

Over 50% of construction activity is concentrated in the Kanto and Kinki regions which encompass Tokyo and Osaka, Japan's two biggest conurbations.

The *Housing Survey of 1988* shows that Japan has an adequate number of dwellings related to the number of households, but the average size is only 89 square metres (about half that of the USA). The government recognizes that the country's social capital stock lags behind that of other industrialized nations and that the nation's economic strength is not reflected in its housing and other social capital. In 1990, a *Public Investment Basic Plan* was formulated to bring these facilities up to the level of other industrialized countries by the year 2000. In particular, it hopes to increase the average house floor area to 100 square metres. The achievement of the Japanese to date to improve housing has been quite remarkable. The dwelling stock has nearly doubled over the past thirty years. 41 million dwellings have been built while 20 million have been demolished.

Although the basic materials and methods of construction used in Japan are similar to those of other developed countries, there are considerable differences in detail. Generally, structures consist of heavy reinforced concrete, steel framed reinforced concrete, or steel frame with spray-applied fireproofing for large buildings, whereas for housing, timber frame is mostly used.

Characteristics and structure of the industry

Construction companies in Japan usually carry out both design and construction for private projects. Design departments of contractors may have as many as 1,000 professionals.

For public sector projects design is normally undertaken by public in-house design departments and the construction contract is then let. In particular most civil engineering work is publicly sponsored and the public sector offices either have their own design sections or hire specialist consultant firms to design their projects. It is quite usual for firms of consultant engineers to employ over 500 people. The largest architectural consultancy firm has over 1,000 employees and many have several hundreds. There is co-operation as well as competition between consultants and contractors; contractors may be invited to participate in consultants' design work or vice versa.

In 1991, there were about 515,000 construction contractors licensed either by the Ministry of Construction or by the Governors of Prefectures. Most contractors are small but there are five large companies: Shimizu Corporation, Kajima Corporation, Taisei Corporation, Takenaka Corporation, and Obayashi Corporation (see table next page). Kumagai Gumi Company used to be very large in the past but it has decreased in size due to problems encountered on overseas contracts. Each of these major contractors has an annual turnover of over ¥ 1,000 billion. They all provide a comprehensive range of construction services in building, civil and heavy engineering; they can find construction sites for clients, help finance and then design, construct and maintain high quality buildings and engineering projects. Takenaka Corporation undertakes 60%-70% of its work as design and build. The other large contractors do less than half of their work in design and build. Below these few top contractors are many smaller contractors with broadly similar capabilities.

MAJOR JAPANESE CONTRACTORS, 1993

Company	Place in ENR's Top 225 International Contractors	Total contracts US$ bn	Foreign contracts as % of work obtained	Work breakdown
Kajima Corporation	38	12.2	8	Building 57% Civil 17% Industrial 27%
Obayashi Corporation	41	10.8	9	Building 54% Civil 18% Industrial 12%
Shimizu Corporation	42	13.7	7	Building 50% Civil 11% Industrial 14%
Takenaka Corporation	45	11.6	7	Building 45% Civil 8% Industrial 47%
Taisei Corporation	51	11.1	6	Building 44% Civil 40% Industrial 5%
Kumagai Gumi Company	71	7.4	6	Building 11% Civil 86% Industrial 3%

Source: Personal contacts

For the last few decades local contractors have had an expanding domestic market because Japan lags behind western developed countries in the provision of infrastructure, most notably roads, sewerage, housing and the city environments. During the 1980s the economy expanded more or less continuously. Government policy is used to regulate the economy and this helps to give the construction industry a relatively even work flow.

The *Contract Construction Business Law* requires contractors to obtain a licence to start a construction business. Nearly all site work in Japan is undertaken by trade contractors who maintain a special relationship with a general contractor, known as a *zenecon*. Under this relationship the general contractor will endeavour to provide continuous employment for his subcontractors, in return for which each subcontractor will allow the general contractors to stipulate a contract price, and to monitor both his financial and project performance. The very large companies do not have a permanent workforce, but a family of subcontractors who are loosely connected to them.

Major Japanese construction firms are developing in a number of directions: internationally; diversifying into other businesses in some way linked to construction; strengthening the total engineering competence by research and development; and providing construction related finance. The Japanese have both the expertise and experience to compete with western European and American contractors. During the 1980s Japanese international contractors have increasingly directed their efforts to the industrialized regions of the world.

According to the *Engineering News Record*, in 1992, 27 Japanese contractors had 8.5% of the world construction export market of the top 225 contractors compared to 32 Japanese contractors with 14% of the market of the top 250 contractors in 1990. In the top 100 there were 17 Japanese contractors in 1992 compared with 15 in 1990. Some of these are very specialized, for example, in petrochemicals, but most have a broad range of operations. However it may be seen from the table opposite that overseas turnover is under 10% of the overall turnover of large contractors. Japanese contractors have worked abroad to service Japanese investors, though usually they use mostly local construction companies and suppliers. To ensure a constant work load, they have then become developers abroad gradually gaining non-Japanese clients, often for 'design and build' projects

One of the features of contracting organizations in Japan is that they undertake a considerable amount of research and development work. The range of research is very wide, from soil testing to air-supported domes. Earthquake engineering is important and the Japanese are generally regarded as world leaders in both research on the use of robots in construction and the development of intelligent buildings. Direct expenditure on research and development by the large construction firms is about 1% of turnover, but they also fund a considerable amount of outside research.

For private sector projects, the law requires that the contractor checks all designs and products to be used in the project and reports to the client any possible failures. For public sector projects the public authorities are in charge of design and bear responsibility. The high degree of responsibilty placed on the contractor for the success of projects is one reason why in-house research and development departments are needed.

The Ministry of Construction (MOC) oversees all aspects of construction. Research institutes and other organizations are under its control although each research institute has a large degree of autonomy. Construction is also monitored by other ministries such as the Ministry of Agriculture and Transport. The government is concerned that a number of sub-standard unqualified construction companies have entered the market. Smaller companies tend to have less stable management due to the shortage of young Japanese workers.

Only recently have foreign contracting firms been allowed a licence to operate in Japan. As a result of pressure from the USA in 1988 the first Japan-US Construction Agreement permitted registration of foreign firms. By May 1992, contractor permits have been issued to 27 foreign contractors: 13 from the USA, 10 from South Korea and one each from France, Australia, Switzerland and the Netherlands.

There are three types of architects in Japan: first class architects, second class architects and wooden building architects. First class architects must have passed an examination set by the Ministry of Construction and be licensed. The other two categories are dealt with on a similar basis by prefectural governors. A contractor with at least one architect can register as an architectural office and offer design services. About 50% of first class architects and most second class architects work for contractors.

The Japanese Institute of Architects limits its membership to independent architects and has not extended it to those employed by contractors. The Kenchikushi is a unique qualification of combined architect and building engineer, held by a number of construction supervisors as well as designers.

Clients and finance

The table showing construction completion by type of work (see earlier page) indicates that in 1993, 58% of all new construction work was funded privately, including over 95% of overall housing, 80% of overall non-housing building and about 23% of overall civil engineering. In 1993 the clients for new housing construction were as indicated in the table on the next page.

OWNERSHIP OF NEW DWELLINGS 1990

Type	% dwelling units	Average floor areas
Private rented accommodation	43	50m²
Company housing for rent	3	79m²
Private speculative housing for sale or rent	19	91m²
Owner occupied housing	35	140m²
All housing	100	90m²

Selection of design consultants

For projects not based on design and build, architects, engineers and cost consultants are usually appointed by the client either directly or after some form of competition. Other consultants are chosen by one of the main consultants. The most important basis for selection is track record with price a secondary factor. Personal contacts and recommendations are sometimes relevant in the private sector but rarely in the public sector. In some cases, however, where the contractor is appointed first, he will ask the client to appoint an architect - often one of his selection. The architect would still be paid by the client.

The Ministry of Construction publication - *Public Announcement No 1206* includes guidelines for the appointment of consultants. The professional associations publish recommended - but not mandatory - fee scales. If the price for the design is fixed fee it is sometimes altered during the course of the project. Designers normally retain copyright.

Contractual arrangements

In the public sector, construction companies of the appropriate category and experience are invited to bid. In selecting those invited, central and local governments rank construction firms according to past orders obtained, sales, financial status and technological capabilities. The contract is then awarded to the lowest bidder. In the private sector the client may appoint a specific contractor or invite selected contractors to bid - the latter is the more common system. Many projects - some 30%-40% of work - are also undertaken on a design and build basis where the architect is employed by the contractor. There is little use of construction management.

The Japanese contractual system is based on trust and mutual understanding. It is very important for both parties to maintain a good and long-term relationship. The Japanese rarely bring in a lawyer into negotiations - that implies mistrust - and litigation is only undertaken as a last resort. Clients tend to work regularly with a contracting firm, and will often have in-house staff with knowledge of building design and construction who will have prepared outline drawings of the proposed works. The contractor generally prepares the working drawings, except for building services, which are prepared by the specialist contractor.

The two most commonly used contract forms are the *Standard Form of Agreement and General Conditions of Government Contract for Works of Building and Civil Engineering*, prepared and recommended by the Construction Industry Council of Japan, and the *General Conditions of Construction Contracts (GCCC)* approved by a number of architects' and contractors' associations. Contract documents, which are relatively short, normally consist of the written contract, general conditions, the design drawings and the specification. There is no bill of quantities but the contractor submits an itemized list of prices (including quantities) with his tender. Liquidated damages are payable if a project is delayed, and there is a guarantee period of two years for brick or concrete buildings and one year for timber structures. The employer is given express rights to vary the work and negotiations take place on dates and costs. Claims are rare.

Liability and insurance

Although the designer has primary responsibility for defects, in practice, the contractor will normally correct the defects in order to retain the confidence of the client. Architects do not therefore normally carry insurance.

The Registration Organization for Warrantied Houses, administered by the Construction Ministry, provides a warranty scheme. This gives a ten year guarantee on the durability of structural components, including foundations, floors, walls and roofs plus a five year warranty on the weather resistance of roofs. The scheme is available to single unit housebuilders using traditional Japanese housebuilding techniques. Prefabricated house builders, who compete with the single unit home builders, also provide a ten year protection on structural components. Some condominium builders have recently started a similar ten year guarantee. In response, the Housing and Urban Development Corporation, the government-managed house supplier, has, since 1983, developed a long-term warranty programme for some condominiums, with warranties of ten years for structural elements, including the roof, and five to ten years for other elements.

Before this long-term warranty of houses and buildings can apply to all builders, a number of problems must be solved regarding such issues as design responsibilities, insurance systems, business profitability and so on. The principle behind long-term warranty is not to guarantee free repair services for ten years, but to build structures in which defects will not occur for at least ten years. Since this puts greater importance on quality, a long-term warranty is a necessity for all construction companies and an inevitable outcome in today's quality-conscious market. Those companies unable to offer such a warranty will eventually lose out in a competitive market.

Materials and construction methods

Although the basic materials and methods of construction used in Japan are similar to those of other developed countries, there are considerable differences in detail. Generally, structures are heavy reinforced concrete, steel framed reinforced concrete, or steel frame with spray applied fireproofing for large buildings, whereas for housing, timber frame is mostly used. Although there is some prefabrication of components for smaller elements, a considerably greater amount of skilled trade work (for example, cutting, fitting and welding of steelwork, cutting and threading of steel pipes, and the preparation of natural stone cladding) takes place on site. The use of tower cranes is unusual; instead materials are either distributed by hoists at the perimeter of buildings, or by small cranes mounted on the top construction level through holes left in the floors.

CONSTRUCTION COST DATA

Cost of labour

The figures next page are typical of labour costs in the Tokyo area as at the third quarter of 1995. The wage rate is the basis of an employee's income.

	Wage rate (per day) ¥
Site operatives	
Mason/bricklayer	29,737
Carpenter	25,835
Plumber	18,559
Electrician	18,725
Structural steel erector	20,411
HVAC installer	17,105
Semi-skilled worker	15,115
Unskilled labourer	12,607
Equipment operator	20,891
Watchman/security	16,000
Site supervision	
General foreman	27,000
Trades foreman	25,000
Contractors' personnel	
Site manager	42,000
Resident engineer	32,000
Resident surveyor	32,000
Junior engineer	13,000
Junior surveyor	13,000
Planner	13,000
Consultants' personnel	
Senior architect	49,000
Senior engineer	49,000
Senior surveyor	49,000
Qualified architect	42,000
Qualified engineer	42,000
Qualified surveyor	42,000

Cost of materials

The figures that follow are the costs of main construction materials, delivered to site in the Tokyo area, as incurred by contractors in the third quarter of 1995. These assume that the materials would be in quantities as required for a medium sized construction project and that the location of the works would be neither constrained nor remote.

	Unit	Cost ¥
Cement and aggregates		
Ordinary portland cement in 40kg bags	tonne	16,000
Coarse aggregates for concrete	m³	5,700
Fine aggregates for concrete	m³	5,500
Ready mixed concrete (210kg cement/cm²)	m³	13,400
Steel		
Mild steel reinforcement	tonne	31,500
High tensile steel reinforcement	tonne	36,300
Precompressing tendons	tonne	33,000
Structural steel sections	tonne	37,000
Bricks and blocks		
Common bricks (210 x 100 x 60mm)	1,000	80,000
Good quality facing bricks (210 x 100 x 60mm)	each	180
Hollow concrete blocks (190 x 190 x 390mm)	each	244
Solid concrete blocks (190 x 190 x 200mm)	each	800
Precast concrete cladding units with exposed aggregate finish	m²	10,300
Timber and insulation		
Softwood sections for carpentry	m³	55,000
Softwood for joinery	m³	103,000
Hardwood for joinery	m³	130,000
Exterior quality plywood (12mm)	m²	1,030
Plywood for interior joinery (5mm)	m²	660
Softwood strip flooring (15mm)	m²	10,500
Chipboard sheet flooring (15mm)	m²	3,000
Softwood internal door complete with frames and ironmongery	each	79,500
Glass and ceramics		
Float glass (5 mm)	m²	1,990
Sealed double glazing units (FL3+A6+FL3) 12mm thick	m²	5,700
Good quality ceramic wall tiles	m²	3,400
Plaster and paint		
Plaster in 25 kg bags	tonne	45,000
Plasterboard (9mm thick)	m²	150
Emulsion paint in 5 litre tins	kg	335
Gloss oil paint in 5 litre tins	kg	380

	Unit	Cost ¥
Tiles and paviors		
Clay floor tiles (200 x 200mm)	m²	4,820
Vinyl floor tiles (2 x 300 x 300mm)	m²	10,000
Precast concrete paving slabs (300 x 300 x 60mm)	m²	4,780
Clay roof tiles	1,000	126,000
Precast concrete roof tiles	1,000	104,000
Drainage		
WC suite complete	each	39,300
Lavatory basin complete	each	49,400
100mm diameter clay drain pipes	m	2,360
150mm diameter stainless steel drain pipes	m	6,770

Unit rates

The descriptions below are generally shortened versions of standard descriptions listed in full in section 4. Where an item has a two digit reference number (e.g. 05 or 33), this relates to the full description against that number in section 4. Where an item has an alphabetic suffix (e.g. 12A or 34B) this indicates that the standard description has been modified. Where a modification is major the complete modified description is included here and the standard description should be ignored; where a modification is minor (e.g. the insertion of a named hardwood) the shortened description has been modified here but, in general, the full description in section 4 prevails.

The unit rates below are main work items on a typical construction project in the Tokyo area in the third quarter of 1995. The rates include all necessary labour, materials and equipment. Allowances to cover preliminary and general items and contractors' overheads and profit have been added to the rates.

		Unit	Rate ¥
Excavation			
01	Mechanical excavation of foundation trenches	m³	6,070
02	Hardcore filling making up levels	m²	1,430
03	Earthwork support	m²	17,080
Concrete work			
04	Plain insitu concrete in strip foundations in trenches	m³	17,780
05	Reinforced insitu concrete in beds	m³	17,780

		Unit	*Rate* ¥
06	Reinforced insitu concrete in walls	m³	17,780
07	Reinforced insitu concrete in suspended floors or roof slabs	m³	17,780
08	Reinforced insitu concrete in columns	m³	17,780
09	Reinforced insitu concrete in isolated beams	m³	17,780
10	Precast concrete slabs	m²	10,610

Formwork

11A	Softwood formwork to concrete walls	m²	4,860
12A	Softwood formwork to concrete columns	m²	4,860
13	Softwood or metal formwork to horizontal soffits of slabs	m²	4,860

Reinforcement

14	Reinforcement in concrete walls	tonne	103,780
15	Reinforcement in suspended concrete slabs	tonne	103,780

Steelwork

17	Fabricate, supply and erect steel framed structure	tonne	246,870
18	Framed structural steelwork in universal joist sections	tonne	139,230
19	Structural steelwork lattice roof trusses	tonne	155,610

Brickwork and blockwork

20	Precast lightweight aggregate hollow concrete block walls	m²	5,970
21A	Solid (perforated) common bricks	m²	16,030

Roofing

24	Concrete interlocking roof tiles 430 x 380mm	m²	8,510
25	Plain clay roof tiles 260 x 160mm	m²	10,500
26	Fibre cement roof slates 600 x 300mm	m²	4,450
27	Sawn softwood roof boarding	m²	2,050
28	Particle board roof coverings	m²	3,080
29	3 layers glass-fibre based bitumen felt roof covering	m²	8,920
30	Bitumen based mastic asphalt roof covering	m²	6,380
31	Glass-fibre mat roof insulation 160mm thick	m²	1,640
33	Troughed galvanized steel roof cladding	m²	4,780

Woodwork and metalwork

34	Preservative treated sawn softwood 50 x 100mm	m	5,030
37	Two panel glazed door in hardwood size 850 x 2000mm	each	297,180
38	Solid core half hour fire resisting hardwood internal flush door, size 800 x 2000mm	each	81,900

		Unit	Rate ¥
39	Aluminium double glazed window, size 1200 x 1200mm	each	111,760
40	Aluminium double glazed door, size 850 x 2100mm	each	90,440
41	Hardwood skirtings	m	2,280

Plumbing

42	UPVC half round eaves gutter	m	1,740
43	UPVC rainwater pipes	m	4,070
44	Light gauge copper cold water tubing	m	2,410
45	High pressure plastic pipes for cold water supply	m	1,460
46	Low pressure plastic pipes for cold water distribution	m	1,770
47	UPVC soil and vent pipes	m	6,370
48	White vitreous china WC suite	each	78,860
49	White vitreous china lavatory basin	each	72,310
51	Stainless steel single bowl sink and double drainer	each	90,210

Electrical work

52	PVC insulated and copper sheathed cable	m	340
53	13 amp unswitched socket outlet	each	4,260
54	Flush mounted 20 amp, 1 way light switch	each	4,380

Finishings

55A	2 coats gypsum based plaster on concrete walls 20mm thick	m²	5,470
56	White glazed tiles on plaster walls	m²	11,060
57	Red clay quarry tiles on concrete floors	m²	12,250
58A	Cement and sand screed to concrete floors 30mm thick	m²	2,380
59	Thermoplastic floor tiles on screed	m²	2,170
60	Mineral fibre tiles on concealed suspension system	m²	4,380

Glazing

61	Glazing to wood	m²	4,680

Painting

62	Emulsion on plaster walls	m²	910
63	Oil paint on timber	m²	1,300

Approximate estimating

The building costs per unit area given below are averages incurred by building clients for typical buildings in the Tokyo area as at the third quarter of 1995. They are based upon the total floor area of all storeys, measured between external walls and without deduction for internal walls. Approximate estimating costs generally include mechanical and electrical installations but exclude furniture, loose or special equipment, and external works; they also exclude fees for professional services. The costs shown are for specifications and standards appropriate to Japan and this should be borne in mind when attempting comparisons with similarly described building types in other countries. A discussion of this issue is included in section 2. Comparative data for countries covered in this publication including construction cost data are presented in Part Three.

Approximate estimating costs must be treated with reserve; they cannot provide more than a rough guide to the probable cost of building.

	Cost m² ¥	Cost ft² ¥
Industrial buildings		
Factories for letting	210,000	19,500
Warehouses, low bay (6 to 8m high) for letting (no heating)	170,000	15,800
Administrative and commercial buildings		
Civic offices, fully air conditioned	315,000	29,300
Offices for letting, high rise, air conditioned	340,000	31,600
Prestige/headquarters office, high rise, air conditioned	380,000	35,300
Health and education buildings		
General hospitals (300 beds)	450,000	41,800
Secondary/middle schools	270,000	25,100
Recreation and arts buildings		
Theatres (over 500 seats) including seating and stage equipment	520,000	48,400
Residential buildings		
Social/economic apartment housing, high rise (with lifts)	280,000	26,000
Private sector apartment buildings (luxury)	360,000	33,500
Hotel, 5 star, city centre	450,000	41,900
Hotel, 3 star, city/provincial	370,000	34,400

Regional variations

The approximate estimating costs are based on projects in Tokyo. These costs should be adjusted by the following factors to take account of regional variations:

Nagoya	:	-9%	Fukuoka:	-9%
Osaka	:	-4%	Sapporo :	-7%
Hiroshima :		-7%		

EXCHANGE RATES AND INFLATION

The combined effect of exchange rates and inflation on prices within a country and price comparisons between countries is discussed in section 2.

Exchange rates

The graph below plots the movement of the Japanese yen against sterling and the US dollar since 1985. The values used for the graph are quarterly and the method of calculating these is described and general guidance on the interpretation of the graph provided in section 2. The average exchange rate in the third quarter of 1995 was yen 145.39 to pound sterling and yen 91.73 to US dollar.

THE JAPANESE YEN AGAINST STERLING AND US DOLLAR

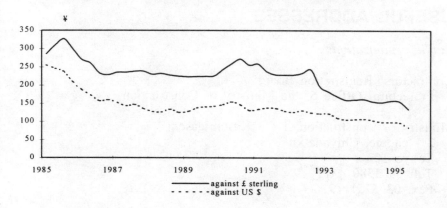

Price inflation

The table below presents consumer price and building cost inflation in Japan since 1980.

CONSUMER PRICE AND BUILDING COST INFLATION

Year	Consumer price inflation		Building cost index	
------	average index	average change %	average index	average change %
1980	100		100	
1981	105	5.0	103	3.0
1982	108	2.9	104	1.0
1983	110	1.9	103	-1.0
1984	112	1.8	103	0.0
1985	115	2.7	103	0.0
1986	115	0.0	102	-1.0
1987	115	0.0	104	2.0
1988	116	0.9	111	6.7
1989	119	2.6	118	6.3
1990	122	2.5	127	7.6
1991	126	3.3	135	6.3
1992	128	1.6	136	0.8
1993	130	1.3	132	-3.4
1994	131	0.7	126	-4.7

USEFUL ADDRESSES

Public organizations

Contractors' Registration Board
    Prefectural Office of the Ministry of Construction

Ministry of Construction, 1 - 3 Kasumigaseki
    2 - chome, Chiyoda-ku
    Tokyo 100
    Tel: 03 3580 4311
    Fax: 03 5251 1926

Housing and Urban Development
1 - 14 - 6 Kudankita, Chiyoda-ku
Tokyo 100
Tel: 03 3263 8111
Fax: 03 3263 8177

Japanese Industrial Standards
4 - 1 - 24, Akasaka, Minato-ku
Tokyo 107
Tel: 03 3583 8005
Fax: 03 3586 2014

Kanto Regional Construction Bureau (6 other locations)
1 - 3 1 Otemachi, Chiyoda-ku
Tokyo 100
Tel: 03 3211 6261
Fax: 03 3285 0287

Management and Coordination Agency
The Statistics Bureau
19 - 1 Wakamatsu-cho, Shinjuku-ku
Tokyo
Tel: 03 3202 1111
Fax: 03 5273 1180

Ministry of Transport
2 - 1 - 3 Kasumigaseki, Chiyoda-ku
Tokyo 100
Tel: 03 3580 3111
Fax: 03 3593 0474

National Land Agency
1 - 2 - 1 Kasumigaseki, Chiyoda-ku
Tokyo 100
Tel: 03 3593 3311
Fax: 03 3501 5349

Trade and professional associations

Japan Civil Engineering Contractors' Association, Inc
    Tokyo Kensetsu Building, 5 - 1 Hacchobori
    2 - chome, Chuo-ku
    Tokyo 104
    Tel: 03 3553 3201
    Fax: 03 3552 3206

Japan Construction Consultants Association
    Shin Kudan Building, 2 - 4 Kudan Minami
    2 - chome, Chiyoda-ku
    Tokyo 102
    Tel: 03 3239 7992

Japan Federation of Construction Contractors, Inc
    Tokyo Kensetsu Building, 2 - 5 - 1 Hacchobori
    Chuo-ku
    Tokyo 104
    Tel: 03 3553 0701
    Fax: 03 3552 2360

Japan Institute of Architects
    2 - 3 - 16 Jingumae
    Shibuya-ku
    Tokyo 150
    Tel: 03 3408 8291
    Fax: 03 3408 8294

Japan Structural Consultants Association
    Ohashi Building, 1 - 3 - 2 Kudan Kita
    Chiyoda-ku
    Tokyo
    Tel: 03 3262 8498
    Fax: 03 3262 8486

Management Research Society (Construction Industry)
    11 - 8 Nihonbashi - Odenmachou
    Chuo-ku
    Tokyo
    Tel: 03 3663 2411
    Fax: 03 3663 2417

The Associated General Contractors of Japan, Inc
2 - 5 - 1 Hacchobori
Chuo-ku
Tokyo
Tel: 03 3551 9396
Fax: 03 3555 3218

The Building Centre of Japan
No. 30 Mori Building, 3 - 2 - 2 Toranomon
Minato-ku
Tokyo
Tel: 03 3434 7161
Fax: 03 3431 3301

The Building Surveyors' Institute of Japan
2 - 26 - 20 Shiba, Minato-ku
Tokyo 108
Tel: 03 3453 9591
Fax: 03 3453 9597

The Japan Chamber of Commerce and Industry
3 - 2 - 2 Marunouchi
Chiyoda-ku
Tokyo 100
Tel: 03 3283 7823
Fax: 03 3211 4859

DAVIS LANGDON & SEAH MALAYSIA
JURU UKUR BAHAN MALAYSIA
J.U.B.M. SDN. BHD.
DLS MANAGEMENT (M) SDN. BHD.

The strategic and integrated management of cost, time and quality - the client "risk" areas of a contract - are essential functions, which are necessary to ensure the satisfactory planning, procurement, execution and operation of construction projects.

We specialise in the financial management of construction projects and their risk areas, from project inception to completion and we concentrate on:

- being positive and creative in our advice, rather than simply reactive;

- providing value for money via efficient management, rather than on superficial cost monitoring;

- giving advice that is matched to the client's requirements, rather than imposing standard or traditional solutions;

- paying attention to the life-cycle costs of constructing and occupying a building, rather than to the initial capital cost only.

Our aim is to provide our clients with risk assurance, cost control and value for money, via effective advice, cost planning and management.

Kuala Lumpur	**Kota Kinabalu**	**Penang**
Jalan Kasah	Wisma Pendidikan	9 Jalan Padang Victoria
Damansara Heights	Suite 84 Jalan Padang	10400 Penang
50490 Kuala Lumpur	PO Box 1598	Tel : (6004) 2287630
Tel : (6003) 2543411	Tel : (6088) 223369	Fax : (6004) 2298031
Fax : (6003) 2559600	Fax : (6088) 2216537	

Johore Bahru	**Kuching**
49-01 Jalan Tun Abdul Razak	2nd Floor Lot 142
Susur 1/1 Medan Cahaya	Bangunan WSK Jalan Abell
80000 Johore Bahru	93100 Kuching
Tel : (6007) 2236229	Tel : (6082) 417357
Fax : (6007) 2235975	Fax : (6082) 426416

DAVIS LANGDON & SEAH INTERNATIONAL

Malaysia

KEY DATA

Population

Population	19.0mn
Urban population	52%
Population under 15	36%
Population 65 and over	4%
Average annual growth rate (1980 to 1993)	2.5%

Geography

Land area	330,000 km²
Agricultural area	39%
Capital city	Kuala Lumpur
Population of capital city	1.34mn

Economy

Monetary unit	Malaysian ringgit (RM)
Exchange rate (average third quarter 1995) to:	
the pound sterling	RM3.91
the US dollar	RM2.47
the yen x 100	RM2.69
Average annual inflation (1980 to 1993)	2.2%
Inflation rate (1994)	3.7%
Gross Domestic Product (GDP) at market prices	RM166.0bn
GDP per capita	RM8,735
Average annual real change in GDP (1980 to 1993)	6.2%
Private consumption as a proportion of GDP	49%
General government consumption as a proportion of GDP	13%
Gross domestic investment as a proportion of GDP	33%
Central government expenditure as a proportion of Gross National Product	27%

Construction

Gross value of construction output *	RM25.0bn
Net value of construction output *	RM11.6bn
Net value of construction output as a proportion of GDP*	7%
Cement production	9 mn tonnes

All data relate to 1993 unless otherwise indicated

* *authors' estimate*

THE CONSTRUCTION INDUSTRY

Construction output

Gross construction output in 1993 is estimated to be 15% of GDP or RM25 billion, equivalent to US$9 billion. The net value of construction output in 1993 is estimated to be 7% of GDP or RM11.6 billion, equivalent to US$4 billion. The construction industry is expected to sustain a robust growth of 12.7% in 1995 (1994 : 13.0%) with the implementation of large infrastructural projects as well as the construction of residential, commercial and industrial buildings.

The figures for gross and net output are not from official statistics. Official statistics indicate that gross construction output in 1993 was of the order of RM22 billion or 13% of GDP. This is very low in relation to an investment level of 33% of GDP. Construction investment is normally about half total investment. The percentage of gross construction output of GDP seems unlikely to be less than 15%. Official data are available for net output of construction as a proportion of GDP but are quoted mainly at constant 1978 prices, at which date the relative prices of construction could have been very different from those 15 years later. In any case, net output would be expected to be at least a third and in many countries nearer a half of gross output. Net output in the official statistics is about 4% of GDP; the authors estimate it to be 7%.

The Malaysian construction industry has seen strong growth since 1989. Growth in construction output has been supported by large infrastructure and civil engineering projects. Buoyancy in the residential housing sector is expected to continue as sustained economic development over the past seven years has led to a higher level of net disposal income for the population.

It is expected that a total of 41,500 new jobs will be created in the construction industry in 1995, increasing the number employed to 635,500. This represents about 8.1% of the country's employment in 1995. As a result of the rapid development of projects, the construction industry faces acute shortages of skilled and semi-skilled workers. Construction companies have become increasingly dependent on foreign labourers. Recognizing the labour shortage, the Malaysian Government has issued a longer period of foreign labour work permits from two years to three years to ease the situation.

The breakdown by type of construction is shown below :

PERCENTAGE OF VALUE OF NEW WORK DONE BY TYPE OF CONSTRUCTION, 1992

Type of construction	Public % of total	Private % of total	Total % of total
Building			
Residential building	2	25	27
Factories and related structures	<1	12	13
Office and commercial buildings	2	12	13
Schools and other educational buildings	1	<1	2
Hospitals and other health service buildings	<1	<1	<1
Other buildings	1	3	3
Total building construction	9	52	60
Civil engineering			
Roads, streets, viaducts, etc.	4	6	11
Bridges, excluding railway bridges	<1	2	2
Railways, including railway bridges	<1	<1	<1
Airports	<1	<1	<1
Harbours, piers	<1	<1	<1
Dams, drainage and irrigation	1	<1	2
Water mains	1	<1	2
Sewerage	<1	<1	<1
Power plant construction, transmission lines, etc.	<1	2	2
Land improvement, levelling, excavating and earthworks	1	5	5
Other civil engineering works	5	8	14
Total civil engineering	14	25	39
Total	23	77	100

Totals do not always sum exactly due to rounding
Source : Department of Statistics, Malaysia

Public sector work is about 23% of the total, the remainder being funded by the private sector. Building construction accounts for 52% of private sector construction work, nearly half of which is related to residential building. Factories, office and commercial building are also important types of construction work undertaken by the private sector.

Civil engineering construction is 14% of public sector construction work. Roads projects form a significant share. The involvement of the private sector in infrastructure projects has been increasing, again with roads projects forming an important part. Also of importance in the private sector is work related to excavating, levelling and the improvement of land.

Repair and maintenance according to official statistics was about 5% of total output in 1992.

The residential construction activity is well supported by strong demand for housing as a result of improved disposable incomes, low interest rates, more affordable repayment terms and the relaxation of eligibility conditions for housing loans. In line with the Sixth Malaysian Plan, the Malaysian government has launched the Low Cost Housing Plan (LCHF) and Abandoned Housing Project Fund (AHPF) to speed up the construction of low cost houses. Recently, the central bank has imposed a monthly-based interest calculation system to ease the burden of home-buyers. This will indirectly increase the demand of houses. The net lettable purpose built office space in Klang Valley takes up about 60% of the national total. In 1994, an increase of 170,854 m^2 in total supply of office space has firmed up the rental rate in Klang Valley. Several mega projects incorporating office space are under construction and hence, further rental adjustment can be expected in the coming years. However, demand for office space is expected to be released from the influx of foreign companies, tenants who had traditionally occupied shops offices and bungalows and domestic new investment. Currently, the average occupancy rate of offices in Klang Valley is about 90%.

The commercial and retail sub-sector is performing well and the selling rate has achieved a 10-year level high in 1995. The current ratio of retail space to population in the Klang Valley is three square feet per capita. The estimated ratio is eight square feet per capita by 1998. Retail space is expected to double in the next three years despite the talk of over supply of retail space in Klang Valley. The current market size of retail space in the Klang Valley is RM4.8 billion.

More golf courses, tourist resorts, hotels and theme parks are planned and/or under construction. This is in line with the government objective to boost the tourist industry. Currently, the hotel occupancy rate is about 85% in Klang Valley. More five star hotels are expected to come on stream before the Commonwealth Games scheduled to be held in 1998. This upsurge will likely increase the competitiveness of the hotel industry to provide better service. However, the government has tightened the regulations to build golf courses following public environmental awareness.

The civil engineering sub-sector remains buoyant due to development and upgrading of infrastructure facilities especially for transportation projects. This sub-sector is expected to perform well in the next 10 years following a few mega projects such as the Kuala Lumpur International Airport (KLIA), metropolitan rail commuter systems and Light Rail Transit (LRT). The government spending on planned roads between 1996 and 2010 is budgeted at RM58 billion. Forecast for infrastructure spending alone in 1996 is around RM20 billion.

Characteristics and structure of the industry

In 1992 there were some 6,991 large contracting companies in Malaysia. Large contracting companies are those reporting RM100,000 and over value of work per annum. The breakdown by numbers for large firms, according to type of construction undertaken, is 1,492 (residential), 1,247 (non-residential), 2,194 (civil engineering) and 2,058 (special trade). The gross value output by these firms is RM19.63 million.

The professions are regulated by the appropriate professional bodies - Pertubuhan Akitek Malaysia (PAM), Institution of Engineers Malaysia, the Association of Consulting Engineers Malaysia, and the Institution of Surveyors Malaysia. Individual professional consultants have to register with their respective professional boards.

The table below shows the breakdown of professional consulting firms in 1991.

PROFESSIONAL CONSULTING FIRMS IN MALAYSIA, 1991

Location	Architectural firms	Engineering firms	Surveying firms
Peninsular Malaysia	306	338	300
Sabah	30	31	39
Sarawak	44	50	38
Total	380	419	377

Source : Monthly Statistical Bulletin, Department of Statistics, Malaysia

Clients and finance

One third of the total construction investment is made up by the public sector and the balance by the private sector. Private sector is promoted by property developers whereas public sector is planned under the *Sixth and Seventh Malaysia Plans* which cover five years each.

Most of the building projects are privately funded where the financing is arranged through banks, trust and insurance companies. Private funding is increasing due to increased privatization of the public organizations. However, the majority of the civil engineering and infrastructure projects are financed by public funding.

Selection of design consultants

In the private sector, most consultants are selected and appointed by the developers based on track record and personal relationships besides cost consideration. In the public sector, the selection criteria of project consultants are based on experience, quota, contacts and cost. Design and build projects are getting popular and more construction firms are building up unit design capabilities.

Contractual arrangements

In the public sector, the JKR (Jabatan Kerja Raya or Public Works Department) form of contract is used for tender bid. The Public Works Department usually invites contracting companies to tender through open advertisements in the major newspapers. Sometimes, tenderers are selected through a pre-qualification exercise for larger jobs. In the private sector, the PAM (Pertubuhan Akitek Malaysia) form of contract is widely adopted. Bill of Quantities, drawings and specification are commonly used as the bases for tender.

Development control and standards

Buildings are required to comply with the *Uniform Building By Laws and Streets, Drainage & Buildings Act 1974*. Local authorities and statutory bodies are responsible for the compliance with standards. Construction firms are required to comply with the *Safety and Health Act* which was enacted in 1994.

There are three pieces of planning registration that are enforced namely *City of Kuala Lumpur (Planning) Act No. 107, 1973, Town and Country (Planning) Act No. 172, 1976* and *Federal Territory (Planning) Act No. 267, 1982*.

Research

The Construction Industry Development Board (CIDB) is one of the government institutions that undertake research, development and training and manpower training in the construction industry. The Public Works Department also undertakes some research on the tender price movement and schedule of rates. The professional body of surveyors, the Institute of Surveyors Malaysia also conducts some research on cost analysis and basic material prices on a quarterly basis. Awareness of the need for research and development has increased within the industry over the last few years and a higher budget has been allocated for this area in the private sector.

CONSTRUCTION COST DATA

Cost of labour

The figures below are typical of labour costs in Kuala Lumpur as at the third quarter of 1995. Cost of labour indicates the cost to a contractor of employing that employee.

Labour rate (per day = 8 hr)

	Wage rate (per day) RM
Site operatives	
Mason/bricklayer	60
Carpenter	70
Plumber	65
Electrician	65
Structural steel erector	85
HVAC installer	65
Semi-skilled worker	45
Unskilled labourer	31
Equipment operator	60
Watchman/security	32
	(per month)
Site supervision	
General foreman	2,200
Trades foreman	1,800
Clerk of works	1,500

	(per month)
Contractors' personnel	
Site manager	6,600
Resident engineer	5,200
Resident surveyor	3,100
Junior engineer	2,500
Junior surveyor	1,700
Consultants' personnel	
Senior architect	6,800
Senior engineer	6,500
Senior surveyor	3,700
Qualified architect	4,800
Qualified engineer	4,500
Qualified surveyor	4,200

Cost of materials

The figures that follow are the costs of main construction materials, delivered to site in the capital area, as incurred by contractors in the third quarter of 1995. These assume that the materials would be in quantities as required for a medium sized construction project and that the location of the works would be neither constrained nor remote.

	Unit	*Cost RM*
Cement and aggregate		
Ordinary portland cement in 50kg bags	tonne	192.00
Coarse aggregates for concrete in 20mm granite	m³	46.20
Fine aggregates for concrete	m³	13.50
Ready mixed concrete (mix 1:2:4)	m³	135.00
Ready mixed concrete (mix 1:1:2)	m³	148.00
Steel		
Mild steel reinforcement 10mm - 40mm diameter	tonne	1,120.00
High tensile steel reinforcement 10mm - 40mm diameter	tonne	1,200.00
Structural steel sections	tonne	2,000.00
Bricks and blocks		
Common bricks (215 x 102 x 65mm)	pc	0.25
Good quality facing bricks (210 x 100 x 70mm)	pc	0.56
Hollow concrete blocks (190 x 390 x 190mm)	pc	1.43
Solid concrete blocks (190 x 390 x 190mm)	pc	1.75

	Unit	Cost RM
Timber and insulation		
Softwood sections for carpentry	m³	350.00
Softwood for joinery	m³	450.00
Hardwood for joinery	m³	640.00
Exterior quality plywood	m²	14.00
Plywood for interior joinery	m²	13.00
Softwood strip flooring	m²	120.00
100mm thick quilt insulation	m²	9.00
100mm thick rigid slab insulation	m²	20.00
Softwood internal door complete with frames and ironmongery	each	200.00
Glass and ceramics		
Float glass (5 mm)	m²	43.00
Good quality ceramic wall tiles (150 x 150mm)	m²	24.00
Plaster and paint		
Plasterboard (5mm thick)	m²	9.00
Emulsion paint in 5 litre tins	litre	11.00
Gloss oil paint in 5 litre tins	litre	15.00
Tiles and paviors		
Clay floor tiles (200 x 200 x 13mm)	m²	35.00
Vinyl floor tiles (300 x 300 x 2mm)	m²	28.50
Precast concrete paving slabs (300 x 300 x 60mm)	m²	37.50
Clay roof tiles	pc	3.80
Precast concrete roof tiles	pc	1.20
Drainage		
WC suite complete	each	500.00
Lavatory basin complete	each	250.00
100mm diameter clay drain pipes	m	25.00
150mm diameter stainless steel drain pipes	m	32.00

Unit rates

The descriptions below are generally shortened versions of standard descriptions listed in full in section 4. Where an item has a two digit reference number (e.g. 05 or 33), this relates to the full description against that number in section 4. Where an item has an alphabetic suffix (e.g. 12A or 34B) this indicates that the standard description has been modified. Where a modification is major the complete modified description is included here and the standard description should be ignored; where a modification is minor (e.g. the insertion of a named hardwood) the shortened description has been modified here but, in general, the full description in section 4 prevails.

The unit rates below are for main work items in a typical construction project in the Kuala Lumpur area in the third quarter of 1995. The rates include all necessary labour, materials and equipment. Allowances of 6% - 8% to cover preliminary and general items and 15% to cover contractors' overheads and profit have been included in the rates.

		Unit	Rate RM
Excavation			
01	Mechanical excavation of foundation trenches	m³	12.00
02	Hardcore filling making up levels	m²	36.00
Concrete work			
04A	Plain insitu concrete in strip foundations in trenches (C25)	m³	150.00
05A	Reinforced insitu concrete in beds (C35)	m³	170.00
06A	Reinforced insitu concrete in walls (C35)	m³	170.00
07A	Reinforced insitu concrete in suspended floors or roof slabs (C35)	m³	170.00
08A	Reinforced insitu concrete in columns (C35)	m³	170.00
09A	Reinforced insitu concrete in isolated beams (C35)	m³	170.00
Formwork			
11	Softwood formwork to concrete walls	m²	25.00
12	Softwood formwork to concrete columns	m²	25.00
13	Softwood to horizontal soffits of slabs	m²	25.00
Reinforcement			
14	Reinforcement in concrete walls	tonne	1,530.00
15	Reinforcement in suspended concrete slabs	tonne	1,530.00
16	Fabric reinforcement in concrete beds	m²	13.50

		Unit	Rate RM

Steelwork

17	Fabricate, supply and erect steel framed structure	tonne	3,800.00
18	Framed structural steelwork in universal joist sections	tonne	3,380.00
19	Structural steelwork lattice roof trusses	tonne	3,940.00

Brickwork and blockwork

20	Precast lightweight aggregate hollow concrete block walls	m²	23.50
21	Solid (perforated) common bricks	m²	28.00
22	Sand lime bricks	m²	26.00
23	Facing bricks	m²	50.00

Roofing

24	Concrete interlocking roof tiles 430 x 380mm	m²	28.00
25	Plain clay roof tiles 260 x 160mm	m²	74.00
26	Fibre cement roof slates 600 x 300mm	m²	25.00
27A	Sawn softwood roof boarding (12mm)	m²	18.50
28	Particle board roof coverings	m²	28.00
29	3 layers glass-fibre based bitumen felt roof covering	m²	28.00
30	Bitumen based mastic asphalt roof covering	m²	25.00
31	Glass-fibre mat roof insulation 160mm thick	m²	10.00
33	Troughed galvanized steel roof cladding	m²	30.00

Woodwork and metalwork

34	Preservative treated sawn softwood 50 x 100mm	m³	1,800.00
35	Preservative treated sawn softwood 50 x 150mm	m³	1,800.00
36	Single glazed casement window in hardwood, size 650 x 900mm	each	150.00
37	Two panel glazed door in hardwood size 850 x 2000mm	each	740.00
38	Solid core half hour fire resisting hardwood internal flush doors, size 800 x 2000mm	each	640.00
39	Aluminium double glazed window, size 1200 x 1200mm	each	850.00
40	Aluminium double glazed door, size 850 x 2100mm	each	848.00
41	Hardwood skirtings	m	10.00

		Unit	Rate RM
Plumbing			
42	UPVC half round eaves gutter	m	15.30
43	UPVC rainwater pipes	m	20.00
44	Light gauge copper cold water tubing	m	32.00
45	High pressure plastic pipes for cold water supply	m	12.00
46	Low pressure plastic pipes for cold water distribution	m	10.00
47	UPVC soil and vent pipes	m	23.00
48	White vitreous china WC suite	each	590.00
49	White vitreous china lavatory basin	each	420.00
51	Stainless steel single bowl sink and double drainer	each	180.00
Electrical Work			
52	PVC insulated and copper sheathed cable	m	6.00
53	13 amp unswitched socket outlet	each	98.00
54	Flush mounted 20 amp, 1 way light switch	each	105.00
Finishings			
55A	2 coats gypsum based plaster on concrete walls 20mm thick	m²	22.00
56	White glazed tiles on plaster walls	m²	42.00
57	Red clay quarry tiles on concrete floors	m²	57.00
58A	Cement and sand screed to concrete floors 30mm thick	m²	11.00
59	Thermoplastic floor tiles on screed	m²	30.00
60	Mineral fibre tiles on concealed suspension system	m²	60.00
Glazing			
61A	6mm clear float glass; glazing to wood	m²	60.00
Painting			
62	Emulsion on plaster walls	m²	2.80
63	Oil paint on timber	m²	4.00

Approximate estimating

The building costs per unit area given below are averages incurred by building clients for typical buildings in the capital area as at the third quarter of 1995. They are based upon the total floor area of all storeys, measured between external walls and without deduction for internal walls.

Approximate estimating costs generally include mechanical and electrical installations but exclude furniture, loose or special equipment, and external works; they also exclude fees for professional services. The costs shown are for specifications and standards appropriate to Malaysia and this should be borne in mind when attempting comparisons with similarly described building types in other countries. A discussion of this issue is included in section 2. Comparative data for countries covered in this publication, including construction cost data, are presented in Part Three.

Approximate estimating costs must be treated with reserve; they cannot provide more than a rough guide to the probable cost of building.

	Cost m^2 RM	Cost ft^2 RM
Industrial buildings		
Factories for letting	592.00	55.00
Factories for owner occupation (light industrial use)	700.00	65.00
Factories for owner occupation (heavy industrial use)	1,023.00	95.00
Factory/office (high-tech) for letting (shell and core only)	904.00	85.00
Factory/office (high-tech) for letting (ground floor shell, first floor offices)	1,184.00	110.00
Factory/office (high tech) for owner occupation (controlled environment, fully finished)	2,045.00	190.00
High tech laboratory workshop centres (air conditioned)	484.00	45.00
Administrative and commercial buildings		
Civic offices, non air conditioned	807.00	75.00
Civic offices, fully air conditioned	1,076.00	100.00
Offices for letting, 5 to 10 storeys, non air conditioned	968.00	90.00
Offices for letting, 5 to 10 storeys, air conditioned	1,184.00	110.00
Offices for letting, high rise, air conditioned	1,722.00	160.00
Offices for owner occupation, 5 to 10 storeys, non air conditioned	1,184.00	110.00
Offices for owner occupation, 5 to 10 storeys, air conditioned	1,400.00	130.00
Offices for owner occupation, high rise, air conditioned	1,938.00	180.00
Prestige/headquarters office, 5 to 10 storeys, air conditioned	1,615.00	150.00
Prestige/headquarters office, high rise, air conditioned	2,153.00	200.00
Health and education buildings		
General hospitals (excluding specialist equipment and installation)	bed	80,000
Private hospitals (excluding specialist equipment and installation)	bed	120,000

	Cost m² RM	Cost ft² RM
Primary/junior schools (m²)	484.00	45.00
Secondary/middle schools (m²)	538.00	50.00

Recreation and arts buildings

	Cost m² RM	Cost ft² RM
Theatres (over 500 seats) including seating and stage equipment	seat	4,000
Theatres (less than 500 seats) including seating and stage equipment	seat	5,000
Concert halls including seating	1,399.00	130.00
Sports hall including changing and social facilities	968.80	90.00
Swimming pools (international standard) including changing and social facilities	each	900,000
Swimming pools (schools standard) including changing facilities	each	300,000
National museums including full air conditioning and standby generator	1,076.00	100.00
Local museums including air conditioning	1,023.00	95.00

Residential buildings

	Cost m² RM	Cost ft² RM
Social/economic single family housing (multiple units)	538.00	50.00
Private/mass market single family housing 2 storey detached/semidetached (multiple units)	646.00	60.00
Purpose designed single family housing 2 storey detached (single unit)	807.00	75.00
Social/economic apartment housing, low rise (no lifts)	430.50	40.00
Social/economic apartment housing, high rise (with lifts)	753.50	70.00
Private sector apartment building (standard specification)	850.00	79.00
Private sector apartment buildings (luxury)	1,200.00	111.50
Student/nurses halls of residence	646.00	60.00
Homes for the elderly (shared accommodation)	538.00	50.00
Homes for the elderly (self contained with shared communal facilities)	646.00	60.00
Hotel, 5 star, city centre	3,229.00	300.00
Hotel, 3 star, city/provincial	2,260.00	210.00
Motel	1,399.00	130.00

Regional variations

The approximate estimating costs are based on projects in the capital.
Adjust these costs by the following factors to take account of regional
variations:

Selangor	0%
Penang	+5%
Johore	+15%
Kota Kinabalu	+15%
Kuching	+15%

EXCHANGE RATES AND INFLATION

The combined effect of exchange rates and inflation on prices within a
country and price comparisons between countries is discussed in section 2.

Exchange rates

The graph below plots the movement of the Malaysian ringgit against
sterling, the US dollar and 100 Japanese yen since 1985. The values used
for the graph are quarterly and the method of calculating these is described
and general guidance on the interpretation of the graph provided in section
2. The average exchange rate in the third quarter of 1995 was RM3.91
to the pound sterling and RM2.47 to the US dollar and RM2.93 to 100
Japanese yen.

THE MALAYSIAN RINGGIT AGAINST STERLING,THE US DOLLAR AND
THE JAPANESE YEN

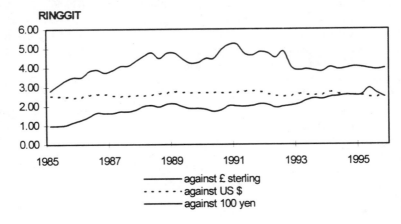

Price inflation

The Government has expressed concern over price escalation of building materials over the last three years. The Ministry of Domestic Trade and Consumer Affairs has conducted a study on the demand and supply of major building materials in Malaysia to monitor the price hike in building materials.

The table below shows consumer price and building price inflation in Malaysia since 1980.

CONSUMER PRICE AND BUILDING PRICE INFLATION

Year	Consumer price inflation average index	average change %	Building price index average index	average change %
1980	100		100	
1981	109	9.0	114	14.0
1982	116	6.4	123	7.9
1983	122	5.2	125	1.6
1984	125	2.5	124	-0.8
1985	126	0.8	125	0.8
1986	126	0.0	124	-0.8
1987	128	1.6	123	-0.8
1988	131	2.3	126	2.4
1989	135	3.1	131	4.0
1990	140	3.7	140	6.7
1991	146	4.4	143	2.1
1992	153	4.7	147	2.8
1993	158	3.6	152	3.4
1994	164	3.7	158	3.9

USEFUL ADDRESSES

Principal Central Government Construction Ministry(ies)

The Ministry of Works
    Kementerian Kerjaraya Malaysia
    Jalan Sultan Salahuddin
    50580 Kuala Lumpur
    Tel: (03) 2919011
    Fax: (03) 2936954/2986612
    Cable: MINWORK, KUALA LUMPUR
    Telex: KRT MA 30415

Regional Government Development Departments

Department of National Housing
    Jabatan Perumahan Negara
    Tingkat 5&6 Exchange Square
    Off Jalan Sumanthan
    Damansara Heights
    50490 Kuala Lumpur
    Tel: (03) 2540222
    Fax: (03) 2530709

The Ministry of Housing and Local Government
    Kementerian Perumahan dan Kerajaan Tempatan
    Paras 4 & 5 Block K
    Pusat Bandar Damansara
    50644 Kuala Lumpur
    Tel: (03) 2547470/7332/7033
    Fax: (03) 2554066

The Public Works Department
    Jabatan Kerja Awam
    (in every state there is a State Public Works Department)

Urban Development Authority (UDA)
    Perbadanan Pembangunan Bandar
    Perbadanan Pembangunan Bandar Ibu Pejabat
    Menara Bukit Bintang
    Lot 111 Jalan Bukit Bintang
    55100 Kuala Lumpur
    Tel: (03) 2428022
    Fax: (03) 2441171

Other Relevant Ministries/Departments

The Malaysian Highway Authority
    Lembaga Lebuhraya Malaysia
    KM 6 Jalan Kajang Serdang
    Peti Surat 22 43000 Kajang
    43000 Kuala Lumpur
    Tel: (03) 8366211
    Fax: (03) 8370822

The Ministry of Land and Regional Development
Kementerian Kemajuan Tanah dan Kemajuan Wilayah
T.13 Wisma Tanah
Jalan Semarak
50574 Kuala Lumpur
Tel: (03) 2921566

The Ministry of Public Enterprises
Kementerian Perusahaan Awam
Tingkat 24 Bangunan Medan Mara
Jalan Raja Laut
50625 Kuala Lumpur
Tel: (03) 2985022
Fax: (03) 2917623

The Ministry of Science, Technology and the Environment
Kementerian Sains, Teknologi dan Alam Sekitar Malaysia
Tingkat 14 Wisma Sime Darby
Jalan Raja Laut
50662 Kuala Lumpur
Tel: (03) 2938955
Fax: (03) 2936006

Town and Country Planning Department
Jabatan Perancang Bandar dan Desa
Jabatan Perancang Department
Jalan Cenderasari
50464 Kuala Lumpur
Tel: (03) 2989211
Fax: (03) 2929994

Contractors' Association

Master Builders Association Malaysia
13C Jalan Gereja (3rd Floor)
50100 Kuala Lumpur
Tel: (03) 2321636, 2382433
Fax: (03) 2383228

Contractors' Registration Board

Board of Architects Malaysia
  Lembaga Akitek Malaysia
  2nd Floor Block C
  Cawangan Bangunan, Ibu Pejabat JKR
  Jalan Tun Ismail, P O Box 12695
  50786 Kuala Lumpur
  Tel: (03) 2982978

Pusat Khidmat Kontraktor
  Kementerian Perusahan Awam
  Medan Mara Tkt 15&16
  Jalan Raja Laut
  50502 Kuala Lumpur
  Tel: (03) 2937088
  Fax: (03) 2922009

New Zealand

KEY DATA

Population
Population	3.5mn
Urban population	86%
Population under 15 (1991)	23%
Population over 65 and over (1991)	11%
Average annual growth rate (1980 to 1993)	0.9%

Geography
Land area	271,000 km²
Agricultural area	53%
Capital city	Wellington
Population of capital city (1991)	325,680
Largest city	Auckland
Population of largest city	885,600

Economy
Monetary unit	New Zealand dollar (NZ$)
Exchange rate (average third quarter 1995) to:	
the pound sterling	NZ$2.38
the US dollar	NZ$1.50
the yen x 100	NZ$1.63
Average annual inflation (1980 to 1993)	8.5%
Inflation rate (1994)	1.7%
Gross Domestic Product (GDP) at market price	NZ$79.4bn
GDP per capita	NZ$26,685
Average annual real change in GDP (1980 to 1993)	1.5%
Private consumption as a proportion of GDP	60%
General government consumption as a proportion of GDP	15%
Gross domestic investment as a proportion of GDP	21%
Central government expenditure as a proportion of Gross National Product	37%

Construction
Gross value of construction output	NZ$7.1bn
Net value of construction output +	NZ$3.2bn
Net value of construction output as a proportion of GDP +	4%

All data relate to 1993 unless otherwise indicated
+ EIU Country Report estimate

THE CONSTRUCTION INDUSTRY

Construction output

The value of gross construction output for 1993 is estimated at NZ$7.1 billion, equivalent to US$3.9 billion, or 9% of GDP. The net value of construction output in 1993 has been estimated by the *Economist Intelligence Unit* to be 4% of GDP or NZ$3.2 billion, equivalent to US$1.7 billion. This figure is low as is the gross output as a percentage of GDP. There may have been an increase by 1995. In the early part of 1995, manufacturing and construction were the key industries underpinning growth in the economy. Building work in 1993 accounted for 43% of total investment in fixed assets.

The breakdown by type of work is shown below:

VALUE OF BUILDING WORK PUT IN PLACE

Type of building	1993/94* NZ$ million	% of total
New dwellings	2,231	50
Alterations and additions	561	13
Total dwellings	2,792	63
Commercial buildings	600	14
Factories	289	7
Hotels and boarding houses	76	2
Schools	190	4
Hospitals	113	3
Other	331	7
Total non-residential buildings	1,599	37
Total	4,391	100

Source: Statistics New Zealand, Key Statistics
* *year ending 31 March*

Characteristics and structure of the industry

Major legislative reforms have occurred in 1991/92 which are having a significant impact on the characteristics and structure of the industry. The former Ministry of Works has been privatized along with many other government departments.

The industry is just beginning to feel the impact of several other reforms - the *Resource Management Act 1991* (which replaces all land, water and air legislation and subsumes the *Town & Country Planning Act 1977*); the *Employment Contracts Act 1992* (which allows individual bargaining rather than national awards); and more generally the requirement for all public and private sector dealings to uphold the principles of the *Treaty of Waitangi* in recognizing the Maori people of New Zealand.

The principles of the *Resource Management Act* are 'sustainable development and minimal adverse environmental effects' but the definitions and implications are unclear and there is expected to be considerable litigation.

Because of the serious falls in building output since 1987/88 contractors have cut staff to minimal levels. The number of persons employed in the industry has fallen dramatically since early 1990. Between June quarter 1990 and June quarter 1991 the construction industry lost around 22% of its workers. Presumably some of these emigrated to Australia and may return if business picks up. However, even with the modest increases in activity some developers have suggested that there are already some capacity constraints with contractors reporting they are too busy even to price jobs.

The Fletcher Construction Company Ltd is number 20 in the 1991 *Engineering News Record* with contracts of nearly US$2 billion of which over 90% were abroad.

Development control and standards

In December 1991, the new *Building Act* reformed the building control system, generally in line with the 1990 recommendations of the NZ Building Industry Commission. There is now a national performance-based *New Zealand Building Code* (NZBC) replacing all local building bylaws and including energy efficiency requirements. The Building Industry Authority (BIA), established under the new Act, now monitors NZBC administration by Territorial Authorities (amalgamated from 231 local councils in 1989 to 81 local and 14 district councils) that issue determinations, grant national accreditation of products and systems, and approve private certifiers. The Act also limits latent defects liability to 10 years from contract completion and introduces durability requirements. Approved documents issued by the BIA contain non-mandatory examples of compliance. The transition period from the old control system ended on 31 December 1992.

CONSTRUCTION COST DATA

Cost of labour

The figures below are typical of labour costs in Auckland as at the third quarter of 1995. The wage rate is the basis of an employee's income.

	Wage rate (per hour) NZ$	Number of hours worked per year
Site operatives		
Mason/bricklayer	24	2,068
Carpenter	24	2,068
Plumber	28	2,068
Electrician	28	2,068
Structural steel erector	24	2,068
HVAC installer	20	2,068
Semi-skilled worker	20	2,068
Unskilled labourer	18	2,068
Equipment operator	21	2,068
Watchman/security	18	2,068
Site supervision		
General foreman	32	2,068
Trades foreman	30	2,068
Clerk of works	35	2,068
Contractors' personnel		
Site manager	38	2,068
Resident engineer	50	1,762
Resident surveyor	50	1,762
Junior engineer	14	1,762
Junior surveyor	18	1,762
Planner	18	1,762

	Wage rate (per hour) NZ$	Number of hours worked per year
Consultants' personnel		
Senior architect	50	1,762
Senior engineer	45	1,762
Senior surveyor	48	1,762
Qualified architect	48	1,762
Qualified engineer	48	1,762
Qualified surveyor	48	1,762

Cost of materials

The figures that follow are the costs of main construction materials, delivered to site in the Auckland area, as incurred by contractors in the third quarter of 1995. These assume that the materials would be in quantities as required for a medium sized construction project and that the location of the works would be neither constrained nor remote.

All the costs in this section exclude Goods and Services tax (GST - see below).

	Unit	Cost NZ$
Cement and aggregate		
Ordinary portland cement in 40kg bags	tonne	315.00
Coarse aggregates for concrete	m^3	79.00
Fine aggregates for concrete	m^3	75.00
Ready mixed concrete (17.5 MPa)	m^3	148.00
Ready mixed concrete (30.0 MPa)	m^3	182.00
Steel		
Mild steel reinforcement (16mm)	tonne	1,400.00
High tensile steel reinforcement (16mm)	tonne	1,450.00
Structural steel sections	tonne	1,400.00
Bricks and blocks		
Common bricks (190 x 90 x 90mm)	1,000	970.00
Good quality facing bricks (190 x 90 x 90mm)	1,000	980.00
Hollow concrete blocks	1,000	230.00
Solid concrete blocks	m^2	250.00
Precast concrete cladding units with exposed aggregate finish (200mm thick)	m^2	240.00

	Unit	Cost NZ$
Timber and insulation		
Softwood sections for carpentry	m³	800.00
Softwood for joinery	m³	900.00
Hardwood for joinery	m³	1400.00
Exterior quality plywood (9mm)	m²	13.00
Plywood for interior joinery (9mm)	m²	11.00
Softwood strip flooring (50mm)	m	4.00
Chipboard sheet flooring (20mm)	m²	22.00
100mm thick quilt insulation	m²	10.00
100mm thick rigid slab insulation	m²	40.00
Softwood internal door complete with frames and ironmongery	each	400.00
Glass and ceramics		
Float glass (6mm)	m²	130.00
Sealed double glazing units (two layers laminated glass)	m²	450.00
Plaster and paint		
Good quality ceramic wall tiles (150 x 150mm)	m²	120.00
Plaster in 50kg bags	tonne	352.00
Plasterboard (12.5mm thick)	m²	16.00
Emulsion paint in 5 litre tins	m²	7.50
Gloss oil paint in 5 litre tins	m²	10.50
Tiles and paviors		
Clay floor tiles (200 x 200mm)	m²	90.00
Vinyl floor tiles (2mm thick)	m²	30.00
Precast concrete paving slabs (100mm)	m²	60.00
Precast concrete roof tiles	m²	33.00
Drainage		
WC suite complete	each	680.00
Lavatory basin complete	each	265.00
100mm diameter clay drain pipes	m	28.00

Unit rates

The descriptions below are generally shortened versions of standard descriptions listed in full in section 4. Where an item has a two digit reference number (e.g. 05 or 33), this relates to the full description against that number in section 4. Where an item has an alphabetic suffix (e.g. 12A or 34B) this indicates that the standard description has been modified. Where a modification is major the complete modified description is included here and the standard description should be ignored; where a modification is minor (e.g. the insertion of a named hardwood) the shortened description has been modified here but, in general, the full description in section 4 prevails.

The unit rates below are for main work items on a typical construction project in the Auckland area in the third quarter of 1995. The rates include all necessary labour, materials and equipment. Allowances to cover preliminary and general items and contractors' overheads and profit should be added to these rates. All the rates in this section exclude Goods and Services tax (GST - see below).

		Unit	*Rate NZ$*
Excavation			
01	Mechanical excavation of foundation trenches	m³	32.50
02	Hardcore filling making up levels	m³	81.00
03	Earthwork support	m²	54.20
Concrete work			
04	Plain insitu concrete in strip foundations in trenches	m³	243.60
05	Reinforced insitu concrete in beds	m³	277.30
06	Reinforced insitu concrete in walls	m³	261.00
07	Reinforced insitu concrete in suspended floors or roof slabs	m³	239.00
08	Reinforced insitu concrete in columns	m³	249.60
09	Reinforced insitu concrete in isolated beams	m³	243.60
10	Precast concrete slab	m²	116.00
Formwork			
11	Softwood or metal formwork to concrete walls	m²	95.20
12	Softwood or metal formwork to concrete columns	m²	98.60
13	Softwood or metal formwork to horizontal soffits of slabs	m²	104.40

		Unit	Rate NZ$
Reinforcement			
14	Reinforcement in concrete walls	tonne	2,204.00
15	Reinforcement in suspended concrete slabs	tonne	2,146.00
16	Fabric reinforcement in concrete beds	m²	11.00
Steelwork			
17	Fabricate, supply and erect steel framed structure	tonne	4,176.00
18	Framed structural steelwork in universal joist sections	tonne	2,726.00
19	Structural steelwork lattice roof trusses	tonne	5,150.00
Brickwork and blockwork			
20	Precast lightweight aggregate hollow concrete block walls	m²	92.80
21A	Solid (perforated) concrete blocks	m²	139.20
23	Facing bricks	m²	167.00
Roofing			
24	Concrete interlocking roof tiles 430 x 380mm	m²	52.80
26	Fibre cement roof slates 600 x 300mm	m²	141.50
27	Sawn softwood roof boarding	m²	160.00
29	3 layers glass-fibre based bitumen felt roof covering	m²	121.80
30	Bitumen based mastic asphalt roof covering	m²	71.90
31A	Glass-fibre mat roof insulation 100mm thick	m²	18.60
33	Troughed galvanized steel roof cladding	m²	51.00
Woodwork and metalwork			
34	Preservative treated sawn softwood 50 x 100mm	m	2.70
35	Preservative treated sawn softwood 50 x 150mm	m	4.30
36	Single glazed casement window in hardwood, 650 x 900mm	m²	852.60
37	Two panel glazed door in hardwood, 850 x 2000mm including ironmongery	each	510.40
38A	Solid core half hour fire resisting hardwood internal flush doors, size 800 x 2000mm including ironmongery	each	1,276.00
39	Aluminium double glazed window, size 1200 x 1200mm	m²	467.50
40	Aluminium double glazed door, size 850 x 2100mm	each	2,030.00
41	Hardwood skirtings	m	13.00
Plumbing			
42	UPVC half round eaves gutter	m	16.50
43	UPVC rainwater pipes	m	25.00
44	Light gauge copper cold water tubing	m	12.40
45	High pressure plastic pipes for cold water supply	m	9.75
46	Low pressure plastic pipes for cold water distribution	m	11.95

	Unit	Rate NZ$
47 UPVC soil and vent pipes	m	42.50
48 White vitreous china WC suite	each	919.90
49 White vitreous china lavatory basin	each	540.60
51 Stainless steel single bowl sink and double drainer	each	690.20

Electrical work

52 PVC insulated and copper sheathed cable	m	5.90
53A 15 amp switched socket outlet	each	15.95
54 Flush mounted 20 amp, 1 way light switch	each	13.30

Finishings

55 2 coats gypsum based plaster on brick walls	m²	51.85
56 White glazed tiles on plaster walls	m²	133.40
57 Red clay quarry tiles on concrete floors	m²	110.20
58 Cement and sand screed to concrete floors	m²	38.30
60 Mineral fibre tiles on exposed two way suspension system	m²	39.45

Glazing

61A 6mm clear float glass; glazing to wood	m²	78.90

Painting

62 Emulsion on plaster walls	m²	10.45
63 Oil paint on timber	m²	12.80

Approximate estimating

The building costs per unit area given below are averages incurred by building clients for typical buildings in the Auckland area as at the third quarter of 1995. They are based upon the total floor area of all storeys, measured between external walls and without deduction for internal walls.

Approximate estimating costs generally include mechanical and electrical installations but exclude furniture, loose or special equipment, and external works; they also exclude fees for professional services. The costs shown are for specifications and standards appropriate to New Zealand and this should be borne in mind when attempting comparisons with similarly described building types in other countries. A discussion of this issue is included in section 2. Comparative data for countries covered in this publication including construction cost data is presented in Part Three.

Approximate estimating costs must be treated with caution; they cannot provide more than a rough guide to the probable cost of building. All the rates in this section exclude general sales tax (GST - see opposite).

	Cost m^2 NZ$	Cost ft^2 NZ$
Industrial buildings		
Factories for letting	390	36
Factories for owner occupation (light industrial use)	410	38
Factories for owner occupation (heavy industrial use)	480	45
Factory/office (high-tech) for letting (shell and core only)	570	53
Factory/office (high-tech) for letting (ground floor shell, first floor offices)	620	58
Factory/office (high tech) for owner occupation (controlled environment, fully finished)	750	70
High tech laboratory workshop centres (air conditioned)	1,800	167
Warehouses, low bay (6 to 8m high) for letting (no heating)	400	37
Warehouses, low bay for owner occupation (including heating)	500	46
Warehouses, high bay for owner occupation (including heating)	650	60
Administrative and commercial buildings		
Civic offices, non air conditioned	1,400	131
Civic offices, fully air conditioned	1,580	147
Offices for letting, 5 to 10 storeys, non air conditioned	1,500	139
Offices for letting, 5 to 10 storeys, air conditioned	1,750	162
Offices for letting, high rise, air conditioned	2,000	186
Offices for owner occupation 5 to 10 storeys, non air conditioned	1,700	158
Offices for owner occupation high rise, air conditioned	2,000	186
Prestige/headquarters office, 5 to 10 storeys, air conditioned	2,200	204
Prestige/headquarters office, high rise, air conditioned	2,400+	223+
Health and education buildings		
General hospitals (100 beds)	2,400	223
Teaching hospitals (100 beds)	2,400	223
Private hospitals (100 beds) aged persons	1,400	131
Health centres	1,600	149
Nursery schools	950	88
Primary/junior schools	950	88
Secondary/middle schools	1,100	102
University (arts) buildings	1,400	131
University (science) buildings	1,650	153
Management training centres	1,450	135
Recreation and arts buildings		
Theatres (over 500 seats) including seating and stage equipment	1,500	139
Theatres (less than 500 seats) including seating and stage equipment	1,700	158

	Cost m² NZ$	Cost ft² NZ$
Concert halls including seating and stage equipment	1,600	149
Sports halls including changing and social facilities	1,300	121
Swimming pools (international standard) including changing and social facilities	2,000	186
Swimming pools (schools standard) including changing facilities	1,800	167
National museums including full air conditioning and standby generator	2,500+	232+
Local museums including air conditioning	2,100	195

Residential buildings

	Cost m² NZ$	Cost ft² NZ$
Social/economic single family housing (multiple units)	830	77
Private/mass market single family housing 2 storey detached/semidetached (multiple units)	850	79
Purpose designed single family housing 2 storey detached (single unit)	1,100	102
Social/economic apartment housing, low rise (no lifts)	1,650	153
Private sector apartment building (standard specification)	1,800	167
Private sector apartment buildings (luxury)	2,200	204
Student/nurses halls of residence	1,500	140
Homes for the elderly (shared accommodation)	1,800	168
Homes for the elderly (self contained with shared communal facilities)	1,300	121
Hotel, 5 star, city centre	2,800	260
Hotel, 3 star, city/provincial	2,200	204
Motel	1,500	139

Goods and Services Tax (GST)

The standard rate of Goods and Services tax (GST) is currently 12.5%, chargeable on building work.

EXCHANGE RATES AND INFLATION

The combined effect of exchange rates and inflation on prices within a country and price comparisons between countries is discussed in section 2.

Exchange rates

The graph below plots the movement of the New Zealand dollar against sterling, US dollar and 100 Japanese yen since 1985. The values used for the graph are quarterly and the method of calculating these is described and general guidance on the interpretation of the graph provided in section 2. The average exchange rate in the third quarter of 1995 was NZ$2.38 to the pound sterling and NZ$1.50 to US dollar and NZ$1.63 to 100 Japanese yen.

THE NEW ZEALAND DOLLAR AGAINST STERLING, US DOLLAR AND JAPANESE YEN

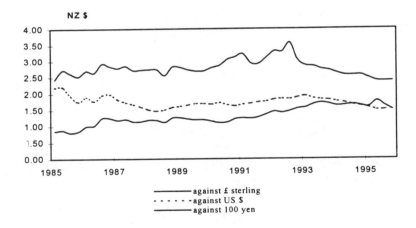

Price inflation

The table below presents consumer price, house price and construction price inflation in New Zealand since 1980.

CONSUMER PRICE, HOUSE PRICE AND CONSTRUCTION COST INFLATION

Year	Consumer price index		House price index		Construction cost index	
	average index	average change %	average index	average change %	average index	average change %
1980	100		100		100	
1981	116	16.0	110	10.0	130	17.6
1982	134	15.5	143	30.0	156	7.5
1983	157	17.2	176	23.1	179	1.5
1984	165	5.1	191	8.5	181	13.7
1985	177	7.3	216	13.1	195	13.4
1986	205	15.8	247	14.4	215	5.3
1987	228	9.0	265	7.3	237	7.6
1988	267	4.0	323	21.9	257	5.0
1989	282	9.0	346	7.1	273	4.5
1990	302	4.5	372	7.5	285	4.3
1991	317	0.8	400	7.5	296	0.3
1992	324	0.9	393	-1.8	302	1.8
1993		1.3		6.1		2.1
1994		4.0		11.1		2.5

USEFUL ADDRESSES

Public organizations

Building Industry Commission
    PO Box 11-846
    Wellington
    Tel: 4 471 0794
    Fax: 4 471 0798

Department of Scientific and Industrial Research
    Director General
    PO Box 1378
    Wellington
    Tel: 4 472 9979
    Fax: 4 472 4025

Department of Statistics
    Marketing Manager
    PO Box 2822
    Wellington
    Tel: 4 472 9119
    Fax: 4 472 9135

Housing Corporation of New Zealand
    PO Box 5009
    Wellington
    Tel: 4 472 1293
    Fax: 4 472 3152

Ministry of Commerce (Building Issues Unit)
    PO Box 173
    Wellington
    Tel: 4 474 2921
    Fax: 4 471 2658

Ministry of Transport
    PO Box 3175
    Wellington
    Tel: 4 472 1253
    Fax: 4 495 0565

Standards Association of New Zealand
    Executive Director
    Private Bag
    Wellington
    Tel: 4 384 2108
    Fax: 4 384 3936

Trade and professional associations

Architectural Aluminium Association of New Zealand
    Director General
    PO Box 11-543
    Wellington
    Tel: 4 473 3000
    Fax: 4 473 3004

Auckland Building Exhibition Centre
Centre Manager
Downtown Centre
Auckland
Tel: 9 309 0976
Fax: 9 379 2988

Building Industry Authority
PO Box 11-846
Wellington
Tel: 4 471 0794
Fax: 4 471 0798

Building Research Association of New Zealand
PO Box 50908
Porirua
Tel: 4 235 7600
Fax: 4 235 8070

Cement and Concrete Association of New Zealand
Private Bag 50902
Porirua
Tel: 4 232 8379
Fax: 4 235 4393

Designers Institute of New Zealand
Administrator
PO Box 5521
Auckland
Tel: 9 377 6012
Fax: 9 388 4713

Electrical Contractors Association of New Zealand Inc
Secretary
PO Box 6372
Wellington
Tel: 4 385 9657
Fax: 4 385 4645

Institute of Professional Engineers
    Chief Executive Director
    PO Box 12-241
    Wellington
    Tel: 4 473 9444
    Fax: 4 473 3011

National Contractors' Association
    Chief Executive
    New Zealand Contractors Federation
    PO Box 12-013
    Wellington
    Tel: 4 473 6514
    Fax: 4 473 2730

New Zealand Heavy Engineering Research Association
    Director
    PO Box 76-134
    Manukau City
    Tel: 9 262 2885
    Fax: 9 262 2858

New Zealand Institute of Architects
    Secretary
    PO Box 483
    Wellington
    Tel: 4 473 53476
    Fax: 4 472 0182

New Zealand Institute of Quantity Surveyors
    Executive Director
    PO Box 3635
    Wellington
    Tel: 4 473 5521
    Fax: 4 473 2918

New Zealand Institute of Surveyors
    Secretary
    PO Box 831
    Wellington
    Tel: 4 471 1774
    Fax: 4 471 1907

DAVIS LANGDON & SEAH PHILIPPINES INC

The strategic and integrated management of cost, time and quality - the client "risk" areas of a contract - are essential functions, which are necessary to ensure the satisfactory planning, procurement, execution and operation of construction projects.

We specialise in the financial management of construction projects and their risk areas, from project inception to completion and we concentrate on:

- being positive and creative in our advice, rather than simply reactive;

- providing value for money via efficient management, rather than on superficial cost monitoring;

- giving advice that is matched to the client's requirements, rather than imposing standard or traditional solutions;

- paying attention to the life-cycle costs of constructing and occupying a building, rather than to the initial capital cost only.

Our aim is to provide our clients with risk assurance, cost control and value for money, via effective advice, cost planning and management.

DAVIS LANGDON & SEAH PHILIPPINES INC
4/F King's Court 1
2129 Pasong Tamo
Makati City
Philippines
Tel : (632) 8112971
Fax : (632) 8112071

DAVIS LANGDON & SEAH INTERNATIONAL

Philippines

KEY DATA

Population

Population	64.8mn
Urban population	52%
Population under 15	37%
Population 65 and over	4%
Average annual growth rate (1980 to 1993)	2.3%

Geography

Land area	300,000 km²
Agricultural area	24%
Capital city	Manila
Population of capital city	1.8mn

Economy

Monetary unit	Philippines peso (P)
Exchange rate (average third quarter 1995) to:	
the pound sterling	P40.73
the US dollar	P25.70
the yen x 100	P28.01
Average annual inflation (1980 to 1993)	13.6%
Inflation rate (1994)	9.3%
Gross Domestic Product (GDP) at market price	P1,475bn
GDP per capita	P22,760
Average annual real change in GDP (1980 to 1993)	1.4%
Private consumption as a proportion of GDP	76%
General government consumption as a proportion of GDP	9%
Gross domestic investment as a proportion of GDP	24%
Central government expenditure as a proportion of Gross National Product	18%

Construction

Gross value of construction output *	P192bn
Net value of construction output	P79.6bn
Net value of construction output as a proportion of GDP	5.4%
Cement production	8mn tonnes

All data relate to 1993 unless otherwise indicated

* *Authors' estimate*

THE CONSTRUCTION INDUSTRY

Construction output

The value of gross construction output in 1993 is estimated at P192 billion, equivalent to US$7 billion, or 13% of GDP. The value of net construction output in 1993 was P79.6 billion, equivalent to US$3.0 billion, or 5.4% of GDP. The net value of construction output in 1994 was P93 billion, equivalent to US$3.5 billion, or 5.6% of GDP.

The figures for gross output of construction are not from official statistics. Official data indicate that construction output was P146.5 billion or 10.1% of GDP. This is very low in relation both to the level of net output of 5.4% of GDP and also very low in relation to an investment of 24% of GDP. A figure of 13% of GDP seems more likely. The discrepancy could be accounted for by the difficulty of counting construction activity in the Philippines.

The Construction Industry Authority of the Philippines (CIAP) cited lower interest rates and general stability in the supply of construction materials, particularly cement products, as helping boost residential and non-residential construction activities.

The gross value added (GVA) in construction reached P38.67 billion, accounting for the highest growth rate (6.6%) in the industrial sector.

In 1994 the construction industry continued to play a significant role in the growth of the economy. A 10.9% growth in the net value of construction output was exceeded only by growth in the electricity, gas and water sectors. A healthy business climate encouraged growth of 10.5% in the level of domestic investment in construction, a contribution of 42% to investment in fixed capital. There was an increase in construction activity both in the public and private sectors. Public work accounted for 44% of gross construction output and private work for 56%.

A breakdown of new building starts is shown in the table opposite. The table shows a large increase from 1993 to 1994 in residential and industrial building. Indeed there was a surge in activity in the construction of residential buildings (particularly housing for low and middle income groups), high rise offices, condominiums, hotels, restaurants and industrial buildings as well as implementation of government flagship projects.

VALUE OF NEW BUILDING STARTS, 1993 AND 1994

Type of work	1993		1994	
	P billion	% of total	P billion	% of total
Resident	17.0	47	21.5	46
Commercial	12.4	34	12.1	25
Industrial	2.5	7	9.2	20
Institutional	3.5	10	3.4	7
Others	0.6	2	0.9	2
Total	36.0	100	47.1	100

Source : Construction Division, National Statistics Office, July 1995

The regional distribution of net value of construction in 1994 in relation to the distribution of population is shown below.

REGIONAL DISTRIBUTION OF CONSTRUCTION COMPARED TO POPULATION

Region	Population (1990) %	Construction (1994) %
National Capital Region (NCR)		
Metro Manila	13	28
I Ilocos Region	6	4
II Cagayan Valley	4	2
III Central Luzon	10	13
IV Southern Tagalog	14	18
V Bicol Region	7	4
VI Western Visayas	9	5
VII Central Visayas	8	6
VIII Eastern Visayas	5	3
IX Western Mindanao	2	3
X Northern Mindanao	6	4
XI Southern Mindanao	7	6
XII Central Mindanao	4	3
XIII Cordillera Autonomous Region (CAR)	2	1
XIV Autonomous Region for Muslim Mindanao (ARMM)	3	-
Total	100	100

Source: Regional Accounts of the Philippines, July 1995

Each of the regions of the greatest construction activity - the Capital Region, Metro Manila, Central Luzon and Southern Tagalog has a larger proportion of national construction output than of the national population.

Characteristics and structure of the industry

The majority of owners commission their own design with a separate planning or architectural firm and invite contractors to bid for its construction. Design and build is used only for small scale projects such as low cost housing projects. In recent years, management contracting has developed considerably in the Philippines especially for large projects. It is however gaining in popularity for the larger projects. The larger general companies include:

1 A.M. Oreta & Company Inc
2 Asiakonstrukt
3 Atlantic, Gulf & Pacific Company, Manila
4 D.M. Consuji Inc
5 F.F. Cruz & Company Inc
6 Filipinas Systems Inc
7 Makati Development Corporation
8 Shimizu Philippine Contractors, Inc
9 W. Golangco Construction Corporation

Clients and finance

The National Statistical Coordination Board (NSCB) data for 1993 showed that over half of the construction output is financed by the private sector and that it turned in P38.385 billion in gross value, cornering 55.1% of the construction industry's total. While the public sector exhibited a growth rate of 15.6%, its gross value amounting to P31.327 billion represented only 44.9% of the total.

Moreover, public and private construction are expected to accelerate at an average annual rate of 9.8% and 6.0%, respectively, from 1995-1998 citing the government's *Core Public Investment Program*, which has 85 flagship projects worth P223 billion for implementation in the medium term as of end 1994.

Selection of design consultants

Generally, professional consultants are appointed directly by the client though sometimes another consultant will make the appointment and occasionally some form of competition is held. Both for private and public work, price is the most important criterion followed by track record, personal contacts and recommendations. There are no recommended fee scales.

Contractual arrangements

In almost all cases building work is undertaken by general contractors. Selection is by competitive tender and the contract is awarded to the contractor who submits the lowest and most comprehensive bid. The principal contract documents comprise conditions of contract, general agreement, schedule of works and bills of quantities.

The selected contractor normally provides all construction materials, manpower, and other inputs. However, in some cases the owner supplies certain materials. Some major contracting companies nominate subcontractors to undertake specialized works such as prestressed concrete, plumbing, electrical, mechanical and drainage.

Development control and standards

The National Housing and Land Use Regulatory Board is responsible for controlling land use and building operations in the industry. The board is responsible for issuing development permits and for ensuring that developers comply with the required standards. Guidelines and procedures for obtaining permits are enumerated in their handbooks, *PD 957* for high cost housing and *BP 225* for low cost housing. The request for a permit is processed only after all requirements are met. It takes about one to three months before a certificate of registration and licence to sell is issued.

All new construction in the Philippines has to comply with the provisions set out in the third edition of the *National Structural Code of the Philippines* or *NSCP,* the *ACI-1989 edition*, the 1985 edition of the *Uniform Building Code* and the 1985 edition of the *AISC Steel Manual.* Deviation from the codes may be allowed by the building officials, provided it is shown and verified by tests that such deviation is within the scope of the code. The *ACI-1989* edition covers the proper design and construction of reinforced concrete buildings. It covers subjects such as permits, inspections, specifications, materials, concrete quality, mixing, formwork, embedded pipes, strength and serviceability, loads, specifications and provisions for seismic design. The quality and testing of materials used in construction are covered by the *American ASTM standard specification* and the welding of reinforcement by the *American AWS standard.*

Liability

The contractor, according to the contract, guarantees the materials and workmanship for a minimum period of one year and is therefore responsible for making good any defects in construction. This is usually supported by a Guarantee Bond to the value of the contract. Main contractors, where relevant, will obtain guarantees from subcontractors. All disputes, claims or questions are settled according to the provisions of the Construction Industry Arbitration Commission.

CONSTRUCTION COST DATA

Cost of labour

The figures below are typical of labour costs in Metro Manila as at the third quarter of 1995. The wage rate is the basis of an employee's income, while the cost of labour indicates the cost to a contractor of employing that employee. The difference between the two covers a variety of mandatory and voluntary contributions - a list of items which could be included is given in section 2.

	Wage rate (per day) P	Cost of labour (per day) P	Number of hours worked per year
Site operatives			
Mason/bricklayer	200	250	2,496
Carpenter	212	265	2,496
Plumber	212	265	2,496
Electrician	233	291	2,496
Structural steel erector	215	267	2,496
HVAC installer	250	350	2,496
Semi-skilled worker	180	225	2,496
Unskilled labourer	145	181	2,496
Equipment operator	226	283	2,496
Watchman/security	183	229	2,496
Site supervision			
General foreman	500	625	2,496
Trades foreman	357	446	2,496
Clerk of works	238	298	2,496

	Wage rate (per day) P	Cost of labour (per day) P	Number of hours worked per year
Contractors' personnel			
Site manager	675	844	2,496
Resident engineer	550	688	2,496
Resident surveyor	550	688	2,496
Junior engineer	300	375	2,496
Junior surveyor	300	375	2,496
Planner	375	469	2,496
Consultants' personnel			
Senior architect	480	844	2,080
Senior engineer	500	688	2,080
Senior surveyor	400	688	2,080
Qualified architect	350	397	2,080
Qualified engineer	350	375	2,080
Qualified surveyor	330	375	2,080

Cost of materials

The figures that follow are the costs of main construction materials, delivered to site in the Metro Manila area, as incurred by contractors in the third quarter of 1995. These assume that the materials would be in quantities as required for a medium sized construction project and that the location of the works would be neither constrained nor remote. All the costs in this section exclude value added tax (VAT).

	Unit	Cost P
Cement and aggregate		
Ordinary portland cement in 40kg bags	bag	109
Coarse aggregates for concrete	m³	500
Fine aggregates for concrete	m³	360
Ready mixed concrete (A: 34 MPa)	m³	2,690
Ready mixed concrete (B: 27 MPa)	m³	2,316
Steel		
Mild steel reinforcement	tonne	14,778
High tensile steel reinforcement	tonne	17,944
Structural steel sections	tonne	38,500

	Unit	Cost P
Bricks and blocks		
Common bricks (2" x 4" x 8")	1,000	4,300
Good quality facing bricks (2" x 4" x 8")	1,000	10,400
Hollow concrete blocks (6" x 8" x 16")	1,000	6,700
Solid concrete blocks (6" x 8" x 16")	1,000	12,000
Precast concrete cladding units with exposed aggregate finish	m²	4,550
Timber and insulation		
Softwood sections for carpentry	m³	16,102
Softwood for joinery	m³	16,526
Hardwood for joinery	m³	21,187
Exterior quality plywood (10mm)	m²	256
Plywood for interior joinery (10mm)	m²	202
Softwood strip flooring (10mm)	m²	480
Chipboard sheet flooring (25mm)	m²	1,300
100mm thick quilt insulation	m²	342
100mm thick rigid slab insulation	m²	1,334
Softwood internal door complete with frames and ironmongery	each	4,770
Glass and ceramics		
Float glass	m²	475
Plaster and paint		
Good quality ceramic wall tiles (108 x 108mm)	m²	350
Plaster in 50 kg bags	tonne	2,350
Plasterboard (13mm thick)	m²	672
Emulsion paint	gallon	240
Tiles and paviors		
Clay floor tiles (4.25" x 4.25" x 0.125")	m²	146
Vinyl floor tiles (300 x 300 x 3mm)	m²	290
Precast concrete paving slabs (400 x 185 x 50mm)	m²	1,580
Drainage		
WC suite complete	each	4,500
Lavatory basin complete	each	4,500
150mm diameter cast iron drain pipes	m	2,475

Unit rates

The descriptions below are generally shortened versions of standard descriptions listed in full in section 4. Where an item has a two digit reference number (e.g. 05 or 33), this relates to the full description against that number in section 4. Where an item has an alphabetic suffix (e.g. 12A or 34B) this indicates that the standard description has been modified. Where a modification is major the complete modified description is included here and the standard description should be ignored; where a modification is minor (e.g. the insertion of a named hardwood) the shortened description has been modified here but, in general, the full description in section 4 prevails.

The unit rates below are for main work items on a typical construction project in the Metro Manila area in the third quarter of 1995. The rates include all necessary labour, materials and equipment. Allowances of 5%-10% to cover preliminary and general items and 3%-5% to cover contractors' overheads and profit have been included in the rates. All the rates in this section exclude value added tax.

		Unit	Rate P
Excavation			
01	Mechanical excavation of foundation trenches	m³	198
02	Hardcore filling making up levels	m³	405
03	Earthwork support	m²	72
Concrete work			
04	Plain insitu concrete in strip foundations in trenches	m³	1,278
05	Reinforced insitu concrete in beds	m³	2,646
06	Reinforced insitu concrete in walls	m³	2,646
07	Reinforced insitu concrete in suspended floors or roof slabs	m³	2,646
08	Reinforced insitu concrete in columns	m³	2,664
09	Reinforced insitu concrete in isolated beams	m³	2,628
10	Precast concrete slab	each	7,254
Formwork			
11	Softwood or metal formwork to concrete walls	m²	315
12	Softwood or metal formwork to concrete columns	m²	315
13	Softwood or metal formwork to horizontal soffits of slabs	m²	342
Reinforcement			
14	Reinforcement in concrete walls	kg	18
15	Reinforcement in suspended concrete slabs	kg	18
16	Fabric reinforcement in concrete beds	m²	45

		Unit	*Rate*
Steelwork			
17	Fabricate, supply and erect steel framed structure	tonne	51,300
18	Framed structural steelwork in universal joist sections	tonne	55,800
19	Structural steelwork lattice roof trusses	tonne	49,050
Brickwork and blockwork			
20	Precast lightweight aggregate hollow concrete block walls	m²	441
21A	Solid (perforated) concrete blocks	m²	337
22	Sand lime bricks	m²	45
Roofing			
24	Concrete interlocking roof tiles 430 x 380mm	m²	1,476
25	Plain clay roof tiles 260 x 160mm	m²	936
28	Particle board roof coverings	m²	756
29	3 layers glass-fibre based bitumen felt roof covering	m²	459
30	Bitumen based mastic asphalt roof covering	m²	531
31	Glass-fibre mat roof insulation 160mm thick	m²	468
32	Rigid sheet loadbearing roof insulation 75mm thick	m²	432
33	Troughed galvanized steel roof cladding	m²	477
Woodwork and metalwork			
34	Preservative treated sawn softwood 50 x 100mm	m	144
35	Preservative treated sawn softwood 50 x 150mm	m	144
36	Single glazed casement window in hardwood, size 650 x 900mm	each	702
37	Two panel glazed door in hardwood, size 850 x 2000mm	each	9,900
38	Solid core half hour fire resisting hardwood internal flush doors, size 800 x 2000mm	each	10,800
39	Aluminium double glazed window, size 1200 x 1200mm	each	14,850
40	Aluminium double glazed door, size 850 x 2100mm	each	15,750
41	Hardwood skirtings	m	171
Plumbing			
42	UPVC half round eaves gutter, 12"x8"	m	234
43	UPVC rainwater pipes, 4" diameter	m	324
44	Light gauge copper cold water tubing	m	207
45	High pressure plastic pipes for cold water supply	m	234
46	Low pressure plastic pipes for cold water distribution	m	36
47	UPVC soil and vent pipes, 4" diameter	m	324
48	White vitreous china WC suite	each	5,040

		Unit	Rate P
Electrical work			
52	PVC insulated and copper sheathed cable	m	1,080
53	13 amp unswitched socket outlet	each	239
54	Flush mounted 20 amp, 1 way light switch	each	162
Finishings			
55	2 coats gypsum based plaster on brick walls	m²	270
56	White glazed tiles on plaster walls	m²	630
57	Red clay quarry tiles on concrete floors	m²	351
58	Cement and sand screed to concrete floors	m²	135
59	Thermoplastic floor tiles on screed	m²	450
60	Mineral fibre tiles on concealed suspension system	m²	675
Glazing			
61	Glazing to wood	m²	540
Painting			
62	Emulsion on plaster walls	m²	48
63	Oil paint on timber	m²	135

Approximate estimating

The building costs per unit area given opposite are averages incurred by building clients for typical buildings in the Metro Manila area as at the third quarter of 1995. They are based upon the total floor area of all storeys, measured between external walls and without deduction for internal walls.

Approximate estimating costs generally include mechanical and electrical installations but exclude furniture, loose or special equipment, and external works; they also include professional services. The costs shown are for specifications and standards appropriate to the Philippines and this should be borne in mind when attempting comparisons with similarly described building types in other countries. A discussion in this issue is included in section 2. Comparative data for countries covered in this publication, including construction cost data, is included in Part Three.

Approximate estimating costs must be treated with caution; they cannot provide more than a rough guide to the probable cost of building. All the rates in this section exclude value added tax.

	Cost m² P	Cost ft² P
Industrial buildings		
Factories for letting	8,370	780
Factories for owner occupation (light industrial use)	10,170	950
Factories for owner occupation (heavy industrial use)	12,150	1,130
Factory/office (high-tech) for letting (shell and core only)	11,340	1,060
Factory/office (high-tech) for letting (ground floor shell, first floor offices)	10,350	970
Factory/office (high tech) for owner occupation (controlled environment, fully finished)	9,600	890
High tech laboratory workshop centres (air conditioned)	16,470	1,530
Warehouses, low bay (6 to 8m high) for letting (no heating)	7,490	700
Warehouses, low bay for owner occupation	8,550	800
Warehouses, high bay for owner occupation	9,180	860
Cold stores/refrigerated stores	11,700	1,090
Administrative and commercial buildings		
Civic offices, non air conditioned	13,050	1,220
Civic offices, fully air conditioned	14,850	1,380
Offices for letting, 5 to 10 storeys, non air conditioned	13,500	1,260
Offices for letting, 5 to 10 storeys, air conditioned	15,750	1,470
Offices for letting, high rise, air conditioned	19,800	1,840
Offices for owner occupation 5 to 10 storeys, non air conditioned	18,900	1,760
Offices for owner occupation 5 to 10 storeys, air conditioned	20,700	1,930
Offices for owner occupation high rise, air conditioned	22,500	2,090
Prestige/headquarters office, 5 to 10 storeys, air conditioned	23,400	2,180
Prestige/headquarters office, high rise, air conditioned	25,200	2,350
Health and education buildings		
General hospitals (230 beds)	27,630	2,570
Teaching hospitals (100 beds)	31,500	2,930
Private hospitals (100 beds)	29,340	2,730
Health centres	9,900	920
Nursery schools	9,900	920
Primary/junior schools	10,800	1,010
Secondary/middle schools	11,970	1,120
University (arts) buildings	13,050	1,220
University (science) buildings	14,850	1,380
Management training centres	14,850	1,380

	Cost m^2P	Cost ft^2P
Recreation and arts buildings		
Theatres (over 500 seats) including seating and stage equipment	22,680	2,110
Theatres (less than 500 seats) including seating and stage equipment	23,850	2,220
Concert halls including seating and stage equipment	23,850	2,220
Sports halls including changing and social facilities	14,670	1,370
National museums including full air conditioning and standby generator	21,420	1,990
Local museums including air conditioning	18,450	1,720
City centre/central libraries	15,480	1,440
Branch/local libraries	13,590	1,270
Residential buildings		
Social/economic single family housing (multiple units)	5,130	480
Private/mass market single family housing 2 storey detached/semidetached (multiple units)	6,480	610
Purpose designed single family housing 2 storey detached (single unit)	8,280	770
Social/economic apartment housing, low rise (no lifts)	9,720	910
Social/economic apartment housing, high rise (with lifts)	11,700	1,090
Private sector apartment building (standard specification)	15,300	1,430
Private sector apartment buildings (luxury)	18,900	1,760
Student/nurses halls of residence	14,670	1,370
Homes for the elderly (shared accommodation)	14,670	1,370
Hotel, 5 star, city centre	30,800	2,870
Hotel, 3 star, city/provincial	26,100	2,430
Motel	21,150	1,970

Value added tax (VAT)

The standard rate of value added tax (VAT) is currently 10%, chargeable on general building work.

EXCHANGE RATES AND INFLATION

The combined effect of exchange rates and inflation on prices within a country and price comparisons between countries is discussed in section 2.

Exchange rates

The graph below plots the movement of the Filipino peso against sterling,
US dollar and 100 Japanese yen since 1985. The values used for the graph
are quarterly and the method of calculating these is described and general
guidance on the interpretation of the graph provided in section 2. The
average exchange rate in the third quarter of 1995 was P40.73 to pound
sterling, P25.70 to US dollar and P28.01 to 100 Japanese yen.

THE FILIPINO PESO AGAINST STERLING, US DOLLAR AND
JAPANESE YEN

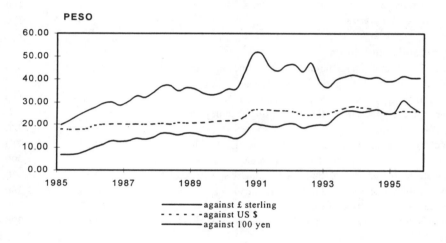

Consumer price inflation

The table below presents consumer price inflation in Philippines since 1989.

CONSUMER PRICE INFLATION

Year	Consumer price index	Inflation average change %
1989	112.2	12.2
1990	128.0	14.1
1991	152.0	18.7
1992	165.6	8.9
1993	178.2	7.6
1994	194.3	9.0
1995	209.8	8.0 (anticipated)

USEFUL ADDRESSES

Public organizations

Construction Industry Arbitration Commission
    Finman Building, Makati
    Tel: 8150709

Construction Industry Authority of the Philippines (CIAP)
    Finman Building
    Makati
    Tel: 8171230

Department of Public Works and Highways (DPWH)
    Bonifacio Drive, Port Area
    Tel: 472663

Department of Trade and Industry (DTI)
    361 Buendia Avenue, Makati
    Tel: 8185701

National Housing Authority
    Elliptical Road, Q.C.
    Tel: 994561

National Statistics Office
    R Magsaysay Blvd
    Sta Mesa
    Manila
    Tel : 7140822

Professional Regulation Commission (PRC)
    P Paredes St, Sampaloe, M.M.
    Tel: 7416061

Trade and professional associations

Association of Structural Engineers of the Philippines (ASEP)
    Unit T-10 New Manila Condominium
    21N Domingo
    New Manila
    Quezon City
    Tel : 795410

Philippine Chamber of Commerce and Industry
    ODC Building
    City of Makati
    Tel: 8176981

Philippine Contractors Accreditation Board (PCAB)
    DTI Building, Buendia Ave,
    Makati, M.M.
    Tel: 8150705

Philippine Contractors Association (PCA)
    INC The Padilla Building, Pasig
    Tel: 6313135

Philippine Institute of Civil Engineers (PICE)
    Room 2402 Cityland 10 Tower II
    6817 dela Costa Cor Ayala Ave
    Makati
    Tel : 8171979

United Architects of the Philippines (UAP)
    CCP Complex, Roxas Blvd, M.M.
    Tel: 8323711

DAVIS LANGDON & SEAH SINGAPORE PTE LTD
DAVIS LANGDON & SEAH PROJECT MANAGEMENT PTE LTD
DAVIS LANGDON & SEAH QUALITY MANAGEMENT PTE LTD

The strategic and integrated management of cost, time and quality - the client "risk" areas of a contract - are essential functions, which are necessary to ensure the satisfactory planning, procurement, execution and operation of construction projects.

We specialise in the financial management of construction projects and their risk areas, from project inception to completion and we concentrate on:

- being positive and creative in our advice, rather than simply reactive;

- providing value for money via efficient management, rather than on superficial cost monitoring;

- giving advice that is matched to the client's requirements, rather than imposing standard or traditional solutions;

- paying attention to the life-cycle costs of constructing and occupying a building, rather than to the initial capital cost only.

Our aim is to provide our clients with risk assurance, cost control and value for money, via effective advice, cost planning and management.

DAVIS LANGDON & SEAH SINGAPORE PTE LTD
135 Cecil Street #12-00
LKN Building
Singapore 069356
Tel : (65) 2223888
Fax : (65) 2247089

DAVIS LANGDON & SEAH INTERNATIONAL

Singapore

KEY DATA

Population
Population	2.8mn
Urban population	100%
Population under 15	23%
Population 65 and over	7%
Average annual growth rate (1980 to 1994)	1.1%

Geography
Land area	639 km2
Agricultural area	2%
Capital city	Singapore

Economy
Monetary unit	Singapore dollar (S$)
Exchange rate (average third quarter 1995) to:	
the pound sterling	S$2.23
the US dollar	S$1.41
the yen x 100	S$1.53
Average annual inflation (1980 to 1993)	2.5%
Inflation rate (1994)	3.1%
Gross Domestic Product (GDP) at market prices	S$89.0bn
GDP per capita	S$31,790
Average annual real change in GDP (1980 to 1993)	6.9%
Private consumption as a proportion of GDP	43%
General government consumption as a proportion of GDP	9%
Gross domestic investment as a proportion of GDP	44%
Central government expenditure as a proportion of Gross National Product	20%

Construction
Gross value of construction output*	S$16.9bn
Net value of construction output	S$6.6bn
Net value of construction output as a proportion of GDP	7.4%
Annual cement consumption	3.5mn tonnes

All data relate to 1993 unless otherwise indicated

* Authors' estimate

THE CONSTRUCTION INDUSTRY

Construction output

The gross value of construction output in 1993 is estimated at S$16.9 billion, equivalent to US$10.6 billion, or 19% of GDP. The net value of construction output in 1993 was S$6.6 billion, equivalent to US$4.1 billion, or 7.4% of GDP. The net value of construction output for 1994 was 7.5% of GDP or S$7.9 billion, equivalent to US$5.1 billion.

The table below presents the value of construction contracts awarded (including a forecast for 1995) and a measure of the completion of construction work in the public and the private sector.

CONSTRUCTION CONTRACTS AWARDED 1993-94 WITH A FORECAST FOR 1995 (S$ MILLION, CURRENT PRICES)

Sector	1993	1994+	1995*
Private			
Residential	1,812	3,091	1,910
Commercial	999	1,272	950
Industrial	1,205	1,544	1,370
Institutional	296	277	210
Civil engineering	64	891	110
Total	4,376	6,326	4,550
Public			
Residential	2,827	3,048	3,260
Commercial	265	167	240
Industrial	229	334	270
Institutional	1,056	1,217	1,930
Civil engineering	1,834	891	1,820
Total	6,211	5,657	7,520
Total	10,587	11,983	12,070

Source : DLSI

+ *Forecast*

* *Estimate*

BUILDING COMPLETIONS IN THE PUBLIC AND PRIVATE SECTORS

Year	Public 000 m²	Private 000 m²
1990	2,589	2,309
1991	2,250	2,013
1992	3,979	2,602
1993	3,397	3,109
1994*	3,428	2,784

* estimate

There has been a shift both in the value of contracts awarded and in the floor area completed from the private to the public sector.

Residential building contracts account for the largest percentage of public sector contracts awarded. A rise in contracts awarded for this type of work has been generated as part of the Housing and Development Board's building programme.

An increase in institutional building for the public sector is largely caused by the redevelopment and expansion of national health facilities. It is expected that the public sector will continue to generate work in civil engineering. Construction work involving the development and maintenance of the road network is part of national policy to improve access between different parts of the island. The Public Works Department (PWD) plans to spend S$2 billion on roads, including upgrading work and the construction of an expressway network.

Characteristics and structure of the industry

The industry in Singapore is supported by the Construction Industry Development Board (CIDB). It is concerned with all aspects of the industry: business management, technology, training and quality.

In 1984, CIDB established a Contractors' Registry to register contractors under various categories and grades for public sector procurement. Only CIDB registered contractors are permitted to tender for public sector construction projects. Contractors intending to be registered under the CIDB Contractors' Registry must have relevant experience. In addition, they are required to prove their financial, technical and management capability in executing construction projects. This includes the employment of technically qualified personnel. In September 1995, the Contractors' Registry covered more than 3,890 contractors and construction related specialist firms. It is used not only by government agencies but also by private sector clients. Of the registered contractors:

- 50% were building and civil engineering contractors

- 6% construction firms were registered in the top grade (G8)

In 1990, CIDB in conjunction with the major public sector agencies developed the Construction Quality Assessment System (CONQUAS). CONQUAS was designed to provide a yardstick for the measure of the level of quality achieved in a completed building project. The system sets out the standards for the various categories of work. Points are awarded for work which falls within the acceptance standards or tolerances to derive the total quality score for the building. CONQUAS has been widely used and accepted not just by the public sector but also by the private sector of the construction industry.

The Preferential Margin Scheme for Construction Quality was introduced in 1990 to encourage local contractors to consistently deliver high quality products. CONQUAS has been used to grade the overall quality of completed projects. In addition, from July 1999, the government will make the ISO 9000 certificate a prerequisite requirement for tenders of public projects worth S$30 million or more. The ISO 9000 certification scheme was promulgated in 1992 and is administered by jointly CIDB and the Singapore Productivity and Standards Board (PSB) for the construction industry in Singapore. Since its launch, more than 50 companies have been certified. From July 1995, those contractors who have already secured the ISO 9000 certificate have been given an additional half percent premium on top of their existing CONQUAS premium.

In the private sector developers are using CONQUAS as well, setting targeted CONQUAS scores for their development projects.

The 20 largest local construction firms ranked by turnover are as follows:

TOP TWENTY CONSTRUCTION FIRMS IN SINGAPORE

Rank	Name of company	Total turnover 1994 S$m
1	L&M Group Investments Ltd	313,366,000
2	Jurong Engineering Ltd	256,448,415
3	Econ International Ltd	231,408,527
4	Lum Chang Building Contractors Pte Ltd	196,982,621
5	Woh Hup Holdings Pte Ltd	184,315,990
6	Bored Piling Pte Ltd	150,144,618
7	Sim Lian Construction Pte Ltd	144,377,490
8	Sembawang Construction Pte Ltd	143,158,000
9	Singapore Piling & Civil Engineering Pte Ltd	141,602,953
10	Singapore Technologies Construction Pte Ltd	141,752,148
11	Lee Kim Tah Pte Ltd	126,681,455
12	Neo Corporation Pte Ltd	124,962,806
13	Koh Bros Building & Civil Engineering Contractor Pte Ltd	124,962,806
14	Sembawang Projects Engineering Co Pte Ltd	117,913,794
15	Tiong Aik Construction Pte Ltd	100,434,888
16	Greatearth Construction (S) Pte Ltd	93,662,000
17	Sung Foo Kee Construction (S) Pte Ltd	83,037,785
18	Low Keng Huat (S) Ltd	78,084,773
19	I.R.E. Corporation Pte Ltd	71,527,151
20	Hua Kok Realty (Pte) Ltd	65,324,404

Source : Construction Focus Vol 7 No 5, Sept-Oct 1995

Jurong Engineering Ltd was ranked 156 in the *Engineering News Record* list of top ten international construction firms. Its overseas contracts were around S$100 million - more than double its local contracts. The IPCO Group is also listed in the *Engineering News Record* at number 134. The L&M Group Investments Ltd, not included in the *Engineering News Record*, had overseas contracts in excess of S$250 million according to the Construction Focus newsletter.

Construction design work is undertaken mainly by architects and professional engineers. It is necessary to be registered with the Board of Architects, Singapore (a statutory board governing the practice of architects) before being allowed to practise in Singapore as an architect or use the designation 'architect'. There are currently about 850 registered architects. The Singapore Institute of Architects (SIA) is the only body representing professional architects in Singapore. It serves as a link between the profession and the government and technical authorities on matters affecting the profession.

The designation 'professional engineer' is registered and protected by the Professional Engineers Board (a statutory board governing the practice of engineers) and no one is allowed to practise in Singapore as a professional engineer unless registered with the Board. There are currently about 1,900 registered professional engineers of various disciplines in Singapore. There are also two bodies representing professional engineers: the Institution of Engineers Singapore (IES) and the Association of Consulting Engineers Singapore (ACES). The IES has about 4,500 members all of whom are registered engineers of various disciplines. Membership of ACES is only open to consulting engineers in private practice and the current membership figure stands at about 80.

The Singapore Institute of Surveyors and Valuers (SISV) is the only body representing surveyors and valuers in Singapore with a membership of slightly over 1,000. The main disciplines covered are quantity surveying, land surveying and valuation and general practice.

Clients and finance

Private sector projects are usually undertaken by private developers and institutions and financed in a number of ways. This includes loans from banks and financial institutions and the developer's own funds. Public sector projects are mainly undertaken by the Housing and Development Board (HDB) and the Public Works Department (PWD) of the Ministry of National Development.

HDB was established as a statutory board in 1960. Its main activity is the provision of suitable housing for lower and middle income groups. As of 1994, the HDB stock of flats housed 86% of the population in Singapore. The sources of finance for the HDB for capital expenditure are mainly government financed loans.

Selection of design consultants

There are no prescribed criteria or specific tender or selection procedures for the choice of design consultants in Singapore. In the public sector, a prequalification exercise through the submission of credentials, including relevant experience, followed by interviews is usually adopted. In some instances, a design competition is held. In the private sector, the design competition method of selection is rarely adopted. Clients may select the design consultants known to them or those who have a reputation for a specific type of building. Price is less important than in the public sector.

There are no published guidelines on the selection of consultants. All the professional bodies publish fee scales though these are not mandatory and are rarely used.

Contractual arrangements

Both HDB and the PWD have, in the past, their own standard forms of contract until recently (September 1995) when the *Public Sector Standard Conditions of Contract for Construction Works* was published for use on all public sector construction projects. Most public contracts are awarded on the basis of the lowest tenders submitted by contractors registered with CIDB.

Most private projects use the Singapore Institute of Architects (SIA) forms of contract : a Measurement Contract (for use with bills quantities); a Lump Sum Contract (where quantities are not part of the contract); and a Minor Works Contract.

Liability and insurance

Professional indemnity insurance is compulsory for architectural and engineering firms practising as limited companies. In the case of partnerships, it is not compulsory, but most big practices do hold professional indemnity insurance.

Development control and standards

The Urban Redevelopment Authority (URA) is the National Planning and Conservation Authority regulating and facilitating the physical development of Singapore. Most types of development require written planning permission but certain types are not considered material or are specifically exempted and thus do not require planning permission. The URA published a series of development control handbooks to guide and inform applicants of the procedures to be observed in submitting development applications.

The Building Control Division (BCD) of the Public Works Department (PWD) of the Ministry of National Development is responsible for setting and monitoring building regulations which cover, for example, structural integrity, lighting, ventilation and thermal transmission. In 1989, a new regulation came into effect requiring all structural designs to be checked and endorsed by accredited checkers who are independent registered professional engineers approved by BCD, before such structural designs are lodged for planning approval.

The Fire Safety Bureau (FSB) of the Singapore Civil Defence Force is responsible for all building inspections prior to the issuance of the Temporary Occupation Permit (TOP) or Certificate of Statutory Completion (CSC) by BCD. In 1994, FSB introduced the Registered Inspectors Scheme to speed up such building inspections. Under this scheme, the Registered Inspectors (RI) will inspect the buildings on behalf of the authority.

The Singapore Productivity and Standards Board (PSB) draws up and promulgates the Singapore Standards (SS), the standard specifications for products, and it is usual for manufacturers to comply with these. Architects and other building professionals generally follow the recommendations of the Singapore Standard when specifying building products.

Research and development

The main organizations engaged in construction research are the Construction Industry Development Board (CIDB) and the Singapore Productivity and Standards Board (PSB).

CONSTRUCTION COST DATA

Cost of labour

The figures below are typical of labour costs in Singapore as at the third quarter of 1995. The wage rate is the basis of an employee's income, while the cost of labour indicates the cost to a contractor of employing that employee. The difference between the two covers a variety of mandatory and voluntary contributions - a list of items which could be included is given in section 2.

	Wage rate (per day) S$	Cost of labour (per day) S$	Number of hours worked per year
Site operatives			
Bricklayer	47.80	56.60	2,288
Carpenter	43.30	53.00	2,288
Plumber	52.80	64.70	2,288
Electrician	51.40	63.00	2,288
Structural steel erector	55.70	68.80	2,288
Welder	56.20	57.70	2,288
Labourer	26.20	41.50	2,288
Equipment operator	62.40	76.40	2,288

	Wage rate (per month) S$	Cost of labour (per month) S$	Number of hours worked per year
Site supervision			
General foreman	3,500	5,690	2,288
Trades foreman	3,000	4,880	2,288
Clerk of works	2,800	4,130	2,288
Resident engineer	3,500	5,160	2,280
Contractors' personnel			
Site manager	4,500	7,810	2,280
Site engineer	2,500	4,560	2,280
Site quantity surveyor	2,300	4,240	2,280
Consultants' personnel			
Senior architect	6,000	8,850	2,080
Senior engineer	4,500	6,640	2,080
Senior surveyor	4,500	6,640	2,080
Qualified architect	4,000	5,900	2,080
Qualified engineer	3,500	5,160	2,080
Qualified surveyor	3,500	5,160	2,080

Cost of materials

The figures that follow are the costs of main construction materials, delivered to site in Singapore, as incurred by contractors in the third quarter of 1995. These assume that the materials would be in quantities as required for a medium sized construction project and that the location of the works would be neither constrained nor remote.

	Unit	Cost S$
Cement and aggregate		
Ordinary portland cement in 50kg bags	tonne	150.00
Coarse aggregates for concrete	tonne	17.50
Fine aggregates for concrete	m³	21.00
Ready mixed concrete (Grade 30)	m³	101.00
Ready mixed concrete (Grade 20)	m³	94.00
Steel		
Mild steel reinforcement	tonne	600.00
High tensile steel reinforcement	tonne	603.00
Structural steel sections	tonne	800.00

	Unit	Cost S$
Bricks and blocks		
Common bricks (215 x 102.5 x 65mm)	1,000	250.00
Good quality facing bricks (215 x 102.5 x 65mm)	1,000	350.00
Hollow concrete blocks (390 x 190 x 100mm)	1,000	750.00
Timber and insulation		
Hardwood for joinery	m^3	800.00
Exterior quality plywood (12mm)	m^2	9.40
Plywood for interior joinery (12mm)	m^2	8.80
50mm thick quilt insulation (16kg/m^3)	m^2	3.00
50mm thick rigid slab insulation (60kg/m^3)	m^2	8.00
Hardwood internal door complete with frame and ironmongery	each	750.00
Glass and ceramics		
Float glass (10mm)	m^2	86.00
Sealed double glazing units (6/12/6) including frame	m^2	300.00
Plaster and paint		
Good quality ceramic wall tiles (300 x 300 x 8mm)	m^2	40.00
Plasterboard (13mm thick) - gypsum	m^2	4.00
Emulsion paint in 5 litre tins	litre	3.50
Gloss oil paint in 5 litre tins	litre	6.00
Tiles and paviors		
Clay floor tiles (100 x 200 x 8mm)	m^2	13.00
Vinyl floor tiles (300 x 300 x 2mm)	m^2	6.00
Clay roof tiles	1,000	2,400.00
Precast concrete roof tiles	1,000	1,000.00
Drainage		
WC suite complete	each	220.00
Wash hand basin complete	each	100.00
100mm diameter clay drain pipes	m	16.00
150mm diameter cast iron drain pipes (medium grade)	m	18.00

Unit rates

The descriptions below are generally shortened versions of standard descriptions listed in full in section 4. Where an item has a two digit reference number (e.g. 05 or 3), this relates to the full description against that number in section 4. Where an item has an alphabetic suffix (e.g.12A or 34B) this indicates that the standard decription has been modified.

Where a modification is major the complete modified description is included here and the standard description should be ignored; where a modification is minor (e.g. the insertion of a named hardwood) the shortened description has been modified here but, in general, the full description in section 4 prevails.

The unit rates below are for main work items on a typical construction project in the city area in the third quarter of 1995. The rates include all necessary labour, materials and equipment. An allowance of 10% has been added to the rates to cover preliminary and general items.

		Unit	RateS$
Excavation			
01	Mechanical excavation of foundation trenches	m³	16.50
02	Hardcore filling making up levels	m²	11.00
Concrete work			
04	Plain insitu concrete in strip foundations in trenches (Grade 20)	m³	132.00
05	Reinforced insitu concrete in beds (Grade 30)	m³	145.20
06	Reinforced insitu concrete in walls (Grade 30)	m³	145.20
07	Reinforced insitu concrete in suspended floors or roof slabs (Grade 30)	m³	145.20
08	Reinforced insitu concrete in columns (Grade 30)	m³	145.20
09	Reinforced insitu concrete in isolated beams (Grade 30)	m³	145.20
Formwork			
11A	Waterproof plywood formwork to concrete walls	m²	30.80
12A	Waterproof plywood formwork to concrete columns	m²	31.90
13A	Waterproof plywood formwork to horizontal soffits of slabs	m²	30.80
Reinforcement			
14	Reinforcement in concrete walls	tonne	1,155.00
15	Reinforcement in suspended concrete slabs	tonne	1,155.00
16	Fabric reinforcement in concrete beds	m²	11.00
Steelwork			
17	Fabricate, supply and erect steel framed structure	tonne	2,750.00
18	Framed structural steelwork in universal joist sections	tonne	2,750.00
19	Structural steelwork lattice roof trusses	tonne	2,970.00
Brickwork and blockwork			
20	Precast lightweight aggregate hollow concrete block walls	m²	20.90
21A	Solid (perforated) concrete blocks	m²	51.70
23	Facing bricks (215mm thick)	m²	99.00

		Unit	RateS$
Roofing			
24	Concrete interlocking roof tiles 430 x 380mm	m²	22.00
25	Plain clay roof tiles 260 x 160mm	m²	55.00
29	3 layers glass-fibre based bitumen felt roof covering	m²	30.80
33	Troughed galvanized steel roof cladding	m²	35.20
Woodwork and metalwork			
34	Preservative treated sawn hardwood 50 x 100mm	m	9.90
35	Preservative treated sawn hardwood 50 x 150mm	m	14.30
37	Two panel glazed door in Kapur hardwood, size 850 x 2000mm	each	660.00
38	Solid core half hour fire resisting hardwood internal flush door, size 800 x 2000mm	each	935.00
39	Aluminium double glazed window, size 1200 x 1200mm	each	825.00
41	Hardwood skirtings	m	7.70
Plumbing			
42	UPVC half round eaves gutter	m	24.20
43	UPVC rainwater pipes	m	25.30
44	Light gauge copper cold water tubing	m	19.80
45	High pressure plastic pipes for cold water supply	m	16.50
47	UPVC soil and vent pipes	m	39.60
48	White vitreous china WC suite	each	462.00
49	White vitreous china wash hand basin	each	297.00
51A	Stainless steel double bowl sink and double drainer	each	440.00
Electrical work			
52	PVC insulated and copper sheathed cable	m	2.20
53	13 amp unswitched socket outlet	each	41.80
54	Flush mounted 20 amp, 1 way light switch	each	123.20
Finishings			
55A	2 coats cement and sand (1:4) plaster on brick walls	m²	12.10
56	White glazed tiles on plaster walls	m²	40.70
57	Red clay quarry tiles on concrete floors	m²	71.50
58	Cement and sand screed to concrete floors	m²	13.20
59	Thermoplastic floor tiles on screed	m²	44.00
60	Mineral fibre tiles on concealed suspension system	m²	38.50
Glazing			
61	Glazing to wood	m²	39.60

		Unit	RateS$
Painting			
62	Emulsion on plaster walls	m²	3.30
63	Oil paint on timber	m²	6.60

Approximate estimating

The building costs per unit area given below are averages incurred by buildng clients for typical buildings in Singapore as at the third quarter of 1995. They are based upon the total floor area of all storeys, measured between external walls and without deduction for internal walls.

Approximate estimating costs generally include mechanical and electrical installations but exclude furniture, loose or special equipment, and external works; they also exclude fees for professional services. The costs shown are for specifications and standards appropriate to Singapore and this should be borne in mind when attempting comparisons with similarly described building types in other countries. A discussion of this issue is included in section 2. Comparative data for countries covered in this publication, including construction cost data, is presented in Part Three.

Approximate estimating costs must be treated with caution; they cannot provide more than a rough guide to the probable cost of building.

	Cost m² S$	Cost ft² S$
Industrial buildings		
Factories for letting	900	84
Factories for owner occupation (light industrial use)	950	88
Factories for owner occupation (heavy industrial use)	1,150	107
Factory/office (high tech) for letting (shell and core only)	1,200	111
Factory/office (high tech) for letting (ground floor shell, first floor offices)	1,300	121
Factory/office (high tech) for owner occupation (controlled environment, fully finished)	1,400	130
High tech laboratory workshop centres (air conditioned)	1,200	111
Warehouses, low bay (6 to 8m high) for letting	850	80
Warehouses, low bay for owner occupation	900	84
Warehouses, high bay for owner occupation	950	88
Administrative and commercial buildings		
Offices for letting, 5 to 10 storeys, non air conditioned	1,400	130
Offices for letting, 5 to 10 storeys, air conditioned	1,600	149
Offices for letting, high rise, air conditioned	1,850	172

	Cost m² S$	Cost ft² S$
Offices for owner occupation high rise, air conditioned	1,950	181
Prestige/headquarters office, 5 to 10 storeys, air conditioned	2,100	195
Prestige/headquarters office, high rise, air conditioned	2,300	214

Health and education buildings

	Cost m² S$	Cost ft² S$
General hospitals (100 beds)	1,750	163
Private hospitals (100 beds)	1,900	177
Health centres	1,350	125
Primary/junior schools	900	84
Secondary/middle schools	1,100	102
University	1,450	135

Recreation and arts buildings

	Cost m² S$	Cost ft² S$
Theatres (less than 500 seats)	2,800	260
Sports halls including changing and social facilities	1,200	111
Swimming pools (international standard) (Olympic size)	each	1,500,000
Swimming pools (schools standard) including changing facilities	each	1,300,000
City centre/central libraries	1,300	121
Branch/local libraries	1,200	111

Residential buildings

	Cost m² S$	Cost ft² S$
Private/mass market single family housing 2 storey detached/semi detached (multiple units)	1,800	167
Purpose designed single family housing 2 storey detached (single unit)	2,000	186
Social/economic apartment housing, high rise (with lifts)	1,000	93
Private sector apartment building (standard specification)	1,300	121
Private sector apartment buildings (luxury)	1,600	149
Student/nurses halls of residence	1,300	121
Homes for the elderly (shared accommodation)	1,350	125
Hotel, 5 star, city centre	2,800	260
Hotel, 3 star, city/provincial	2,100	195

EXCHANGE RATES AND INFLATION

The combined effect of exchange rates and inflation on prices within a country and price comparisons between countries is discussed in section 2.

Exchange rates

The graph below plots the movement of the Singapore dollar against sterling, US dollar and 100 Japanese yen since 1985. The values used for the graph are quarterly and the method of calculating this is described and general guidance on the interpretation of the graph provided in section 2. The average exchange rate in the second quarter of 1995 was S$2.23 to pound sterling, S$1.41 to US dollar and S$1.53 to 100 Japanese yen.

THE SINGAPORE DOLLAR AGAINST STERLING, US DOLLAR
AND JAPANESE YEN

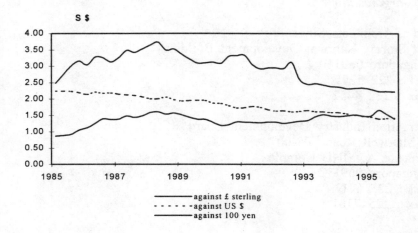

Price inflation

The table below presents building cost price inflation in Singapore since 1988.

BUILDING COST PRICE INFLATION

Year	Building costs average index	Year	Building costs average index
1988	78	1992	105
1989	91	1993	101
1990	100	1994	100
1991	107	1995	100

USEFUL ADDRESSES

Public organizations

Board of Architects, Singapore
1st Storey, National Development Building
Singapore 069110
Tel : 222 5295
Fax : 222 4452

Construction Industry Development Board
9 Maxwell Road #03-00
Annexe A, MND Complex
Singapore 069112
Tel : 225 6711
Fax : 225 7301

Department of Statistics
Ministry of Trade and Industry
8 Shenton Way #10-01
Treasury Building
Singapore 068111
Tel : 225 9111

Ministry of the Environment
  40 Scotts Road
  Singapore 228231
  Tel : 732 7733
  Fax : 731 9456

Ministry of National Development
  5 Maxwell Road #21/22-00
  Tower Block
  MND Complex
  Singapore 069110
  Tel : 222 1211
  Fax : 222 1459

Professional Engineers Board
  c/o Public Works Department
  1st Storey, National Development Building
  Singapore 069110
  Tel : 222 9293

Singapore Productivity and Standards Board
  PSB Building
  2 Bukit Merah Central
  Singapore 159835
  Tel : 2786666
  Fax : 2786665

Urban Redevelopment Authority
  URA Building
  45 Maxwell Road
  Singapore 069118
  Tel : 221 6666
  Fax : 224 8752

Trade and professional associations

Association of Consulting Engineers Singapore
  50 Jalan Sultan #07-08
  Jalan Sultan Centre
  Singapore 198974
  Tel : 292 4660
  Fax : 292 4628

Institution of Engineers Singapore
  70 Bukit Tinggi Road
  Singapore 289758
  Tel : 469 5000
  Fax : 467 1108

Real Estate Developers' Association of Singapore (REDAS)
  190 Clemenceau Avenue #07-01
  Singapore Shopping Centre
  Singapore 239924
  Tel : 336 6655
  Fax : 337 2217

Singapore Contractors' Association Ltd
  Construction House
  1 Bukit Merah Lane 2
  Singapore 159760
  Tel : 278 9577
  Fax : 273 3977

Singapore Federation of Chambers of Commerce and Industry
  47 Hill Street #03-01
  Chinese Chambers of Commerce and Industry Building
  Singapore 179365
  Tel : 338 9761
  Fax : 339 5630

Singapore Institute of Arbitrators
  170 Upper Bukit Timah Road #09-04
  Bukit Timah Shopping Centre
  Singapore 588179
  Tel : 468 4317
  Fax : 468 8510

Singapore Institute of Architects
  20 Orchard Road #02-00
  SMA House
  Singapore 238830
  Tel : 338 8977
  Fax : 336 8708

Singapore Institute of Building Ltd
   Block 134 Jurong East Street 13
   #04-307K
   Singapore 600134
   Tel : 566 2296
   Fax : 566 8369

Singapore Institute of Landscape Architects
   617 Bukit Timah Road
   Singapore 269718
   Tel : 466 9211
   Telex: GARCEN RS 35451

Singapore Institute of Surveyors and Valuers
   20 Maxwell Road #10-09B
   Maxwell House
   Singapore 069113
   Tel : 222 3030
   Fax : 225 2453

South Korea

KEY DATA

Population

Population	44.1mn
Urban population	78%
Population under 15	25%
Population 65 and over	6%
Average annual growth rate (1980 to 1993)	1.1%

Geography

Land area	99,000 km²
Agricultural area	23%
Capital city	Seoul
Population of capital city (1990)	10.4mn

Economy

Monetary unit	South Korean Won (W)
Exchange rate (average third quarter 1995) to:	
the pound sterling	W 1,209
the US dollar	W 763
the yen x 100	W 814
Average annual inflation (1980 to 1993)	6.3%
Inflation rate (1994)	6.2%
Gross Domestic Product (GDP) at market prices	W 265,500bn
GDP per capita	W 6,020,400
Average annual real change in GDP (1980 to 1993)	9.1%
Private consumption as a proportion of GDP	54%
General government consumption as a proportion of GDP	11%
Gross domestic investment as a proportion of GDP	34%
Central government expenditure as a proportion of Gross National Product	17%

Construction

Gross value of construction output *	W 50,000bn
Net value of construction output *	W 21,250bn
Net value of construction output as a proportion of GDP *	8%

All data relate to 1993 unlesss otherwise indicated

* *Authors' estimate*

THE CONSTRUCTION INDUSTRY

Construction output

The gross output of construction in 1993 is estimated at about W50,000 billion, equivalent to US$63 billion, or 19% of GDP. The net output of construction in 1993 is estimated at W21,250 billion, equivalent to US$26.7 billion, or 8% of GDP.

Indicators of the level of construction activity in recent years according to type of construction work are presented in the tables below.

PERMITS ISSUED, 1993 AND 1994

Type of building	1993 million m²	%	1994 million m²	%
Dwellings	69.3	59	63.3	54
Factories	11.4	10	13.3	11
Commercial	24.8	21	27.6	24
Other	12.3	10	12.0	11
Total	117.8	100	116.2	100

Source: Bank of Korea Monthly Statistical Bulletin, 1995

VALUE OF DOMESTIC ORDERS, 1993 AND 1994 (CURRENT PRICES)

Type of work	1993 W billion	1994 W billion
Building	23,246	24,606
Civil engineering	9,721	12,303
Total	32,967	36,909

Source: Bank of Korea Monthly Statistical Bulletin, 1995

Both the above tables may not be all-inclusive. Other partial data suggest that the public sector commissions about 36% of work, the remainder being private.

A high level of investment in fixed assets for the economy as a whole in 1994 was dominated by investment in machinery and transport equipment rather than in construction. Investment in residential building had declined over the previous year. The prospects for construction are expected to improve in 1995 since it is anticipated that there will be higher growth in the level of construction spending compared with that in machinery and equipment. In the first five months of 1995 the number of building permits issued was 30% higher than the corresponding period in 1994. The value of construction orders, at current prices, rose by 19.5% over the same period. It should be noted that movements in the level of permits are generally more volatile than other indicators because there is a tendency to build up and run down 'stocks' of permits.

Permits issued for dwellings have fallen dramatically in 1994 by 31.5% but in 1995 it is expected to increase by about 17.1%. In the coming three years, it seems unlikely that the rate will be further increased. The figures for 1993 and 1994 are as follows:

INDICATORS OF CONSTRUCTION ACTIVITY, SOUTH KOREA, 1993 AND 1994

Indicators	1993	1994	Percentage of total 1994	% change
Permits issued, million m²				
Dwellings	72.1	54.8	45	- 31.5
Factories	11.6	12.4	10	+ 6.9
Commercial	38.9	39.5	32	+ 1.5
Other	20.6	16.2	13	- 27.2
Total	143.2	122.9	100	- 11.5
Domestic orders, billion Won				
Manufacturers private	2,612	3,865	10	+ 48.0
Non-manufacturers private	17,862	18,364	49	+ 2.8
Public	12,752	14,954	40	+ 17.2
Other	20	13	1	- 53.8
Total	33,248	37,197	100	+ 11.8

Source: Monthly Statistical Bulletin (September 1995), Bank of Korea

Under its New Economic Plan, the South Korean government intends to direct investment into transport-related infrastructure. Spending of about US$70 billion will be undertaken on major road, railway, airport and port projects as well as water supply and sewerage projects.

Overseas work has been a very important component for Korean contractors. It has grown rapidly since 1991 after being on the decline in the mid 1980s. In 1995 it is expected to be around US$10 billion worth of new projects. The top ten Korean contractors focus their businesses on overseas markets and are fairly aggressive in such countries as China and in South-East and South-West Asia.

Characteristics and structure of the industry

The top ten contracting companies in South Korea account for 35% of the work in the country and around 80% of the work overseas. The top ten contractors in terms of turnover are as follows:

MAJOR KOREAN CONTRACTORS, 1995 (ESTIMATION)

Company	No of Employees	Work abroad % turnover
Hyundai	5,970	24
Daewoo	3,290	38
Donga	3,250	27
Samsung	3,020	17
Daelim	3,120	8
Hyundai Industries	1,890	-
Ssangyong	1,870	22
Lg	1,670	2
Korea Heavy Industry Co.	2,560	-
Lotte	1,460	-
Total	28,100	14

Source: The International Contractors Association of Korea

Donga Construction Ind Co Ltd was ranked 22nd, Daewoo Corporation 48th while Ssangyong 83rd in *Engineering News Record's 1995* ranking of *The World's Top 225 International Contractors*. Seven other Korean contractors were ranked in the above list. All top Korean contractors have their own design surveying and planning divisions. The primary objective is to consolidate and simplify all engineering and construction sectors within the business group for better efficiency and synergy effect.

Clients and finance

Of the work undertaken by the top 10 contractors, about 60% is for private sector clients and the remainder for public sector clients. Private work has increased rapidly since 1992.

Selection of design consultants

In the public sector, consultants are selected in competition. And in the private sector, the client himself usually chooses the designer, but for large projects a competition may be held which may include foreign consultants. Design is generally separated from construction but in housing it is normally carried out on a design-build basis.

Contractual arrangements

There are three methods of selecting contractors. Selective tendering is most common and contractors are shortlisted according to their record and financial ratings. However, where a special technology or construction method is required, a limited competition of those contractors prequalified for the project is preferred.

At the pre-tender stage contractors must submit a number of documents verifying their bona fides including, for example, certificates of tax clearance, technical expert log book and financial status of their business. At the tendering stage following public notice of the tender, detailed information on the project is given. The contract documents include specifications, tax certificates, written guarantees, etc. and the contract itself covers the normal contractual arrangements including provisions for delay and defects.

Liability and insurance

Various insurances and guarantees are compulsory; those relating to performance in bidding, carrying out the work, maintenance, and also for protection against dumping. It is also obligatory to insure against workers' compensation and fire. Some contractors have other additional insurance arrangements.

Development control and standards

In each city and town, there is an area zoning for overall and regional development planning. While alterations to the plans are possible, they are very unusual and difficult to comply.

Each project is assessed in terms of its traffic impact and then in terms of the building itself - its energy usage, structure and aesthetics. The speed of the approval process depends on the region, the size of the project and its purpose but the whole process normally takes six to eight months. Sophisticated buildings such as hotels, condominiums, sports centres or fire stations may take longer. There are laws on requirements for building structures and facility standards which must be rigidly adhered to. *Korean Standards* (KS) also exist for building materials such as bricks, glass, steel and aggregates.

CONSTRUCTION COST DATA

Cost of labour

The figures below are typical of labour costs in South Korea as at the third quarter of 1995. The wage rate is the basis of an employee's income, while the cost of labour indicates the cost to a contractor of employing that employee.

	Wage rate (daily=12hrs) Won	Cost of labour (daily=12hrs) Won	Number of hours worked per year
Site operatives			
Mason/bricklayer	75,600	84,000	3,720
Carpenter	83,500	92,800	3,720
Plumber	60,800	67,600	3,720
Electrician	60,500	67,300	3,720
Structural steel erector	83,000	92,300	3,720
HVAC installer	61,500	88,400	3,720
Semi-skilled worker	58,500	65,000	3,720
Unskilled labourer	45,000	50,000	3,720
Equipment operator	67,600	75,200	3,720
Watchman/security	39,500	43,900	3,720

	Wage rate (daily=12hrs) Won	Cost of labour (daily=12hrs) Won	Number of hours worked per year
Site supervision			
General foreman	74,700	83,000	3,720
Trades foreman	58,500	65,000	3,720
Clerk of works	49,500	55,000	3,720
	(per month)	*(per month)*	
Contractors' personnel			
Site manager	2,690,000	3,000,000	3,190
Resident engineer	2,340,000	2,600,000	3,190
Resident surveyor	2,340,000	2,600,000	3,190
Junior engineer	1,350,000	1,500,000	3,190
Junior surveyor	1,350,000	1,500,000	3,190
Planner	1,350,000	1,500,000	3,190
Consultants' personnel			
Senior architect	2,610,000	2,920,000	3,190
Senior engineer	2,610,000	2,920,000	3,190
Senior surveyor	2,610,000	2,920,000	3,190
Qualified architect	2,750,000	3,210,000	3,190
Qualified engineer	2,810,000	3,310,000	3,190
Qualified surveyor	2,810,000	3,310,000	3,190

Cost of materials

The figures that follow are the costs of main construction materials, delivered to site in the Seoul area, as incurred by contractors in the third quarter of 1995. These assume that the materials would be in quantities as required for a medium sized construction project and that the location of the works would be neither constrained nor remote. All the costs in this section exclude value added tax (VAT - see below).

	Unit	Cost Won
Cement and aggregate		
Ordinary portland cement in 40kg bags	40 kg	2,600
Coarse aggregates for concrete	m³	14,000
Fine aggregates for concrete	m³	14,000
Ready mixed concrete (40-135-8)	m³	35,400
Ready mixed concrete (25-210-12)	m³	42,800
Precast concrete piles D350 x 65 x 10m	each	110,100

	Unit	Cost Won
Steel		
Mild steel reinforcement (over D16)	tonne	280,000
High tensile steel reinforcement (over D16)	tonne	302,000
Structural steel sections (rolled H beam)	tonne	385,000
Bricks and blocks		
Common bricks (190 x 90 x 57mm)	1,000	40,000
Good quality facing bricks (190 x 90 x 57mm)	1,000	200,000
Hollow concrete blocks (150 x 190 x 390mm)	each	500
Autoclaved lightweight concrete blocks (100 x 400 x 600mm)	each	9,000
Precast concrete cladding units with plain surface finish	m²	28,000
Timber and insulation		
Softwood sections for carpentry	m³	269,000
Softwood for joinery	m³	687,700
Exterior quality plywood (15mm)	m²	7,740
Plywood for interior joinery (12mm)	m²	9,910
Softwood strip flooring (22 x 129 x 3700mm)	m²	68,000
Chipboard sheet flooring (18 x 1210 x 2420mm)	m²	60,320
100mm thick quilt insulation	m²	5,100
100mm thick rigid slab insulation (expanded polystyrene)	m²	5,600
Softwood internal door complete with frames and ironmongery	each	115,500
Glass and ceramics		
Float glass (3mm)	m²	2,700
Sealed double glazing units	m²	13,500
Plaster and paint		
Good quality ceramic wall tiles (150 x 150mm)	m²	9,000
Plaster in 25kg bags	bag	1,430
Plasterboard (9mm thick)	m²	1,290
Emulsion paint in 5 litre tins	litre	5,460
Gloss oil paint in 5 litre tins	litre	9,440
Tiles and paviors		
Clay floor tiles (200 x 200 x 10mm)	m²	20,000
Vinyl floor tiles (300 x 300 x 3mm)	m²	3,340
Precast concrete paving slabs (300 x 300 x 60mm)	m²	5,200
Clay roof tiles (300 x 360 x 21mm)	1,000	850,000
Precast concrete roof tiles (400 x 750 x 12mm)	1,000	600,000
Granite 20-24mm thick polished finish medium quality	m²	40,000
Granite 20-24mm thick polished finish high quality	m²	91,000

	Unit	Cost Won
Drainage		
WC suite complete	each	400,000
Lavatory basin complete	each	83,000
100mm diameter PVC drain pipes	m	18,800
150mm diameter cast iron drain pipes	m	22,600

Unit rates

The descriptions below are generally shortened versions of standard descriptions listed in full in section 4. Where an item has a two digit reference number (e.g. 05 or 33), this relates to the full description against that number in section 4. Where an item has an alphabetic suffix (e.g. 12A or 34B) this indicates that the standard description has been modified. Where a modification is major the complete modified description is included here and the standard description should be ignored; where a modification is minor (e.g. the insertion of a named hardwood) the shortened description has been modified here but, in general, the full description in section 4 prevails.

The unit rates below are for main work items on a typical construction project in the Seoul and adjoining areas in the third quarter of 1995. The rates include all necessary labour, materials and equipment. Allowances to cover preliminary and general items and contractor's overheads and profit have been added to the rates. All the rates in this section exclude value added tax (VAT - see below).

		Unit	Rate Won
Excavation			
01	Mechanical excavation of foundation trenches	m³	805
02	Hardcore filling making up levels	m²	3,660
03	Earthwork support	m²	17,320
Concrete work			
04	Plain insitu concrete in strip foundations in trenches	m³	75,480
05	Reinforced insitu concrete in beds	m³	79,738
06	Reinforced insitu concrete in walls	m³	88,938
07	Reinforced insitu concrete in suspended floors or roof slabs	m³	88,938
08	Reinforced insitu concrete in columns	m³	74,358
09	Reinforced insitu concrete in isolated beams	m³	88,938
10	Precast concrete slabs	m²	51,362

		Unit	*Rate Won*

Formwork

		Unit	Rate Won
11	Softwood formwork to concrete walls	m²	24,400
12	Softwood or metal formwork to concrete columns	m²	26,840
13	Softwood or metal formwork to horizontal soffits of slabs	m²	23,180

Reinforcement

14	Reinforcement in concrete walls	tonne	717,360
15	Reinforcement in suspended concrete slabs	tonne	717,360
16	Fabric reinforcement in concrete beds	m²	1,098

Steelwork

17	Fabricate, supply and erect steel framed structure	tonne	789,096
18	Framed structural steelwork in universal joist sections	tonne	1,037,000
19	Structural steelwork lattice roof trusses	tonne	1,159,000

Brickwork and blockwork

20	Precast lightweight aggregate hollow concrete block walls	m²	53,070
21A	Solid (perforated) concrete blocks	m²	12,688
23	Facing bricks	m²	29,036

Roofing

24	Concrete interlocking roof tiles 430 x 380mm	m²	5,734
25	Plain clay roof tiles 260 x 160mm	m²	27,084
26	Fibre cement roof slates 600 x 300mm	m²	43,920
27	Sawn softwood roof boarding	m²	13,542
28	Particle board roof coverings	m²	17,202
29	3 layers glass-fibre based bitumen felt roof covering	m²	14,640
30	Bitumen based mastic asphalt roof covering	m²	14,650
31A	Glass-fibre mat roof insulation 100mm thick	m²	19,520
32	Rigid sheet loadbearing roof insulation 75mm thick	m²	12,200
33	Troughed galvanized steel roof cladding	m²	12,200

Woodwork and metalwork

34	Preservative treated sawn softwood 50 x 100mm	m	9,760
35	Preservative treated sawn softwood 50 x 150mm	m	12,200
36	Single glazed casement window in Lanan hardwood, size 650 x 900mm	each	67,100
37	Two panel glazed door in Lanan hardwood, size 850 x 2000mm	each	268,400
38A	Solid core half hour fire resisting aluminium internal flush doors, size 800 x 2000mm	each	152,500

	Unit	Rate Won
39A Aluminium double glazed window, size 1200 x 1200mm	each	146,400
40A Aluminium double glazed door, size 850 x 2100mm	each	6,100
41A Hardwood skirtings (Lanan)	m	1,159,000

Plumbing

		Unit	Rate Won
42	UPVC half round eaves gutter	m	10,980
43	UPVC rainwater pipes	m	8,784
44	Light gauge copper cold water tubing	m	6,710
45	High pressure plastic pipes for cold water supply	m	5,490
46	Low pressure plastic pipes for cold water distribution	m	6,222
47	UPVC soil and vent pipes	m	14,762
48	White vitreous china WC suite	each	111,142
49	White vitreous china lavatory basin	each	79,300
50	Glazed fireclay shower tray	each	152,500
51	Stainless steel single bowl sink and double drainer	each	111,142

Finishings

		Unit	Rate Won
55	2 coats gypsum based plaster on brick walls	m^2	44,074
56	White glazed tiles on plaster walls	m^2	48,434
56A	Granite veneer 20mm thick for walls, fixed with cement mortar	m^2	13,420
57	Red clay quarry tiles on concrete floors	m^2	55,998
58	Cement and sand screed to concrete floors	m^2	20,740
59	Thermoplastic floor tiles on screed	m^2	21,960
60	Mineral fibre tiles on concealed suspension system	m^2	97,600

Glazing

		Unit	Rate Won
61	Glazing to wood	m^2	21,960

Painting

		Unit	Rate Won
62	Emulsion on plaster walls	m^2	2,684
63	Oil paint on timber	m^2	3,233

Approximate estimating

The building costs per unit area given below are averages incurred by building clients for typical buildings in the Seoul and adjoining areas as at the third quarter of 1995. They are based upon the total floor area of all storeys, measured between external walls and without deduction for internal walls.

Approximate estimating costs generally include mechanical and electrical installations but exclude furniture, loose or special equipment, and external works; they also exclude fees for professional services. The costs shown are for specifications and standards appropriate to South Korea and this should be borne in mind when attempting comparisons with similarly described building types in other countries. A discussion of this issue is included in section 2. Comparative data for countries covered in this publication, including construction cost data, is presented in Part Three.

Approximate estimating costs must be treated with caution; they cannot provide more than a rough guide to the probable cost of building. All the rates in this section exclude value added tax (VAT - see below).

	Cost m² Won	Cost ft² Won
Industrial buildings		
Factories for letting	573,000	53,300
Factories for owner occupation (light industrial use)	611,000	56,900
Factories for owner occupation (heavy industrial use)	650,000	60,400
Factory/office (high-tech) for letting (shell and core only)	841,000	78,200
Factory/office (high-tech) for letting (ground floor shell, first floor offices)	803,000	74,600
Factory/office (high tech) for owner occupation (controlled environment, fully finished)	956,000	88,800
High tech laboratory workshop centres (air conditioned)	1,725,000	159,800
Warehouses, low bay (6 to 8m high) for letting (no heating)	343,000	31,900
Warehouses, low bay for owner occupation (including heating)	382,000	35,500
Warehouses, high bay for owner occupation (including heating)	459,000	42,600
Cold stores/refrigerated stores	1,334,000	124,000
Administrative and commercial buildings		
Civic offices, non air conditioned	611,000	56,900
Civic offices, fully air conditioned	382,000	35,500
Offices for letting, 5 to 10 storeys, non air conditioned	841,000	78,200
Offices for letting, 5 to 10 storeys, air conditioned	918,000	85,300
Offices for letting, high rise, air conditioned	879,000	81,700
Offices for owner occupation 5 to 10 storeys, non air conditioned	956,000	88,800
Offices for owner occupation 5 to 10 storeys, air conditioned	1,071,000	99,500
Offices for owner occupation high rise, air conditioned	994,000	92,400
Prestige/headquarters office, 5 to 10 storeys, air conditioned	841,000	78,200
Prestige/headquarters office, high rise, air conditioned	1,071,000	99,500

	Cost m² Won	Cost ft² Won
Health and education buildings		
General hospitals (100 beds)	1,334,000	124,000
Teaching hospitals (100 beds)	1,147,000	106,000
Private hospitals (100 beds)	764,000	71,100
Health centres	956,000	88,800
Nursery schools	764,000	71,100
Primary/junior schools	688,000	63,900
Secondary/middle schools	688,000	63,900
University (arts) buildings	764,000	71,100
University (science) buildings	879,000	81,700
Management training centres	764,000	71,100
Recreation and arts buildings		
Theatres (over 500 seats) including seating and stage equipment	1,529,000	142,600
Theatres (less than 500 seats) including seating and stage equipment	1,920,000	178,200
Concert halls including seating and stage equipment	2,104,000	195,500
Sports halls including changing and social facilities	1,334,000	124,000
Swimming pools (international standard) including changing and social facilities	956,000	88,800
Swimming pools (schools standard) including changing facilities	956,000	88,800
National museums including full air conditioning and standby generator	764,000	71,100
Local museums including air conditioning	958,000	88,800
Branch/local libraries	764,000	71,100
Residential buildings		
Social/economic single family housing (multiple units)	841,000	78,200
Private/mass market single family housing 2 storey detached/semidetached (multiple units)	688,000	63,900
Purpose designed single family housing 2 storey detached (single unit)	764,000	71,100
Social/economic apartment housing, low rise (no lifts)	497,000	46,200
Social/economic apartment housing, high rise (with lifts)	535,000	49,900
Private sector apartment building (standard specification)	611,000	56,900
Private sector apartment buildings (luxury)	956,000	88,800
Student/nurses halls of residence	497,000	46,200
Homes for the elderly (shared accommodation)	497,000	46,200

	Cost m² Won	Cost ft² Won
Homes for the elderly (self contained with shared communal facilities)	535,000	49,900
Hotel, 5 star, city centre	1,334,000	124,000
Hotel, 3 star, city/provincial	1,147,000	106,600
Motel	956,000	88,800

Regional variations

The approximate estimating costs are based on projects in Seoul and other big cities. For other parts of country, add 5% to these costs.

Value added tax (VAT)

The standard rate of value added tax (VAT) is currently 10%, chargeable on general building work.

EXCHANGE RATES AND INFLATION

The combined effect of exchange rates and inflation on prices within a country and price comparisons between countries is discussed in section 2.

Exchange rates

The graph below plots the movement of the South Korean won against sterling, US dollar and 100 Japanese yen since 1985. The values used for the graph are quarterly and the method of calculating these is described and general guidance on the interpretation of the graph provided in section 2. The average exchange rate at the third quarter of 1995 was W1,209 to pound sterling, W763 to US dollar and W814 to 100 Japanese yen.

THE SOUTH KOREAN WON AGAINST STERLING, US DOLLAR AND JAPANESE YEN

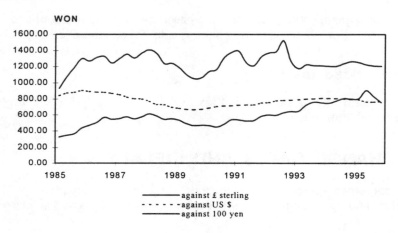

Price inflation

The table below presents retail prices and building price inflation in South Korea since 1990.

RETAIL PRICE AND BUILDING PRICE INFLATION

Year	Retail price index		Building price index	
	average index	average change %	average index	average change %
1990	183	8.3	173	11.6
1991	201	9.8	182	5.2
1992	116	6.1	126	5.6
1993	121	4.2	126	5.6
1994	126	6.2	132	4.6

USEFUL ADDRESSES

Public organizations

Korea Institute of Construction Technology
    142 Umyon-Dong, Socho-Ku
    Seoul, Korea
    Tel: 010 822 577 5006
    Fax: 010 822 572 8714
    Telex Kictex K28878

Korea Land Development Corporation
    164 Samsung-Dong
    Kangnam-Ku
    Seoul, Korea
    Tel: 010 822 550 7000
    Fax: 010 822 539 8176

Korea National Housing Corporation
    254 Nonkyun-Dong
    Kangnam Ku
    Seoul, Korea
    Tel: 010 822 513 3114
    Fax: 010 822 545 1854

Korean Standards Association
13-31 Youido-Dong
Youngdeungpo-Ku
Seoul, Korea
Tel: 010 822 369 8114
Fax: 010 822 780 3440

Ministry of Construction and Transportation
1 Jungang-Dong
Kwachun-Shi
Kyonggi-Do
Republic of Korea
Tel: 010 822 503 7171
Fax: 010 822 503 7409

Ministry of Finance and Economy
1 Jung Aug-Dong
Kwachon
Kyonggi-Do
Tel: 010 822 503 1717
Fax: 010 822 503 9033

Public Information Officer
Tel: 010 822 503 7312

The National Statistical Office
647-15 Yeaksam-Dong
Kangnam-Ku
Seoul, Korea
Tel: 010 822 222 1901/5
Fax: 010 822 538 3874

Trade and professional organizations

Construction Association of Korea
71-2 Nonhyon-Dong
Kangnam-Ku
Seoul, Korea
Tel : 010 822 547 6101
Fax : 010 822 3444 2441

Korea Construction Engineers Association
720-20 Yeaksam-Dong
Kang Nam-Ku
Seoul, Korea
Tel: 010 822 567 5571
Fax: 010 822 558 3936/569 0619

Korea Engineering Services Association
61-5 Nonhyun-Dong
Kangnam-Ku
Seoul, Korea
Tel: 010 822 541 1736
Fax: 010 822 543 5074

Korea Housing Builders Association
15-23 Yoido-Dong
Youngdeungpo-Ku
Seoul, Korea
Tel: 010 822 557 1352
Fax: 010 822 557 7408

Korea Institute of Registered Architecture
1603-55 Seocho-Dong
Seocho-Ku
Seoul, Korea
Tel: 010 822 581 5711
Fax: 010 822 586 8823

Korean Institute of Architects (section Coreenne de L'uia)
1-117 Dongsung-Dong
Chongro-Ku
Seoul, Korea
Tel: 010 822 744 8050/744 3725
Fax: 010 822 743 5363

The Architectural Institute of Korea
1044-34 Dongjak-KU
Sadang-Dong
Seoul, Korea
Tel: 010 822 525 1841-4
Fax: 010 822 525 1845

The International Contractors Association of Korea
    60-1 3-GA Chungmu-Ro Joong-Ku
    Seoul, Korea
    Tel : 010 822 274 1614
    Fax : 010 822 274 0742/3

The Korean Professional Engineers Association
    635-4 Yeoksam-Dong
    Kang Nam-Ku
    Seoul, Korea
    Tel: 010 822 557 1352
    Fax: 010 822 557 7408

Others

Korea Development Bank
    10-2 Kwanchui-Dong
    Chongro-Ku
    Seoul, Korea
    Tel: 010 822 398 6114
    Fax: 010 822 733 2994

Korea Housing Bank
    36/3 Yoido-Dong
    Youngdeungpo-Ku
    Seoul 150-010
    Korea
    Tel: 010 822 769 7114 or 769 8114
    Fax: 010 822 780 2375

The Korea Housing Association
    71-2, Nonhyon-Dong
    Kangnam-Ku
    Seoul, Korea
    Tel: 010 822 547 1835/548 1078
    Fax: 010 822 512 1312/514 3168

Sri Lanka

KEY DATA

Population
Population	17.9m
Urban population	22%
Population under 15 (1991)	32%
Population over 65 and over (1991)	4%
Average annual growth rate (1980 to 1993)	1.5%

Geography
Land area	66,000km²
Agricultural area	32%
Capital city	Colombo
Population of capital city (1991)	2.0mn

Economy
Monetary unit	Sri Lanka Rupee (SLR)
Exchange rate (average third quarter 1995) to:	
the pound sterling	SLR80.28
the US dollar	SLR50.65
the yen x 100	SLR55.22
Average annual inflation (1980 to 1993)	11.1%
Inflation rate (1994)	8.4%
Gross Domestic Product (GDP) at market price	SLR496.0bn
GDP per capita	SLR27,710
Average annual real change in GDP (1980 to 1993)	4.0%
Private consumption as a proportion of GDP	75%
General government consumption as a proportion of GDP	9%
Gross domestic investment as a proportion of GDP	25%
Central government expenditure as a proportion of Gross National Product	27%

Construction
Gross value of construction output *	SLR84bn
Net value of construction output *	SLR36bn
Net value of construction output as a proportion of GDP	7.3%
Cement production (1994)	1.6mn tonnes

All data relate to 1993 unless otherwise indicated
* Author's estimate

THE CONSTRUCTION INDUSTRY

Construction output

The value of net construction output in 1994 was SLR38.3 billion, equivalent to US$0.8 billion, or 7.3% of GDP. The corresponding percentage of gross construction output of GDP is estimated at 17%, 1994 GDP being SLR78.8 billion. Applying these same percentages to 1993 GDP of SLR496 billion, the gross output for that year is SLR84.3 billion or US$1.8 billion and the net output SLR36.2 billion or US$0.8 billion. Because GDP and construction output grew in 1994 by about the same amount this estimate is reasonable.

In 1994, construction output grew by 6%, only a little more than the growth in the economy as a whole. The boom in the economy had resulted in increased construction activity and the start of a number of essential projects to improve the country's infrastructure.

Up-to-date statistics on the breakdown of the workload in the construction sectors are not available. However, Sri Lanka's Institute for Construction Training and Development (ICTAD) estimates building work contributes about 62% of total construction output with the remaining 38% arising from civil engineering. Building work consists of housing (about 42%) and non-residential building (about 20%). Civil engineering work includes roads, water supply and irrigation.

In recent years the overall level of public sector work has generally declined while private sector work has increased. In particular there has been a rise in property development, including the redevelopment and refurbishment of hotels. Recent investment in the Sri Lankan manufacturing sector has also had a positive impact on the level of construction work.

The Sri Lankan government is encouraging private investment in infrastructure projects - water supply, waste water disposal, power generation, roads, industrial estates, car parks and buildings. Both local and foreign private investors are being encouraged to participate. Government policy is also encouraging private investment in property by targeting certain areas of Colombo for development.

A main priority of the government is the provision of social housing. The Urban Development Authority (UDA), a body that promotes intergrated planning and development of urban locations, increased its expenditure to more than SLR1 million in 1994. There was, however, a reduction in the number of housing units completed under the *One Point Five Million Houses Programme (OPFMHP)*. In 1994 the number of housing units completed fell to 41,930 from 50,137 in 1993.

Characteristics and structure of the industry

There are two sectors in the industry, the formal sector and the informal sector. The informal sector's real output is hardly quantified, but according to some analysts may be as high as 35% of the entire industry. This sector constitutes probably 75% of house building. Quite a number of social building and infrastructure work is carried out by the people themselves.

The formal sector of the construction industry was dominated by two state sector contractors till the latter part of the 1970s. The adoption of open economic policies by the government in the latter part of 1970s and early 1980s led to an explosive growth in the number of contractors as well as in the quantum of work. In today's context the bulk of the building work is carried out by general contractors who employ labour-only subcontractors. Specialist subcontractors may be nominated by the client's consultant team or employed by the general contractor.

Building work has been administered by professional consultants appointed by the building client. The consultants are responsible for design and specification of the work, the contractual arrangements and the supervision of the contract. However, since of late, design and build contractors offering a single point of responsibility have also made inroads to the industry, especially in the industrial building sector. Further, other non traditional forms of arrangements are beginning to emerge as the industry is progressing into the doorstep of the next century.

Major players in the industry are privately owned companies and as such the turnover or the workload in hand is not disclosed.

Contractors are graded by a governmental organization named ICTAD (Institute for Construction Training and Development) into five grades, ie. from Grade I to Grade V, according to a host of criteria. As a rough guide, a Grade I contractor is able to handle work up to about SLR600 million in a year, without having to seek joint ventures and like.

Construction design work is undertaken mainly by architects and engineers. A large proportion of the architects are members of the Sri Lanka Institute of Architects (a statutory body governing the practice of architects). A large number of the Institute members are working in the private sector as partners or employed by senior members and the rest work in the government, education or semi governmental bodies.

Civil engineers are normally members of the Institution of Civil Engineers (a statutory body governing the practice of engineering). They too are employed at various institutions along the lines of the architects.

The surveyor is beginning to gain its due prominence in Sri Lanka. The lack of appreciation of the surveyor and his services is due to the fact that there are no professionally qualified personnel in Sri Lanka.

However this situation is fast changing with the introduction of undergraduate programmes in the universities in the mid 1980s, and demand far outstrips the supply. The profession is fast gaining acceptance equal to that of designers and is in the process of gaining statutory approval of its professional body.

Clients and finance

Until the early 1980s the Sri Lankan construction industry has been dominated by the public sector. However since the mid 80s there is a marked shift towards the private sector and a gradual decline of the importance of the state sector. Due to the high level of foreign investment, most of the large clients are foreign.

The Sri Lankan banking sector has had an explosive growth in the past fifteen years and hence their activities have expanded into the construction industry in a marked way. Both development and commercial banks are very involved with the construction sector, and the exposure of merchant banks are less visible.

Selection of design consultants

There are no prescribed criteria or specific tender or selection procedures for the choice of design consultants in Sri Lanka. In the public sector, a pre-qualification exercise through the submission of credentials and relevant experience followed by interviews is usually adopted. In some instances a design competition is held. In the private sector, the design competition method is hardly adopted. Clients may select the design consultants known to them or from those who have a reputation for a specific type of building. The fee is based on a mandatory fee scale stipulated by the Sri Lanka Institute of Architects (SLIA).

Contractual arrangements

The Buildings Department has its own standard form of contract named *BD 11*, which is hardly used by clients. The *ICTAD Standard Form of Contract* is widely accepted by the industry and its use is mandatory for all public sector contracts. This contract assumes the use of measured bills of quantities that are normally prepared by the Quantity Surveyor. The tender documentation under this form might comprise:

- Drawings
- Specifications
- Bills of quantities, schedules of works or schedules of rates

Contracts are usually let on a measure and pay basis. Fluctuations in labour, materials and plant costs are reimbursed. Such increased costs are paid according to a formula, which is based on input percentages and indices which are published by the ICTAD itself.

In addition to these forms of contracts independent consultants have devised their own forms of contract based on the popular forms of contract elsewhere, e.g. JCT, FIDIC, etc.

A number of alternative contractual arrangements are available, most notably management contracting, design and build and construction management. Under management contracting, the client enters into a separate contract with a designer and a management contractor and the management contractor enters into subcontracts with works contractors. However, in construction management, the client enters into separate contracts with a designer, a construction manager and works contractors. This form of contractual arrangement is increasingly being used in preference to management contracting.

Liability and insurance

Almost all professional practices do not carry professional indemnity insurance, probably due to the reason that there have not been any major litigation actions as far as professional practices are concerned.

Development control and standards

The Urban Development Authority (UDA) is the national planning authority regulating and facilitating the physical development of Sri Lanka. Most types of development require written planning permission.

The Sri Lanka Standards Institution draws up and promulgates the *Sri Lanka Standards (SLS)*, the standard specification for products, and it is usual for manufacturers to comply with these. Architects and other building professionals generally follow the recommendations of the *SLS* or in its absence the *BS* specifications when specifying building products.

Research and development

The main organizations engaged in construction research are the ICTAD, the Building Economics Research Unit (BERU) of the University of Moratuwa and the University of Peradeniya. The addresses are given under the Useful Addresses section.

CONSTRUCTION COST DATA

Cost of labour

The figures are typical of labour costs in the Western Province (Colombo and its suburbs) as at the third quarter of 1995. The wage rate is on the basis of an employee's income, while the cost of labour indicates the cost to a contractor of employing that employee. The difference between the two covers a variety of contributions - among them are EPF (Employees Provident Fund), ETF (Employees Trust Fund), holidays, bonus, and any other fringe benefits.

	Wage rate (per day) SLR	Cost of labour (per day) SLR	Number of hours worked per year
Site operatives			
Mason/bricklayer	250	375	2,038
Carpenter	250	375	2,038
Plumber	250	375	2,038
Electrician	275	415	2,038
Structural steel erector	300	450	2,038
HVAC installer	350	525	2,038
Semi-skilled worker	200	300	2,038
Unskilled labourer	175	265	2,038
Equipment operator	200	265	2,038
Watchman/Security	200	300	2,038
	(per month)	*(per month)*	
Site supervision			
General foreman	5,250	7,875	
Trades foreman	4,750	7,125	
Clerk of works	6,500	9,750	

	Wage rate (per month) SLR	Cost of labour (per month) SLR
Contractor's personnel		
Site manager	25,000	49,500
Resident engineer	15,000	22,750
Resident surveyor	15,000	22,750
Junior engineer	8,500	12,400
Junior surveyor	8,500	12,400
Planner	15,000	20,000
Consultants' personnel		
Senior architect	35,000	57,000
Senior engineer	30,000	53,250
Senior surveyor	30,000	49,500
Qualified architect	15,000	22,500
Qualified engineer	15,000	22,500
Qualified surveyor	15,000	22,500

Cost of materials

The figures that follow are the costs of main construction materials, delivered to site in Colombo city area, as incurred by contractors in the third quarter of 1995. These assume that the materials would be in quantities as required for a medium sized construction project and that the location of the works would be neither constrained nor remote.

All the costs in this section exclude business turnover tax (BTT - see below).

	Unit	Cost SLR
Cement and aggregate		
Ordinary portland cement in 50kg bags	tonne	5,200
Coarse aggregate for concrete (20mm)	m^3	1,000
Fine aggregates for concrete	m^3	450
Ready mixed concrete($15N/mm^2$)	m^3	3,750
Ready mixed concrete($20N/mm^2$)	m^3	4,100
Ready mixed concrete($25N/mm^2$)	m^3	4,200
Ready mixed concrete($30N/mm^2$)	m^3	4,600
Ready mixed concrete($35N/mm^2$)	m^3	4,800
Ready mixed concrete($40N/mm^2$)	m^3	4,900

	Unit	Cost SLR
Steel		
Mild steel reinforcement	tonne	35,000
High tensile steel reinforcement	tonne	35,000
Bricks and blocks		
Common bricks (215x102.5x65mm)-hand cut	1,000	1,750
Good quality facing bricks (215x102.5x65mm)	1,000	5,250
Hollow cement blocks (400x200x100mm)	1,000	14,100
Rubble (150mm-225mm)	m³	425
Timber and Insulation		
Formwork timber class III(3/4" thick)	m²	175
Timber class I (25x100mm)	m	100
Plywood sheets (8'x4')-imported (15mm thick)	each	1,350
Plywood doors (2'9"x6'9")	each	1,200
Glass and ceramics		
Plain glass (3mm)	m²	225
Good quality ceramic wall tiles (108x108mm)	m²	470
Plaster and paint		
Lime plaster in 25kg bags	tonne	5,000
Emulsion paint in 4 litre bucket	litre	200
Gloss enamel paint in 4 litre bucket	litre	250
Coloured pigment (Red)	kg	260
Tiles and paviors		
Ceramic floor tiles (300x300mm)-white	m²	625
Insitu terrazzo	m²	900
Granite tiles (300x300mm)	m²	4,600
Calicut roof tiles	1000	10,000
Drainage		
Sanitary ware-imported	3pcs	33,250
110mm diameter PVC pipes	m	800

Unit rates

The descriptions below are generally shortened versions of standard descriptions listed in section 4. Where an item has a two digit reference number (e.g. 05 or 33), this relates to the full descriptions against that number in section 4. Where an item has an alphabetic suffix (e.g. 12A or 34B) this indicates that the standard has been modified.

Where a modification is a major one the complete modified description is included here and the standard description should be ignored, where a modification is minor (e.g. the insertion of a named hardwood) the shortened description has been modified here but, in general, the full description in section 4 prevails.

The unit rates below are for main work items on a typical construction project in the Colombo area in the third quarter of 1995. The rates include all necessary labour, materials and equipment. Allowances to cover preliminary and general items and contractor's overheads and profit have been included in the rates. All the rates in this section exclude business turnover tax (BTT - see below).

		Unit	Rate SLR
Excavation			
01	Mechanical excavation of foundation trenches (not exceeding 1m depth)	m³	180
02	Hardcore filling making up levels	m³	370
Concrete work			
04A	Plain insitu concrete in strip foundation in trenches (15N/m2)	m³	290
05	Reinforced insitu concrete in beds (20N/m2)	m³	6,200
06	Reinforced insitu concrete in walls (20N/m2)	m³	6,300
07A	Reinforced insitu concrete suspended floors or roof slabs (25N/m2)	m³	6,460
08A	Reinforced insitu concrete in columns (30N/m2)	m³	6,825
09A	Reinforced insitu concrete in isolated beams (30N/m2)	m³	6,825
Formwork			
11A	Plywood formwork to concrete walls	m²	525
12A	Plywood or metal formwork to concrete columns	m²	500
13A	Plywood or metal formwork to horizontal soffits of slabs	m²	473
Reinforcement			
14A	Reinforcement in concrete walls (10mm)	tonne	46,200
15A	Reinforcement in suspended concrete slabs (10mm)	tonne	45,675
16A	Fabric reinforcement in concrete (A142 steel mesh)	m²	210
Brickwork and blockwork			
20	Precast lightweight aggregate hollow concrete block walls (100mm thick)	m²	630

	Unit	*Rate SLR*
21A Brickwork in common bricks bedded in 1:5 cement sand mortar (1 brick thick)	m²	814
22A Brickwork in common bricks bedded in 1:5 cement sand mortar (1/2 brick thick)	m²	420
23A Facing bricks bedded in 1:5 cement sand mortar (1 brick thick)	m²	1,208

Roofing

24A Calicut roof tiles 400 x 250mm	m²	137
25 Plain clay roof tiles 200x150mm	m²	315
26A Half round roof tiles	m²	446
27A Lunumidella roof boarding	m²	394
31A Double sided reflective aluminium foil with wool blanket for thermostatic insulation (including sound insulation)	m²	236
33A Zinc/Aluminium steel roof sheeting	m²	1,313

Woodwork and metalwork

34A Preservative treated sawn timber 75x100mm	m	341
35A Preservative treated sawn softwood 50x150mm	m	420
36A Single glazed casement window in class 1 timber size 630 x 900mm	m²	5,250
38A Solid core half hour fire resisting hardwood internal flush door, size 838x1981mm	m²	6,825
39A Aluminium glazed window, size 1200 x 1200mm	m²	7,350
40A Aluminium glazed door, size 8050 x 2100mm	m²	8,400
41A Timber skirtings (class 1 timber) 25x100mm roof trusses	m	289

Plumbing

42 UPVC half round eaves gutter (112mm)	m	210
43A UPVC rainwater pipes (110mm)	m	368
45A High pressure plastic pipes for cold water supply (50mm)	m	236
46A Low pressure plastic pipes for cold water distribution	m	105
47A UPVC soil and vent pipes (110mm/type 600)	m	693
48 White vitreous china WC suite	each	3,150
49 White vitreous china lavatory basin	each	2,625
50 White glazed fireclay shower tray	each	3,150
51 Stainless steel single bowl sink and double drainer	each	3,150

Electrical work

52A PVC insulated and PVC sheathed copper cable core	m	8.40
53 13 amp unswitched socket outlet	each	315
54A Flush mounted 5amp, 1 way light switch	each	184

		Unit	Rates SLR
Finishings			
55A	2 coats cement based plaster on brick walls (rough finish)	m²	147
56	White glazed tiles on plaster walls	m²	1,208
57A	Non slip ceramic floor tiles	m²	1,155
58A	Cement and sand screed to concrete floors (12mm thick)	m²	189
59A	PVC floor tiles on screed	m²	945
Glazing			
61	Glazing to wood	m²	788
Painting			
62	Emulsion on plaster walls	m²	158
63	Oil paint on timber	m²	184

Approximate estimating

The building costs per unit area given below are averages incurred by building clients for typical buildings in Sri Lanka as at the third quarter of 1995. They are based upon the total floor area of all storeys, measured between external walls and without deduction for internal walls.

Approximate estimating costs generally include mechanical and electrical installations but exclude furniture, loose or special equipment, and external works; they also exclude fees for professional services. The costs shown are for specifications and standards appropriate to Sri Lanka and this should be borne in mind when attempting comparisons with similarly described building types in other countries. A discussion on this issue is included in section 2. Comparative data for countries covered in this publication, including construction cost data, is presented in Part Three.

Approximate estimating costs must be treated with caution; they cannot provide more than a rough guide to the probable cost of building. All the rates in this section include business turnover tax (BTT - 6% as at present).

	Cost m2 SLR	Cost ft2 SLR
Industrial buildings		
Factories for owner occupation (light industrial use)	9,500	900
Factories for owner occupation (heavy industrial use)	31,000	2,900
Factory/office (high tech) for owner occupation (controlled environment,fully finished)	23,000	2,140
Warehouse, low bay for owner occupation	15,850	1,475
Warehouse, high bay for owner occupation	9,700	900

	Cost m2 SLR	Cost ft2 SLR
Administrative and commercial buildings		
Civic offices, non air-conditioned	19,700	1,830
Civic offices, fully air conditioned	21,150	1,975
Offices for letting/owner occupation high rise, air-conditioned		
10 to 15 storeys.	30,575	2,850
Headquarters office, 5 to 10 storeys, air-conditioned	28,700	2,675
Prestige office, high rise with air conditioning and parking	32,300	3,000
Health and education buildings		
General hospitals	16,300	1,525
Private hospitals	32,740	3,050
Health centres	21,230	1,975
Nursery schools	4,675	430
University buildings	9,880	925
Management training centres	9,625	900
Recreation and arts buildings		
Concert halls including seating and stage equipment	5,076	475
Swimming pools (international standard) including changing		
and social facilities (surface tension)	8,580	800
Swimming pools (school standard) including changing facilities	9,240	860
Local museums	7,750	720
City centre/shopping complex including parking	75,350	7,000
Book shops/libraries	13,100	1,250
Town development/shopping/bus stands	12,000	1,125
Studio/engineering buildings for television network	16,415	1,500
Shopping arcades	6,500	600
Stadia	8,650	800
Residential buildings		
Social/economic single family housing (single units)	20,300	1,900
Private/Private single family housing 2 storey detached	10,760	1,000
Purpose designed single family housing 2 storey detached (single unit)	9,800	910
Local/economic apartment housing, low rise (no lifts)-low cost	9,850	915
Social/economics apartment housing, low rise (with lifts)	13,275	1,250
Private sector apartment building (standard specification)	31,850	3,000
Private sector apartment building (luxury)	35,000	3,250
Students/nurses hall of residence low cost	9,150	850
Hotel, 5 star, city centre	73,100	6,800
Hotel, 3 star, city	35,875	3,350
Resorts	18,100	1,675
Resorts -cottage type	26,400	2,450
Motel	15,370	1,425

Exchange rates

The graph below plots the movement of the Sri Lankan rupee against sterling, US dollar and 100 Japanese yen since 1985. The values used for the graph are quarterly and the method of calculating these is described and general guidance on the interpretation of the graph provided in section 2. The average exchange rate in the third quarter of 1995 was SLR 80.28 to pound sterling, SLR 50.65 to US dollar and SLR 55.22 to 100 Japanese yen.

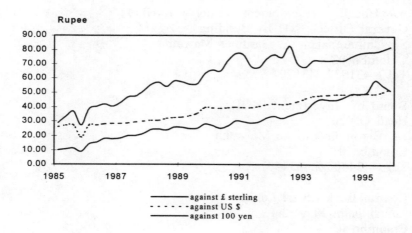

— against £ sterling
- - - - - against US $
— against 100 yen

USEFUL ADDRESSES

Public organizations

Building Economics Research Unit (BERU)
    Department of Building Economics
    Faculty of Architecture
    University of Moratuwa
    Tel : 645301
        645441
        645671 - Ext 263

Department of Buildings
  Sethsiripaya, Jawardenapura
  Battaramulla
  Tel : 862721, 862722

Institute for Construction Training and Development (ICTAD)
  Savsiripaya, Wijerama Mawatha
  Colombo 07
  Tel : 686092

National Housing Development Authority (NHDA)
  General Office , NHDA Building
  Sir Chittampalam A. Gardiner Mawatha
  Colombo 02
  Tel : 431932, 431707

The Board of Investment (BOI)
  Head Office
  14, Baron Jayatillake Mawatha
  Colombo 01
  Tel : 434403-5, 434407-9

The Central Bank of Sri Lanka
  Janadhipathi Mawatha
  Colombo 01
  Tel : 421191, 430991

The Department of Census and Statistics
  06, Albert Crescent
  Colombo 07
  Tel : 692988

The Urban Development Authority
  27, D.R. Wijewardena Mawatha
  Colombo 10
  Tel : 696460

Trade and professional associations

Institute of Quantity Surveyors (IQS)
  185/2, Model Farm Road
  Colombo 08
  Tel : 685599

National Building Research Organisation (NBRO)
99/1, Jawatta Road
Colombo 05
Tel : 500354

Organisation of Professional Association (OPA)
275/5, Baudhaloka Mawatha
Colombo 07
Tel : 697109

Sri Lanka Institute of Architects (SLIA)
120/10, Wijerama Mawatha
Colombo 07
Tel : 697101

Sri Lanka Institute of Engineers
120/15, Wijerama Mawatha
Colombo 07
Tel : 698426, 685490

Taiwan

KEY DATA

Population
Population	21.1mn
Urban population	52%
Population under 15	25%
Population 60 and over	11%
Average annual growth rate (1984 to 1994)	0.9%

Geography
Land area	36,000 km²
Agricultural area	25%
Capital city	Taipei
Population of capital city	2.7mn

Economy
Monetary unit	New Taiwan dollar (NT$)
Exchange rate (average third quarter 1995) to :	
the pound sterling	NT$42.38
the US dollar	NT$26.74
the yen x 100	NT$29.15
Average annual inflation (1990 to 1994)	3.9%
Inflation rate (1994)	4.1%
Gross Domestic Product (GDP) at market prices	NT$5,700bn
GDP per capita	NT$270,140
Average annual real change in GDP (1990 to 1994)	6.8%
Private consumption as a proportion of GDP	57%
General government consumption as a proportion of GDP	17%
Gross domestic investment as a proportion of GDP	24%

Construction
Gross value of construction output*	NT$740bn
Net value of construction output	NT$319.2bn
Net value of construction output as a proportion of GDP	5.6%
Annual cement consumption	25mn tonnes

All data relate to 1993 unless otherwise indicated

* *Author's estimate*

THE CONSTRUCTION INDUSTRY

Construction output

The gross output of construction in 1993 is estimated at NT$740 billion, equivalent to US$28 billion, or 13% of GDP. The net output of construction in 1993 was NT$319.2 billion, equivalent to US$12.2 billion, or 5.6% of GDP. The net output of construction in 1994 was NT$339.2 billion, equivalent to US$13.0 billion, or 5.3% of GDP.

The output of building construction for the years 1990-1992 is as shown in the table below.

OUTPUT OF BUILDING CONSTRUCTION, 1990-92

	New building construction million m²	Proportion of building in concrete construction %
1990	31.3	85
1991	32.0	87
1992	36.9	90

Source: Council for Economic Planning and Development Industry of Free China

The construction industry received a boost in 1990 by the announcement of a Six Year National Plan. This announcement, made by the government, outlined details of a major infrastructure and construction programme aimed at making Taiwan an Asia Pacific Regional Operations Centre. The works were valued in the region of US$300 billion, although at the time of announcement, it was estimated that 60% of the work was already underway. In addition, certain elements of the plan have yet to be realised due to delays in passing the necessary legislation. Upgrading of infrastructure, however, continues to be viewed as a priority if Taiwan is to capitalize on any shift of commerce from Hong Kong after the 1997 handover to China. The government is currently looking to the private sector to invest capital in public works in order to realize the aims of the original Six Year Plan.

The stalling of the National Plan has, however, created a downturn in the construction market. Almost all local contractors had 'geared up' to cope with the anticipated work load. When the new work did not materialize the industry went into recession and competition intensified. The private sector has also suffered from a loss of confidence as a result of the government's policy change. Overall from 1992 - 1993 the construction market has contracted and analysts suggest this may continue for a further 18 - 24 months. The housing sector although not unaffected, is the only sector to remain stable, whilst showing little growth.

The majority of construction output, approximately 91.2% is carried out within the designated Urban Planning Zone i.e. urban sites, the remainder being in rural areas. Taipei Country gets the largest share of construction work followed by Taipei City. Overall the largest construction market is Great Taipei Zone which enjoys more than 30% of the total national construction output.

Characteristics and structure of the industry

It is a legal requirement in Taiwan for construction firms to be registered under a government administered licencing system. There are three types of licence, Class A, B and C. The licences are awarded according to a company's technical ability and experience. The highest category, Class A enables the contractor to tender for any reasonable sized project. Class B enables the contractor to work on projects up to a value of NT$30 million and Class C on projects up to a value of NT$15 million. A contractor's licence can be upgraded after a set period of time and performing satisfactorily at the class in which it is currently operating. Licences can also be transferred. A contractor may purchase a Class A licence from another company which no longer has the technical expertise to carry out large projects. As of 1992 there were 1,147 Class A contractors, 559 Class B and 1,684 Class C.

The tendering of public works is governed by the *Auditing Law* and the *Examination Regulations*. These statutes identify three possible methods for the tendering of public works. They are Public Tendering, Tender Comparison and Tender Negotiation. Each method is outlined in statute defining when it should be used in order to ensure the fairest and most efficient method of tendering in any particular circumstance. Recently, however, the public tendering process has attracted much criticism. The main areas of concern being escalating contract sums, poor workmanship, late completion and corruption. As expenditure on public works is planned to increase and as the market becomes internationalized it is accepted that the current tendering procedures must be reviewed.

Generally major government funded projects are taken by quasi-government organizations such as the Retired Servicemen's Engineering Agency (RSEA) or the Bureau of Engineering Services (BES). Both organizations enjoy special privileges including, in the case RSEA, the right of first refusal on major projects. However, this relationship with the government has resulted in accusations of corruption and there are now proposals to privatize these organizations.

In line with Taiwan's trade protective economic policy there are less major western construction companies operating in Taiwan than in any other country in the region. It is believed that the principal reason for this is the Licencing System, outlined above, which would require major international contractors to operate locally in Taiwan on relatively small projects for many years in order to obtain a Class A licence. This may change as Taiwan seeks entry to the World Trade Organisation. A prerequisite of entry would be to open its doors to foreign competition and to comply with internationally accepted tendering practices.

The construction industry in Taiwan suffers a shortage of skilled labour. This is further exacerbated by restrictions on the import of foreign workers. The availability of unskilled labour may be determined by seasons as many labourers return to the countryside for crop harvesting. Research by the Public Construction Supervisory Committee of the Executive Council has revealed that wages of construction workers in Taiwan are about 50% higher than in other developing countries. However, productivity is comparable with that in other developing countries. This may be due partly to the shortage of labour.

The majority of construction in Taiwan utilizes reinforced concrete and other locally available materials. The preferred height for a building being in the 7m-15m category. Statistical evidence indicates that high rise structures are losing popularity.

It is anticipated that the coming years will be something of a transitional period for the construction industry in Taiwan. Restriction on foreign competition may dropped, standard forms of contract reviewed, and outmoded tendering procedures updated. Local contractors will have to re-organize in order to compete effectively with major international contractors on large scale infrastructure projects.

Clients and finance

According to an independent market analysis the private sector accounts for approximately 45%. The housing market is the largest single sector representing approximately 50% of work carried out. In 1993 licences for 21,769,000m² of housing were approved. Funding comes from both private and public sector.

Further to recent funding difficulties the government has come to believe that the success of the Six Year National Plan will to an extent be dependent upon its ability to attract investment from private sources. Legislation is being drafted which will provide the legal basis on which the government can agree to Build Operate and Transfer projects and similiar schemes for the investment of private (and foreign) capital in public works. It is also proposed, in order to make the scheme more attractive, to offer tax and financial incentives, measures to facilitate land acquisition, and authority to the private sector to develop land adjacent to public projects.

Plans are also being considered for the privatization of the power generation industry which will introduce independent power into the system.

Selection of design consultants

In the case of architects the normal basis of selection would be on their experience. Personal contacts and recommendations also play a part. The profession of architect in Taiwan is split into two categories, Class A and Class B. These classes are used as a basis for establishing their suitability for different types of work. As of 1992 there were 1,993 Class A Architects and 76 Class B Architects.

As with the architects, the structural engineer will normally be selected according to track record and general suitability for the project in question.

The title of quantity surveyor or cost consultant is not formally recognized in Taiwan. The preparation of estimates normally falls within the architect's scope of work.

Contractual arrangements

The tendering of public works is overseen by the Ministry of Audit (MOA). The function of the MOA in the construction field is to ensure that other government agencies comply with the relevant laws and regulations governing the award of construction contracts. The preparation of a tender budget by government bodies is the first step in the process. Tender budgets are normally set very low in order to encourage the tenderers to be more competitive.

Tenders will then be invited from contractors of the appropriate classification. It is necessary at this stage for the contractor to go through a prequalification process. The prequalification will involve the contractor in a process of demonstrating that he can comply with a series of criteria outlined in a prequalification document. An interview may also be requested.

Once a list of suitable tenderers has been prepared, tenders will be invited. If the lowest tender is above the government budget, a period of negotiation will follow in order to try and match the government figure.

Other higher tenderers may be requested to participate in such negotiations in order to heighten competition.

In the private sector the market is very commercial. The employer or client will himself take responsibility for the issue of the tender. He will also conduct any subsequent negotiation.

Generally public contracts will be let under a government standard form of contract. In cases where international bids are being invited, *FIDIC* (an international form of contract), the *British JCT 80*, or the *American Institute of Architects Form of Contract* may be used.

Liability and insurance

Most contracts for public works are let under the government standard forms of contract. These forms set out the risks, rights and obligations of the various parties to the contract. Generally the contracts place most of the risk on the contractor, including loss of profit and liability for consequential damages. Typically the contracts do not offer a facility for the contractor to introduce variations in contract terms. This may lead to disputes.

The preferred method of dispute resolution is by arbitration although recently there have been proposals to delete arbitration clauses from the construction contracts because of the failure of arbitration to resolve a dispute on a recent major contract. Presently, however, it is still considered a quicker, more economic and effective option than recourse to the civil courts. The period for which a contractor remains liable under a contract varies and must be written into the contract before issue,

Also within the standard form of contracts, the contractor is responsible for providing insurances covering the works themselves, people engaged on the works and third party liability. It is also common for the contract to call for a performance bond (bank bond), often a substantial sum of money.

Development control and standards

The Construction and Planning Administration (CPA) was established in March 1981 and is the governmental authority in charge of regional planning, city planning, building regulations and public works, among others. The following departments fall under its auspices.

The Department of Regional Planning is responsible for overall planning of national land use. This will include development and ratification of regional plans, supervision, promotion and co-ordination of affairs related to regional development. On a more local level, the Department of City Planning is responsible for the preparation of urban development policies. City planning laws, new towns planning, urban renewal and co-ordination of metropolitan development also fall under their jurisdiction. All planning applications and licences for construction will be processed through this Department. As of the end of 1990 there were 437 localities covered with city plans, totalling 435,162 hectares. Among them are 138 town plans, 208 countryside plans and 91 special district plans. Currently there are four new towns being planned or developed.

The Department of Building Regulations supervises all new construction and maintains standards within the industry. The main functions of this Department are the drafting, revision and interpretation of building laws, codes and related regulations. Plans must be submitted to this Department for approval before construction can commence.

The Construction and Planning Administration also regulates the industry. This regulation includes approval of applications to establish new construction companies and new subcontracting firms and approval of advancement of construction companies to higher classifications.

CONSTRUCTION COST DATA

Cost of labour

The figures below are typical of labour costs in the Taipei area as at the third quarter of 1995. The wage rate is the basis of an employee's income, while the cost of labour indicates the cost to a contractor of employing that employee. The difference between the two covers a variety of mandatory and voluntary contributions - a list of items which could be included is given in section 2.

	Wage rate (per day) NT$	Cost of labour (per day) NT$	Number of hours worked per year
Site operatives			
Bricklayer	386	425	2,200
Carpenter	414	455	2,200
Plumber	357	393	2,200
Electrician	371	408	2,200

	Wage rate (per day) NT$	Cost of labour (per day) NT$	Number of hours worked per year
Structural steel erector	500	550	2,200
Semi-skilled worker	340	374	2,200
Unskilled labourer	257	283	2,200
Steel bender	414	455	2,200
Scaffolder	471	518	2,200
Plasterer	414	455	2,200

Cost of materials

The figures that follow are the costs of main construction materials, delivered to site in the Taipei area, as incurred by contractors in the third quarter of 1995. These assume that the materials would be in quantities as required for a medium sized construction project and that the location of the works would be neither constrained nor remote.

All the costs in this section exclude value added tax (VAT - see below)

	Unit	Cost NT$
Cement and aggregate		
Ordinary portland cement in 50kg bags	tonne	3,200
Coarse aggregates for concrete	m^3	320
Fine aggregates for concrete	m^3	230
Ready mixed concrete (4000 Psi)	m^3	2,200
Ready mixed concrete (2000 Psi)	m^3	1,650
Steel		
Reinforcement	tonne	8,700
H section (below 700mm)	kg	12
H section (above 700mm)	kg	14
Channel	kg	12
Angle	kg	11
Timber		
Hardwood	m^3	13,000
Softwood	m^3	6,500

Unit rates

The descriptions below are generally shortened versions of standard descriptions listed in full in section 4. Where an item has a two digit reference number (e.g. 05 or 33), this relates to the full description against that number in section 4. Where an item has an alphabetic suffix (e.g. 12A or 34B) this indicates that the standard description has been modified. Where a modification is major the complete modified description is included here and the standard description should be ignored; where a modification is minor (e.g. the insertion of a named hardwood) the shortened description has been modified here but, in general, the full description in section 4 prevails.

The unit rates below are for main work items on a typical construction project in Taipei in the third quarter of 1995. The rates include all necessary labour, materials and equipment. An allowance of 5%-10% to cover preliminary and general items have been added to the rates. All the rates in this section exclude value added tax (see below).

		Unit	Cost NT$
Excavation			
01	Mechanical excavation of foundation trenches including earthwork support	m³	630
02	Hardcore filling in bed; 150mm thick	m²	160
Concrete work			
04A	Plain insitu concrete (2000 psi) in beds	m³	1,900
05	Reinforced insitu concrete (4000 psi) in beds	m³	2,650
06	Reinforced insitu concrete (4000 psi) in walls	m³	2,650
07	Reinforced insitu concrete (4000 psi) in suspended floors	m³	2,650
08	Reinforced insitu concrete (4000 psi) in columns	m³	2,650
09A	Reinforced insitu concrete (4000 psi) in suspended beams	m³	2,650
Formwork			
11	Formwork to sides of wall	m²	580
12	Formwork to sides of columns	m²	580
13	Formwork to soffit of suspended slabs	m²	600
Reinforcement			
14	Reinforcement in concrete walls	kg	18
15	Reinforcement in suspended concrete slabs	kg	18
Steelwork			
17	Fabricate, supply and erect steel frame structure	tonne	65

	Unit	Cost NT$
Brickwork and blockwork		
22A Solid (perforated) sand lime bricks (half brick thick)	m²	620
Roofing		
24A 300 x 300 x 20mm thick concrete tiles	m²	380
30A Waterproof sheet membrane	m²	330
30B Waterproof cement and sand screed; average 90mm thick	m²	430
32A Polystyrene board insulation on roof slabs	m²	400
Woodwork and metalwork		
37A Proprietary plastic laminated door; size 900 x 2100mm (excluding ironmongery)	no	17,500
38A One hour fire rated proprietary plastic laminated door; size 900 x 2100mm (excluding ironmongery)	no	39,000
39A Double glazing aluminium window; size 900 x 2100mm	no	9,800
40A Proprietary steel door; size 2000 x 1400mm	no	31,000
41A 38mm diameter stainless steel tubular rails	m	820
41B 50mm diameter stainless steel tubular rails	m	1,080
Plumbing		
44A 50mm diameter galvanised steel pipes; fixed to wall	m	390
44B 75mm diameter galvanised steel pipes; fixed to wall	m	600
44C 100mm diameter galvanised steel pipes; fixed to wall	m	910
47A 300mm wide x 600mm average depth surface channels	m	3,150
47B Precast concrete channel covers	m	960
47C 600 x 400 x 30mm thick cast iron gratings	no	1,750
Finishings		
55A 20mm thick cement and sand plaster to wall	m²	410
56A 200 x 200 x 5mm white glazed tiles	m²	1,000
56B Metallic lustre ceramic facing tiles to external wall	m²	1,800
56C 100 x 100 x 9mm unglazed porcelain tiles	m²	950
56D Paperhanging; vinyl sheet covering to walls	m²	650
58A 150mm thick lightweight concrete to floors	m²	250
58B 50mm thick cement and sand paving; steel trowelled smooth	m²	320
60 Mineral fibreboard suspended ceiling system	m²	1,150
60A Aluminium suspended ceiling system	m²	3,100
Glazing		
61 6mm thick clear float glass	m²	1,050
61A Reflective double glazing to metal	m²	2,400

	Unit	*Cost NT$*
Painting		
62A Emulsion paint with acrylic alkali resisting primer to ceilings	m²	175
62B Cement paint in two coats to plastered ceilings	m²	90
62C Spraying polyurethane paint to walls	m²	230

Approximate estimating

The building costs per unit area given below are averages incurred by building clients for typical buildings in the Taipei area as at the third quarter of 1995. They are based upon the total floor area of all storeys, measured between external walls and without deduction for internal walls.

Approximate estimating costs generally include mechanical and electrical installations but exclude furniture, loose or special equipment, and external works; they also exclude fees for professional services. The costs shown are for specifications and standards appropriate to Hong Kong and this should be borne in mind when attempting comparisons with similarly described building types in other countries. A discussion of this issue is included in section 2. Comparative data for countries covered in this publication, including construction cost data, is presented in Part Three. Approximate estimating costs must be treated with caution; they cannot provide more than a rough guide to the probable cost of building.

	Cost *m² NT$*	*Cost* *ft² NT$*
Residential buildings		
Low rise (reinforced concrete structure)	18,500	1,720
High rise (reinforced concrete structure)	29,400	2,732
Commercial buildings		
Low rise (reinforced concrete structure)	19,100	1,775
High rise (reinforced concrete structure)	30,000	2,788
High rise (structural steel frame)	33,300	3,095

Regional variations

The approximate estimating costs are based on projects in Taipei. For costs in Kaohsiung and other areas reduce by approximately 7%.

Value added tax (VAT)

The standard rate of value added tax (VAT) is currently 5%, chargeable on general building work.

EXCHANGE RATES AND INFLATION

The combined effect of exchange rates and inflation on prices within a country and price comparisons between countries is discussed in section 2.

Exchange rates

The graph below plots the movement of the New Taiwan Dollar against sterling, US dollar and 100 Japanese yen since 1985. The figures used for the graph are quarterly and the method of calculating these is described and general guidance on the interpretation of the graph provided in section 2. The exchange rates at third quarter 1993 was NT$42.38 to pound sterling, NT$26.74 to US dollar and NT$29.15 to 100 Japanese yen.

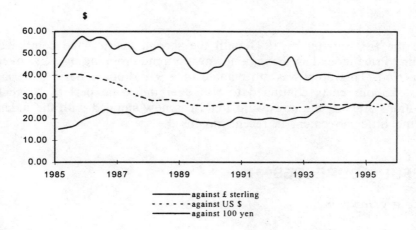

Price inflation

The table below presents consumer price inflation in Taiwan since 1986.

CONSUMER PRICE INFLATION

Year	Consumer Price Index	
	average index	*average change %*
1986	87.19	-
1987	87.64	0.52
1988	88.77	1.29
1989	92.68	4.40
1990	96.51	4.13
1991	100.00	3.62
1992	104.47	4.47
1993	107.54	2.94
1994	111.95	4.10
1995*	115.83	3.46

* *Forecast*

Since the first quarter of 1993 until the second quarter, the combined Building Price index has shown a downward trend dropping by 3.2% over that period. This drop was attributable to a 9% drop in basic material prices. Labour costs continued to rise over the same period. Current indications are that the downward trend has now stopped with the index showing little movement in recent months.

USEFUL ADDRESSES

Public organizations

Bureau of Public Works
  1 Shih Fu Road
  Taipei
  Tel : 759 8898
  Fax : 720 5817

Bureau of Urban Development
  1 Shih Fu Road
  Taipei
  Tel : 759 8889
  Fax : 759 3321

Construction and Planning Administration
Ministry of Interior
  14th Floor
  333 Section 2
  Tunhwas Road
  Taipei
  Tel : 737 4701

Council for Economic Planning and Development
  9th Floor
  87 Nanking East Road
  Section 2
  Taipei
  Tel : 522 5300
  Fax : 551 9011

Department of Rapid Transit Systems
  13th Floor, 16 Nanking East Road
  Section 4
  Taipei
  Tel : 578 5678
  Fax : 578 0999

Housing and Urban Development Bureau
  342 Pa Teh Road
  Section 2
  Taipei
  Tel : 773 1212
  Fax : 772 8503

Office of Building Standards
  1 Shih Fu Road
  Taipei
  Tel : 720 8889
  Fax : 397 9798

Trade organizations

Chinese Association of General Contractors
    10th Floor, 21 Chang-An East Road
    Section 1
    Taipei
    Tel : 581 8014
    Fax : 581 0091

Taiwan Electrical Engineering Association
    11th Floor, 76 Sung Kiang Road
    Taipei
    Tel : 571 9236
    Fax : 523 2996

Taiwan Union Building Materials Association
    Room 4
    7th Floor, 374 Pa Teh Road
    Section 2
    Taipei
    Tel : 751 8834
    Fax : 777 2101

DAVIS LANGDON & SEAH (THAILAND) LTD
LECE (THAILAND) LTD

The strategic and integrated management of cost, time and quality - the client "risk" areas of a contract - are essential functions, which are necessary to ensure the satisfactory planning, procurement, execution and operation of construction projects.

We specialise in the financial management of construction projects and their risk areas, from project inception to completion and we concentrate on:

- being positive and creative in our advice, rather than simply reactive;

- providing value for money via efficient management, rather than on superficial cost monitoring;

- giving advice that is matched to the client's requirements, rather than imposing standard or traditional solutions;

- paying attention to the life-cycle costs of constructing and occupying a building, rather than to the initial capital cost only.

Our aim is to provide our clients with risk assurance, cost control and value for money, via effective advice, cost planning and management.

DAVIS LANGDON & SEAH (THAILAND) LTD
8th Floor, Kian Gwan Building
140 Wireless Road
Bangkok 10330
Thailand
Tel : (662) 2537390
Fax : (662) 2534977

DAVIS LANGDON & SEAH INTERNATIONAL

Thailand

KEY DATA

Population

Population	58.1mn
Urban population	19%
Population under 15	33%
Population 65 and over	2%
Average annual growth rate (1980 to 1993)	1.7%

Geography

Land area	513,000 km²
Agricultural area	41%
Capital city	Bangkok
Population of capital city	7mn

Economy

Monetary unit	Thai baht (Bt)
Exchange rate (average third quarter 1995) to:	
the pound sterling	Bt 39.41
the US dollar	Bt 24.87
the yen x 100	Bt 27.11
Average annual inflation (1980 to 1993)	4.3%
Inflation rate (1994)	5.0%
Gross Domestic Product (GDP) at market prices	Bt 3,150bn
GDP per capita	Bt 54,217
Average annual real change in GDP (1980 to 1993)	8.2%
Private consumption as a proportion of GDP	52%
General government consumption as a proportion of GDP	10%
Gross domestic investment as a proportion of GDP	40%
Central government expenditure as a proportion of Gross National Product	16%

Construction

Gross value of construction output *	Bt 567bn
Net value of construction output	Bt 217.2bn
Net value of construction output as a proportion of GDP	6.9%
Cement production	26mn tonnes

All data relate to 1993 unless otherwise indicated

* *Author's estimate*

THE CONSTRUCTION INDUSTRY

Construction output

The gross output of the construction industry in 1993 is estimated at Bt 567 billion, equivalent to US$22 billion, or 18% of GDP. The value of net output of construction in 1993 was Bt 217.2 billion, equivalent to US$8.7 billion, or 6.9% of GDP.

In 1994 the construction sector is thought to have grown by about 8% and a similar increase was expected for 1995. Growth in 1994 was lower than the 8.3% growth in 1993, primarily due to a slowdown in commercial and office building work in the Bangkok area arising from low occupancy rates. Private sector residential and office construction work is now being affected by the Bank of Thailand's strict control on commercial bank credit to real estate businesses. The cost of construction has also increased owing to higher interest rates, forcing private sector developers to either down-size their projects or slow the rate of development of new projects. Activity in other sector of private sector work has been buoyant, particularly in the regions, in line with an improvement in the level of activity in the general economy.

Public construction work for government and state enterprises grew by 16.6% (13.6% in 1993) as a result of continuing investment in infrastructure and utility projects as part of a policy to promote decentralization and support development in the regions. Important projects include the construction and improvement of irrigation systems, construction of motorways, expansion of other major routes to four-lane highways, electricity generation plants, gas pipelines and the expansion of telephone services. The government's policy to promote growth and the development of basic infrastructure in the regional areas has encouraged the development of several small and medium-sized projects.

BUILDING APPROVALS

Region	Area approved (000 m²)		
	1992	1993	1994
Central region (excluding Bangkok)	4,371	2,931	3,199
Bangkok Metropolis	27,237	29,720	26,108
Northern region	1,469	1,866	2,216
Southern region	1,700	1,625	1,811
North-eastern region	1,451	1,882	2,751
Total	36,227	38,023	35,994

Source: Annual Economic Report, 1994, Bank of Thailand

Growth in investment fuelled an increase in the volume of construction materials sold; the volume of cement increased by 12.6% in 1994 (13.6% in 1993), iron rods by 12.8% in 1994 (25.1% in 1993), galvanised iron sheets by 25.6% (12.0% in 1993). The increase also reflects an expansion in production capacity in a move to substitute the import of construction materials. Machinery for construction, however, still remains one of the country's imports.

The situation described above has not seriously affected major construction firms who have over the past two to three years used Thailand as a base from which to venture into Indochina markets such as Vietnam, Myanmar, Cambodia and Laos.

Characteristics and structure of the industry

The number of contracting companies has increased significantly over the last few years and it is estimated that there are now over 4,500 construction firms. Most of these are small Thai firms and most of the top ten contracting firms are of foreign origin, often joint ventures. Competition from foreign contractors has been increasing in recent years, notably those from South Korea, Japan and European countries.

Clients and finance

The three main categories of clients of the industry are:

- the government consisting of various government departments that are financed by the Treasury;

- state enterprises, that is, government and private sector, joint venture organizations financed by the Treasury and from foreign loans;

- the private sector comprising private property developers, insurance companies, and other financial institutions financed by banks or the developer's own resources.

Selection of design consultants

The government has in-house design teams to undertake its own projects. However, if it is felt that the nature, scope, etc. of a proposed project cannot be adequately undertaken by an in-house design team, then outside consultants are invited to bid. There is a process of pre-qualification based on reputation, past experience, staff capacity, etc. When tenders are invited, a brief is given together with all the predetermined rules and regulations. The level of professional fee is also predetermined. The selection committee seeks the best overall design to satisfy the brief. Design competitions are frequently held to appoint consultants.

In the case of a state enterprise, tenders may be invited. The level of fee quoted is one of the factors taken into consideration when awarding a contract whereas, in the private sector, the design concept and fees are the major considerations in awarding work to consultants. In-house design organizations usually function as project co-ordinators. Depending on the terms of engagement of consultants, in-house design organizations may have an important role.

The method used for selecting consultants is the same for housing, building works and civil engineering.

Contractual arrangements

Construction contract documents may be prepared either in Thai or English. Government works use several versions of the standard form of contract while no standard form of contract exists for the private sector. However, a commonly used form is a simplified version of a contract produced by the Joint Contracts Tribunal in the UK.

Liability and insurance

Contractors may be liable for injury to persons and property caused during the carrying out of the works. Professionals may also be held liable for negligence.

Contractors are usually required to offer a six to twelve month warranty period after project completion during which defects that the contractors are responsible have to be made good at no cost to the Employer. It is usual therefore for a contractor to take out a Contractors' All Risks Insurance Policy.

Consultants do not usually, however, offer the client any design warranty, but foreign investors normally ask for a twelve month warranty period. Insurance is not compulsory for professionals.

It is usual for claims to be settled out of court. Some designers limit claims by clients to an amount not exceeding their fees.

Development control and standards

Land use planning is based on zoning for various types of development. For the application of planning permission, the consultants must submit a set of submission drawings to the city hall. In the case of a factory, an environmental study must also be provided. The submission drawings will be forwarded to the land use department within the city hall to check for compliance with land use requirements. If approved, these drawings are then passed on to the structural, architectural and the mechanical and electrical departments for checking against compliance with by-laws. If the drawings satisfy all these requirements they are endorsed with the signature of either the governor or deputy governor of the city hall for the granting of planning permission.

The whole process of obtaining planning permission takes 45 days and the chances of approval are high. If an application is turned down, an appeal may be made in writing to the city hall. It is to be noted that the city hall might approve a minor departure from the land use requirements if it can be shown that such departure actually benefits the general public.

There is a set of building regulations applicable to the whole country. A building of more then $10,000m^2$ needs an occupancy permit. The city hall officers will inspect the completed building against the approved planning submission. Depending on the type of development, officers from relevant departments will inspect the building. For example, the health authority will inspect a hospital, and the health and fire authority will inspect a hotel.

The national standard for building materials/products is the *TIS (Thai Industrial Standard)*. However, many foreign equivalents (e.g. *BS, ASTM, DIN, JIS*, etc.) are also acceptable.

CONSTRUCTION COST DATA

Cost of labour

The figures below are typical of labour costs in the Bangkok area as at third quarter of 1995.

Cost of labour
(per hour)
Bt

Site operatives

Unskilled labourer	23
Semi-skilled labourer	28
Skilled labourer	39

Cost of materials

The figures that follow are the costs of main construction materials, delivered to site in the Bangkok area, as incurred by contractors in the third quarter of 1995. These assume that the materials would be in quantities as required for a medium sized construction project and that the location of the works would be neither constrained nor remote. All the rates in this section exclude value added tax (VAT - see below).

	Unit	*Cost Bt*
Cement and aggregate		
Ordinary portland cement in 50kg bags	tonne	1,660
Coarse aggregates for concrete	m^3	300
Fine aggregates for concrete	m^3	300
Ready mixed concrete (mix Grade 20)	m^3	1,430
Ready mixed concrete (mix Grade 24)	m^3	1,590
Steel		
Mild steel reinforcement	tonne	11,500
High tensile steel reinforcement	tonne	10,500
Structural steel sections	tonne	18,000

	Units	Cost Bt
Bricks and blocks		
Common bricks (160 x 35 x 70mm)	1,000	550
Good quality facing bricks (220 x 65 x 105mm)	1,000	4,500
Hollow concrete blocks (390 x 105 x 65mm)	1,000	3,750
Precast concrete cladding units with exposed aggregate finish	m^2	1,700
Timber and insulation		
Softwood for carpentry	m^3	10,600
Softwood for joinery	m^3	14,000
Hardwood for joinery	m^3	26,500
Exterior quality plywood (20mm)	m^2	400
Plywood for interior joinery (4mm)	m^2	130
Plywood for interior joinery (20mm)	m^2	400
Softwood strip flooring (19mm)	m^2	700
Chipboard sheet flooring (25mm)	m^2	300
100mm thick quilt insulation	m^2	150
100mm thick rigid slab insulation (solar slab)	m^2	250
Softwood internal door complete with frames and ironmongery	each	3,500
Glass and ceramics		
Float glass (6mm)	m^2	450
Plaster and paint		
Good quality ceramic wall tiles (200 x 200mm)	m^2	300
Plaster in 50kg bags	tonne	1,900
Plasterboard (12mm thick)	m^2	55
Emulsion paint in tins	gallon	270
Gloss oil paint in tins	gallon	545
Tiles and paviors		
Clay floor tiles (100 x 100mm)	m^2	250
Vinyl floor tiles (230 x 230 x 2.0mm)	m^2	160
Precast concrete paving slabs (500 x 500 x 50mm)	m^2	150
Clay roof tiles (255 x 140mm)	1,000	7,000
Precast concrete roof tiles (420 x 330mm)	1,000	13,000
Drainage		
WC suite complete (medium quality)	each	3,500
Lavatory basin complete (medium quality)	each	2,200
100mm diameter PVC drain pipes	m	170
150mm diameter cast iron drain pipes	m	1,350

Unit rates

The descriptions below are generally shortened versions of standard descriptions listed in full in section 4. Where an item has a two digit reference number (e.g. 05 or 33), this relates to the full description against that number in section 4. Where an item has an alphabetic suffix (e.g. 12A or 34B) this indicates that the standard description has been modified. Where a modification is major the complete modified description is included here and the standard description should be ignored; where a modification is minor (e.g. the insertion of a named hardwood) the shortened description has been modified here but, in general, the full description in section 4 prevails.

The unit rates below are for main work items on a typical construction project in the Bangkok area in the third quarter of 1995. The rates include all necessary labour, materials and equipment. Allowance of 10% to cover preliminaries and general items and 10% to cover for Contractor's profit and overheads have been included in the unit rates. All the rates in this section exclude value added tax (VAT - see below).

		Unit	Rate Bt
Excavation			
01A	Mechanical excavation of foundation trenches including earthwork support	m^3	120
02	Hardcore filling making up levels	m^3	400
Concrete work			
04	Plain insitu concrete in strip foundations in trenches	m^3	1,956
05	Reinforced insitu concrete in beds	m^3	1,956
06	Reinforced insitu concrete in walls	m^3	1,956
07	Reinforced insitu concrete in suspended floors or roof slabs	m^3	1,956
08	Reinforced insitu concrete in columns	m^3	1,956
09	Reinforced insitu concrete in isolated beams	m^3	1,956
10	Precast concrete slabs	m^2	475
Formwork			
11	Softwood formwork to concrete walls	m^2	325
12	Softwood formwork to concrete columns	m^2	325
13	Softwood formwork to horizontal soffits of slabs	m^2	325
Reinforcement			
14	Reinforcement in concrete walls	tonne	16,800
15	Reinforcement in suspended concrete slabs	tonne	16,800
16	Fabric reinforcement in concrete beds	m^2	84

	Unit	Rate Bt
Steelwork		
17 Fabricate, supply and erect steel framed structure	tonne	35,000
18 Framed structural steelwork in universal joist sections	tonne	34,000
19 Structural steelwork lattice roof trusses	tonne	33,000
Brickwork and blockwork		
21A Solid (perforated) concrete blocks (70mm thick)	m²	300
23A Local one brick wall	m²	236
Roofing		
24A Concrete interlocking roof tiles 400 x 330mm	m²	200
25A Plain clay roof tiles 255 x 140mm	m²	900
27 Sawn softwood roof boarding	m²	850
31 Glass-fibre mat roof insulation 160mm thick	m²	150
33 Troughed galvanized steel roof cladding	m²	530
Woodwork and metalwork		
34 Preservative treated sawn softwood 50 x 100mm	m	120
35 Preservative treated sawn softwood 50 x 150mm	m	182
36 Single glazed casement window in hardwood, size 650 x 900mm	each	1,850
37 Two panel glazed door in hardwood, size 850 x 2,000mm	each	6,500
38A Solid core two hours fire resisting hardwood internal flush door, size 800 x 2000mm with ironmongery	each	15,000
41 Hardwood skirtings	m	80
Plumbing		
42A Light gauge galvanized sheet box gutter 150 x 100mm	m	280
43A PVC rainwater pipes (100mm diameter) class 8.5	m	340
44A Light gauge copper cold water tubing (50mm diameter)	m	815
45A 100mm diameter high pressure polybutylene pipes for cold water supply	m	910
46A 100mm diameter low pressure polybutylene pipes for cold water distribution	m	690
47 UPVC soil and vent pipes (100mm diameter)	m	350
48 White vitreous china WC suite	each	4,500
49 White vitreous china lavatory basin	each	3,000
50 Glazed fireclay shower tray	each	5,000
51 Stainless steel single bowl sink and double drainer	each	3,500

		Unit	Rate Bt
Electrical work			
52	PVC insulated and copper sheathed cable	m	60
53A	10 amp unswitched socket outlet	each	200
54	Flush mounted 20 amp, 1 way light switch	each	200
Finishings			
55	2 coats gypsum based plaster on brick walls	m²	135
56	White glazed tiles on plaster walls	m²	550
58	Cement and sand screed to concrete floors	m²	180
60	Mineral fibre tiles on concealed suspension system	m²	600
Glazing			
61	Glazing to wood	m²	485
Painting			
62	Emulsion on plaster walls	m²	65
63	Oil paint on timber	m²	75

Approximate estimating

The building costs per unit area given below are averages incurred by building clients for typical buildings in the Bangkok area as at the third quarter of 1995. They are based upon the total floor area of all storeys, measured between external walls and without deduction for internal walls.

Approximate estimating costs generally include mechanical and electrical installations but exclude furniture, loose or special equipment, and external works; they also exclude fees for professional services. The costs shown are for specifications and standards appropriate to Thailand and this should be borne in mind when attempting comparisons with similarly described building types in other countries. A discussion of this issue is included in section 2. Comparative data for countries covered in this publication, including construction cost data, is presented in Part Three.

Approximate estimating costs must be treated with caution; they cannot provide more than a rough guide to the probable cost of building. All the rates in this section exclude value added tax (VAT - see next page).

	Cost m² Bt	Cost ft² Bt
Industrial		
Light duty flatted factories, 150 lb loading	11,500	1,070
Single storey conventional factory of structural steelwork	11,000	1,020
Office/commercial		
Average standard offices, high rise	14,000	1,300
Prestige offices, high rise	20,000	1,860
Domestic		
Detached houses and bungalows	12,500	1,160
Average standard apartments, high rise	13,500	1,260
Luxury apartments, high rise	17,000	1,580
Hotels		
3 star budget hotel inclusive of fixtures and fittings	23,250	2,160
5 star luxury hotels inclusive of fixtures and fittings	31,250	2,900
Others		
Car parks, above ground	6,500	605
Retail/department stores (without finishes)	12,500	1,160

Value added tax (VAT)

The standard rate of value added tax (VAT) is currently 7%.

Regional variations

The approximate estimating costs are based on projects in the Bangkok area. For other parts of Thailand, adjust these costs by the following factors :

North	Chiangmai	+ 10%
South	Phuket/Samui	+ 12%
South Coast	Pattaya/Cha-Am	+ 5%

EXCHANGE RATES

The graph below plots the movement of the Thai baht against sterling, US dollar and 100 Japanese yen since 1985. The figures used for the graph are quarterly and the method of calculating these is described and general guidance on the interpretation of the graph provided in section 2. The exchange rate at the third quarter of 1995 was Bt39.41 to pound sterling, Bt24.87 to US dollar and Bt27.11 to 100 Japanese yen.

THE THAI BAHT AGAINST STERLING, US DOLLAR AND JAPANESE YEN

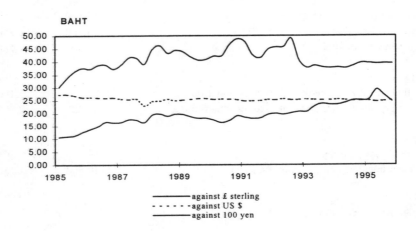

USEFUL ADDRESSES

Public organizations

Department of Commercial Registration
    Ministry of Commerce
    Maharaj Road, Pra Rajawang
    Pra Nakorn
    Bangkok 10200
    Tel: 222 6918, 222 9851, 222 2870

Department of Town and Country Planning
 Ministry of Interior
 224 Rama 9 Road, Huay Kwang
 Bangkok 10310
 Tel: 245 1420
 Fax: 246 0180

Office of Board for the Control of the
Engineering and Architectural Profession
 Visuthkasart Road
 Bangkok 10200
 Tel: 281 1421, 282 2861

Public Works Department
 Ministry of Interior
 218/1 Rama 6 Road
 Bangkok 10400
 Tel: 272 0061, 273 0878, 273 0860
 Fax: 273 0878 Ext 115

Thai Industrial Standard Institution
 Ministry of Industry, Rama 6 Road, Rajthavi
 Bangkok 10400
 Tel: 246 1170
 Fax: 246 4085

Thailand Institute of Scientific and Technological Research
 196 Paholyothin Road, Jat Tu Jak
 Bangkok 10900
 Tel: 579 1121/30 Ext. 2112
 Fax: 561 4771, 579 4940

The Engineering Institute of Thailand
 Faculty of Engineering
 Chulalongkorn University, Anglee Dunan Road
 Bangkok 10330
 Tel: 252 6051

The National Statistical Office
 Larn Luang Road, Pomp Prarp
 Bangkok 10100
 Tel: 282 1535

Trade and professional associations

Thai Contractor Association
110 Wireless Road, Pathumwan
Bangkok 10330
Tel: 251 0697, 252 2953
Fax: 255 3990

The Association of Siamese Architects
under Royal Patronage
248/1 Soi Japanese School
Rama 9 Road, Huay Kwang
Bangkok 10310
Tel: 319 4124, 319 6555
Fax: 319 6419

The Consulting Engineer Association of Thailand
37/1 Soi Petchburi 15, Petchburi Road
Bangkok 10400
Tel: 251 0092
Fax: 253 4283

DAVIS LANGDON & EVEREST
DAVIS LANGDON CONSULTANCY
DAVIS LANGDON MANAGEMENT

The strategic and integrated management of cost, time and quality - the client "risk" areas of a contract - are essential functions, which are necessary to ensure the satisfactory planning, procurement, execution and operation of construction projects.

We specialise in the financial management of construction projects and their risk areas, from project inception to completion and we concentrate on:

- being positive and creative in our advice, rather than simply reactive;

- providing value for money via efficient management, rather than on superficial cost monitoring;

- giving advice that is matched to the client's requirements, rather than imposing standard or traditional solutions;

- paying attention to the life-cycle costs of constructing and occupying a building, rather than to the initial capital cost only.

Our aim is to provide our clients with risk assurance, cost control and value for money, via effective advice, cost planning and management.

London, Bristol, Cambridge, Cardiff, Chester, Edinburgh, Gateshead, Glasgow, Ipswich, Leeds, Liverpool, Manchester, Milton Keynes, Newport, Norwich, Oxford, Plymouth, Portsmouth, Southampton

DAVIS LANGDON & SEAH INTERNATIONAL

United Kingdom

KEY DATA

Population

Population	57.9mn
Urban population	89%
Population under 15	19%
Population 65 and over	16%
Average annual growth rate (1980 to 1993)	0.3%

Geography

Land area	245,000 km²
Agricultural area	76%
Capital city	London
Population of capital city (1990)	6.7mn

Economy

Monetary unit	Pound sterling (£)
Exchange rate (average first quarter 1995) to:	
the US dollar	£0.63
the yen x 100	£0.69
Average annual inflation (1980 to 1993)	5.6%
Inflation rate (1994)	2.4%
Gross Domestic Product (GDP) at market price	£630.0bn
GDP per capita	£10,881
Average annual real change in GDP (1980 to 1993)	2.5%
Private consumption as a proportion of GDP	64%
General government consumption as a proportion of GDP	22%
Gross domestic investment as a proportion of GDP	15%
Central government expenditure as a proportion of Gross National Product	43%

Construction

Gross value of construction output	£46.3bn
Net value of construction output	£33.4bn
Net value of construction output as a proportion of GDP	5.3%
Annual cement consumption	11mn tonnes

All data relate to 1993 unless otherwise indicated

THE CONSTRUCTION INDUSTRY

Construction output

The gross output of construction in 1993 was £46.3 billion or 7.4% of GDP, equivalent to US$70.5 billion. The net output of construction in 1993 was £28.8 billion or 5.3% of GDP, equivalent to US$44.5 billion.

The gross construction output in 1994 was £49.4 billion or 7.4% of GDP, equivalent to US$74.3 billion. The net output in 1994 was £31.0 billion or 5.4% of GDP, equivalent to US$46.7 billion.

The breakdown by type of work is shown below:

OUTPUT OF CONSTRUCTION, 1993 AND 1994 (CURRENT PRICES)

	1993		1994	
	£	% of	£	% of
Type of work	million	total	million	total
New work				
Residential building	6,628	14.3	7,417	15.0
Non-residential building				
Private office and commercial	5,131	11.1	5,642	11.5
Private industrial	2,208	4.8	2,493	5.0
Infrastructure	5,544	12.0	5,140	10.4
Other public	4,045	8.7	4,380	8.9
Total non-residential building	16,927	36.5	17,655	35.8
Total new work	23,556	50.9	25,072	50.8
Repair and maintenance				
Residential	12,809	27.7	13,738	27.8
Other	9,958	21.5	10,560	21.4
Total repair and maintenance	22,767	49.1	24,298	49.2
Total	46,323	100.0	49,370	100.0

Totals do not always sum exactly due to rounding
Source: DoE Housing and Construction Statistics

Based on *Euroconstruct* estimates for 1994, new civil engineering comprised about 14% of construction output and new non-residential construction about 30% of all work.

Following years of decline in (real) construction output, there was a 2.3% growth between 1993 and 1994 in the level of all new construction work. Although the level of growth in output in the construction industry was less than that in the economy as a whole during 1994 (3.8% growth in real GDP at market prices), there were notable changes in the level of activity in a number of the construction sectors.

Increased levels of activity in the private office, commercial and industrial sectors in 1994 marked a turning point in an otherwise downward trend which began in 1989/90. This was also the case in the level of repair and maintenance work.

The trend of declining levels of investment in the public sector work in the UK was clearly in evidence with the decline in the level of infrastructure works in 1994. In real terms, the output of this sector of the industry fell by 12% between 1993 and 1994.

The UK has one of the lowest levels of construction as a proportion of GDP of any West European country. The percentage of work related to housing is also rather low. However, that of repair and maintenance is high. In fact, in the case of the UK, the repair and maintenance is an underestimate since major renovation work on all buildings except for housing is included in new work.

Moreover, maintenance expenditure is actually much higher than indicated in the table above. Expenditure on DIY (do-it-yourself) materials by the residential sector (£4.7 billion in 1989) and substantial expenditure on maintenance in the non-residential sector (undertaken by private direct labour organizations and therefore unrecorded) may increase actual maintenance expenditure by as much as 40%. In addition, it is thought that there is uncounted expenditure for work done by those avoiding tax and insurance obligations.

One of the most marked features of the construction industry over recent years has been the shift in activity by region. Historically, construction work in a region has been closely related to the population in that region. The table overleaf lists percentages showing the 1985 population for the standard economic regions and the construction new orders for 1979, 1986 and 1994.

REGIONAL POPULATION AND CONSTRUCTION NEW ORDERS, 1979-1994

Region	Population 1985 (%)	New Orders		
		1979 (%)	1986 (%)	1994 (%)
North	5.6	5.5	3.8	5.2
Yorks and Humberside	8.9	9.2	7.2	7.8
East Midlands	7.1	5.8	6.3	6.9
East Anglia	3.6	4.6	4.8	4.0
South East	31.2	32.3	42.5	32.7
South West	8.2	7.7	8.5	8.4
West Midlands	9.4	8.1	6.8	8.1
North West	11.6	10.9	8.4	10.8
Wales	5.1	4.7	4.2	5.9
Scotland	9.3	11.2	7.5	10.2
Total	100.0	100.0	100.0	100.0

Sources: DoE Housing and Construction Statistics and CSO Regional Trends

In 1979, four regions had construction new orders 10% above or below their share of population. The East and West Midlands each had less than their shares; Scotland and East Anglia had substantially more than their shares. In 1986 only East Anglia, the South East, and the South West had more than their share. All other regions had significantly less than their share by population. However, by 1994 there was a distinct movement back to the 1979 relationships.

In 1993 British contractors obtained orders abroad totalling £3.2 billion as shown in the table overleaf. This represents a large increase over 1992 levels at current prices. Hong Kong accounted for 63% of the Far East contracts in 1993 and 84% in 1992 compared with an average of 40% from 1989-1991. The Far East and North America between them account for over 60% of the total in 1993. In 1981-1982, the Middle East alone accounted for 37%.

UK CONSTRUCTION WORK OVERSEAS - VALUE OF CONTRACTS OBTAINED (£ MILLION - CURRENT PRICES)

Areas of world	1986	%	1991	%	1993	%
Europe	100	5.9	105	4.8	273	8.4
Middle East	261	15.3	245	11.1	400	12.3
Far East	172	10.1	575	26.1	752	23.2
Africa	174	10.2	234	10.6	225	6.9
North America	789	46.3	781	35.4	1,240	38.2
Rest of America	55	3.2	65	2.9	130	4.0
Oceania	153	9.0	200	9.1	227	7.0
Total	1,704	100.0	2,205	100.0	3,247	100.0

Source: DoE Housing and Construction Statistics 1983-1993

Characteristics and structure of the industry

The bulk of building work in UK is carried out by general contractors who traditionally employed their own labour force but now increasingly use labour-only subcontractors. Specialist subcontractors may be nominated by the client's consultant team or employed by the general contractor.

Traditionally, building work in the UK has been administered by professional consultants appointed by the building client. The consultants are responsible for the design and specification of the work, the contractual arrangements and the supervision of the contract. However, over the last 20 years, design-and-build contractors offering a single point of responsibility have also established a sizeable share of the market as have other less traditional arrangements.

The construction industry in the UK consists of a large number of small firms and a few very large firms. In 1993 there were estimated to be 195,000 construction firms of which 33 employed over 1,200 persons and 182 employed over 300. In 1989, at the height of the boom, there were 46 contractors employing over 1,200 and 267 employing more than 300. This fall can be accounted for by firms having shrunk into a lower category, merged or gone out of business. However, these figures do not reflect the degree of importance of the large firms in industry; the smaller firms in the construction industry often act as subcontractors to the larger firms.

In *Building* magazine's *Top 300 European Contractors* for 1994 there are 51 UK companies and 16 in the top 100. The *Engineering News Record's 1994 Top 225 International Contractors* lists nine UK contractors in the top 100 in 1994 (13 in 1988).

The principal UK contractors with some of their characteristics are shown in the table below.

MAJOR UK CONTRACTORS AND THEIR INTERNATIONAL REVENUE, 1994

Major contractors	Place in Building's 'Top 300 European Contractors' 1994	Place in ENR's 'Top 225 International Contractors' 1994	Main work/types	International revenue 1994 US$ billion
Tarmac	11	-	Construction, materials, quarry	-
AMEC	18	51	Construction, offshore engineering	0.55
Wimpey	22	53	General building, industrial, transportation	0.51
Balfour Beatty (BICC Group)	24	47	Construction	0.58
Bovis Construction Group (P&O Group)	25	14	General building, transportation	1.61
Mowlem	28	72	General building, industrial	0.31
Laing	33	124	General building, transportation	0.10
Taylor Woodrow	35	103	General building, transportation	0.15
Trafalgar House	36	1	Industrial, petrochemical, general building	6.80
Costain	41	78	General building, transportation	0.27

Sources: Building 15.2.95; Engineering News Record 28.8.95

Contractors are listed in the order quoted in the *Building* magazine which is based on total turnover. This does not, however, always reflects their construction or their contracting size as the order is based on all the activities of the named company. The main types of work in which they operate are shown on the table.

One feature of the major British contractors is the extent of their diversification beyond general contracting into property development, speculative housebuilding, material production and other businesses such as mining or airports. This was thought to have enabled the larger contractors to weather the fluctuations in construction demand and gives a better level of profitability for the construction group as a whole. However, as a result of recent recession, some of the non-contracting businesses have been the cause of financial failure for some medium-sized contractors; the larger firms have found it necessary to divest themselves of such subsidiary businesses.

Construction design work in the UK is mainly undertaken by architects and engineers. In April 1994 there were about 28,000 architects in full time employment. However, many are unemployed. Of these 28,000, 82% are believed to be members of the Royal Institute of British Architects (RIBA). In 1994, 69% of architects were employed in private practice - two thirds as principals and one third salaried, 24% were in the public sector and 7% in private sector organizations. Most practices are small but some employ over 100 staff.

Practising civil engineers normally are members of the Institution of Civil Engineers whose membership is about 80,000. Most structural engineers are members of the Institution of Structural Engineers, with a membership of about 23,000 and most building services engineers are members of the Chartered Institution of Building Services Engineers having a membership of over 15,000. All these institutions have substantially increased their membership in the last few years. The title of Chartered Engineer is registered and protected, either by the professional institution or by the Engineering Council.

Most construction design work in the UK is undertaken by private consultancy practices. The amount of in-house work has shrunk considerably in the last ten years and the remaining contractors' design departments are relatively small, being mainly concerned with building rather than civil engineering work. In 1994 there were 750 independently registered consulting engineering firms, some of which are members of the Association of Consulting Engineers. In 1994, seven of the top engineering firms had over 1,000 staff and a further nine between 500 and 1,000. Altogether these firms accounted for about half the 37,000 staff employed in private practice; most of the other half were employed in firms with less than 10 employees.

The surveying profession is very important in the UK. The Royal Institution of Chartered Surveyors is an umbrella organization for quantity surveyors and building surveyors as well as a number of other surveyor disciplines more concerned with property. In total, the membership in the UK is about 63,000 with about 21,000 quantity surveyors and about 6,000 building surveyors. The quantity surveyor plays a key role in the UK construction industry and in countries influenced by UK practices. Originally his role was to prepare a bill of quantities and measure work on site. The profession has, however, developed a range of consultancy services for clients and has achieved a full professional status equivalent to that of designers. In 1994, 46% of UK quantity surveyors worked in private practice, 18% with contractors, 11% in public service, and 5% in commercial organizations. Most quantity surveying practices are small but a number of very large firms do employ several hundred staff.

Clients and finance

Historically, the UK construction industry maintained a fairly even split between orders in the public and private sectors. However, since mid 1970s there has been a marked decline in public sector investment. By 1979, 41% of new construction output was for public sector clients; by 1985 this had reduced to 32%; and by 1991 to 29%. In 1993, however, it rose to 35% because of the steep fall in private sector work. Although the decline in public work has occurred in all types of public construction it has been most dramatic in the public housing sector and infrastructure - the latter largely as a result of the privatization of the public utilities. In 1993, public sector housing starts were only 13.5% of their 1981 levels, whereas private sector housing starts in 1991 were 110% of their 1981 level. Nearly all public sector housing is now undertaken by housing associations. They are replacing local authorities as providers of social housing and in 1993 accounted for 95% of public sector starts.

A large part of the purchase of private housing, both existing and new, is financed by mortgages from building societies, with banks rising in importance as an alternative source.

Non-residential work in the private sector may be financed in a number of ways. It may be built and owned by owner occupiers or may be built by developers/investors and then let. It is estimated, for example, that owner occupiers account for up to 80% of new construction of industrial buildings. However, the amount of other types of private building built and owned by the occupier is much less. Such statistics as are available suggest that the majority of non-residential building and non-housing building is financed by the banking, pension and insurance sectors or by property developers' own funds.

Selection of design consultants

In the last few years there have been major changes in the selection of design consultants in the public sector. Firstly, public sector clients are now required to select on the basis of fee competition. It is not mandatory, however, to accept the lowest tender if greater value for money is achieved by the acceptance of another tender. Secondly, the *EU Directive* relating to the selection of professional consultants came into effect on 1st July 1994 and competitions now have to be advertised. It is possible, however, to have a pre-qualification process to identify a list of suitable consultants and then draw from that list on the basis of fee competition. In fact, most public sector clients do wish to interview potential consultants and will select on the basis of capabilities and experience as well as on price.

A number of the large, regular public sector clients have their own in-house project managers who have their own views as to the way in which they will manage a project. In many cases they appoint an architect, in the first instance, under the traditional process but appoint themselves as the lead consultants. Other public sector clients will appoint other professionals first, perhaps a specialized engineer or a quantity surveyor if cost control is especially important.

In the private sector there is more flexibility as to the method of selection of consultants, with the personal attributes of the main player and the experience and reputation of the firm being of great importance. Fee competition is less usual although it has been used by some and is being considered by others. It is usual for fees to be negotiated. Regular clients rarely adopt the fee scales recommended by the institutions.

In the last few years the whole ethos of the organization of the construction process has changed from one of a well trodden path to one of choice and flexibility.

Contractual arrangements

As in the case of the selection of design consultants, contractual arrangements in the UK are undergoing changes as fast and great as at any time in the past. The 'traditional' system of a main contractor appointed by the client is still used for the majority of projects but the number of alternative contractual arrangements is increasing and the popularity of each one fluctuates according to : the relative bargaining power of the client and other parties to the process, the size, type and complexity of work being undertaken and current fashion. Design and build has become very important - according to a survey undertaken for the RICS by Davis Langdon &

Everest - as 24% of the value of contracts included in the study in 1993 were design and build compared to about 15% in 1991. The number of 'novated design and build' contracts is also increasing. Under this arrangement the preliminary design is undertaken by the architect - working to the client's instruction - whose design is then taken over by the contractor, normally employed by the same architect to complete the design.

There has been a sharp fall in the importance of 'construction management' contracts and a lesser fall in the 'management contracting' methods to 12.5% of the total value of contracts. In 'management contracting', the clients enters into separate contracts with the designer and the management contractor; the 'management contractor' enters into subcontracts with the works contractors.

The National Joint Consultative Committee, which comprises a group of client and consultant bodies, publishes codes for selective tendering. Generally, prices are based on firm bills of quantities although approximate bills of quantities or specifications and drawings are sometimes used.

The predominant form of contract used in the UK is the *Joint Contracts Tribunal (JCT) 1980 Standard Form of Contract with quantities* (known as *JCT80*). This contract assumes the use of measured bills of quantities that are normally prepared by the quantity surveyor. The JCT also produces the 1984 Intermediate Form of Building Contract for works of simpler content. The tender documentation under both these forms of contract might comprise:

- drawings
- specification
- bills of quantities, schedules of works or schedules of rates.

The JCT building contracts are produced in private and local authority editions. Government buildings and civil engineering contracts are placed using the *General Conditions of Government Contracts for Building and Civil Engineering Works,* otherwise known as *Form GC/Works/1.*

For civil engineering, local authority and private clients generally use the *Institution of Civil Engineers Conditions of Contract, fifth edition,* but an amended version of *GC/Works/1* is also sometimes used.

There are separate contract forms prepared by these bodies for the other types of contractual arrangements.

Changes are taking place in these current contractual arrangements. A report by Sir Michael Latham, commissioned jointly by the Government and the construction industry, was published in 1994, entitled *Constructing the Team*. It recommended the increased use of a form of contract originally developed for the British Property Federation and now known as the *New Engineering Contract (NEC)*. This contract form is regarded as less confrontational than the JCT or other forms of contract and is currently being used, on an experimental basis, by some very large clients.

Contracts of up to 18 months duration or less are generally let on a fixed price basis. Fluctuations in labour, materials and plant costs on longer term contracts can be adjusted, where the contract permits. Such increased costs on private contracts may be paid for on the basis of invoices for materials and plant, and time sheets for labour. Local authority government contracts and some private contracts generally involve the use of an adjustment formula based on monthly published indices.

The contractors' quantity surveyors as well as the quantity surveyors representing the client need to have an agreed method for measuring the building works. The first such method was produced in 1922 and a new, completely revised edition *Standard Method of Measurement of Building Works, Seventh Edition*, commonly known as *SMM7*, was issued in 1987. It was prepared by a Development Unit set up by the Royal Institution of Chartered Surveyors and the Building Employers Confederation. It embodies the essentials of good practice and is generally followed for all UK building work. Civil engineers have a similar document.

There are a number of different definitions of the area of commercial offices. Gross External Area (GEA) is an RICS term which describes the office floor space as per the *Town and Country Planning Act 1971*. It is the area on each floor from the outside face of the external walls, i.e, the complete footprint of the building. When calculating this area, the following should be excluded: open balconies and fire escapes; atria and areas with a height of less than 1.50m, e.g. under roof slopes; open covered ways or minor canopies; open vehicle parking areas; terraces, party walls beyond the centre line. Structural elements and spaces such as partitions, columns, lifts wells, plant rooms and the like should be included.

Gross Floor Area (GFA) is an RICS term measured on the same basis as GEA but between the inside faces of the external walls to all enclosed spaces fulfilling the functional requirements of the building including all circulation areas, voids, staircases (to be measured flat on plan) and other non office areas such as plant rooms, toilets and enclosed car parks.

Net Lettable Area (NLA) is another RICS term that refers to the gross internal building area less the building core area and any other common areas. It is measured to the internal finish of external walls and excludes all auxillary and ancillary spaces such as toilets, ducts, plant rooms, staircases, lift wells and major access circulation. This equates with the letting agents lettable floor area.

The Maximum Usable Area (MUA) is the benchmark for comparing empty buildings and their space efficiency and is measured as the net internal area excluding only the minimum primary circulation, i.e. the base minimum circulation which would satisfy the local fire authority. Typically most cases would be covered by assuming routes 1.50m wide, joining vertical routes and fire exits with no point further than 12m from a primary fire route.

The Treated Area is measured on the same basis as GFA but excludes those areas which are not directly heated, i.e. plant and lift motor rooms, carparks, unheated storage rooms, etc.

Liability and insurance

Since the mid 1970s there has been a marked increase in litigation on professional liability. Liability may arise in contract or in tort. In contract, proof is required of a breach of contract. However, contracts do not normally define clearly the limits of work or duties of the professional and are in any case often informal, thus giving plenty of opportunity for litigation. The numbers of claims under tort, which increased in the 1970s, have more recently declined as a result of various legal judgements.

Largely because of the reliance on case law made by the courts, the great problem of the English system is its uncertainty and complexity. There is no certainty as to whether liability exists, on the amount involved, the period of liability or the time lag before any liability is determined.

Not all professional practices carry professional indemnity insurance. However, most of the larger ones are insured. The cost of premiums is now very high.

The proposals of the European Commission for a standard liability throughout the Community may substantially alter the UK position and create greater certainty.

Development control and standards

The system for planning and control of development was introduced by the *Town and Country Planning Act 1947*. Although this has been amended, notably by the *Town and Country Planning Act 1971*, the principles remain the same. Responsibility for planning lies with local authorities: the county councils as well as the district councils. A development plan for each area must be produced and every development needs to receive permission from the relevant authority.

In general, applications for development must be made to the relevant district council. The total volume of applications is about 500,000 a year, of which about 37% are householder applications for very small alterations to dwellings.

Most planning applications are simple and go through a process which varies from district to district but is usually straightforward. However, quite a lot of weight lies on the judgement of the local planning officer and ultimately of the elected council members; there is no certainty that an application will be granted. Nevertheless, there is usually considerable room for negotiation in changes to the original application. In 1990/91, 20% of all planning applications were refused.

About 55% of planning applications in 1991 were dealt with within eight weeks and 78% within 13 weeks.

All new construction in the UK has to comply with Building Regulations, which are couched in terms of a series of technical requirements. These requirements are backed by *Approved Documents* which set out ways in which the requirements can be met. These documents give guidance but are not mandatory. In many areas the *Approved Document* will refer a designer to an appropriate British Standard on complex issues. At present, approval for construction work is given by local authorities except that, in the case of private sector housing, the National House Builders Council (NHBC) can act as an alternative 'Approved Inspector'. The 1985 *Building Act* has provision for other persons or bodies to act as Approved Inspectors, but to date this has not materialized, primarily due to the problem of liability insurance.

CONSTRUCTION COST DATA

Cost of labour

The figures below are typical of labour costs in the London area as at the third quarter of 1995. The wage rate is the basis of an employee's income, while the cost of labour indicates the cost to a contractor of employing that employee. The difference between the two covers a variety of mandatory and voluntary contributions - a list of items which could be included is given in section 2.

	Wage rate (per hour) £	Cost of labour (per hour) £	Number of hours worked per year
Site operatives			
Mason/bricklayer	4.48	5.90	1,802
Carpenter	4.50	5.93	1,802
Plumber	5.12	6.89	1,733

	Wage rate (per hour) £	Cost of labour (per hour) £	Number of hours worked per year
Electrician	7.13	9.17	1,733
Structural steel erector	5.89	8.24	1,771
HVAC installer	6.84	8.90	1,756
Semi-skilled worker	3.79	5.07	1,802
Unskilled labourer	3.68	4.94	1,802
Equipment operator	4.04	5.43	1,802
Watchman/security	3.71	5.00	1,802
Site supervision			
General foreman	5.78	7.58	1,802
Trades foreman	4.82	6.32	1,802

	(per year) £	(per year) £	
Clerk of works	24,421	30,889	
Contractors' personnel			
Site manager	30,136	37,715	
Resident engineer	18,758	24,121	
Resident surveyor	22,941	29,199	
Junior engineer	14,486	16,843	
Junior surveyor	14,768	17,165	
Planner	20,447	26,351	
Consultants' personnel			
Senior architect	28,125	35,119	
Senior engineer	30,450	37,774	
Senior surveyor	29,750	36,975	
Qualified architect	22,980	29,243	
Qualified engineer	23,450	29,780	
Qualified surveyor	24,160	30,590	

Cost of materials

The figures that follow are the costs of main construction materials, delivered to site in the London area, as incurred by contractors in the third quarter of 1995. These assume that the materials would be in quantities as required for a medium sized construction project and that the location of the works would be neither constrained nor remote.

All the costs in this section exclude value added tax (VAT - see below).

	Unit	Cost £
Cement and aggregate		
Ordinary portland cement in 50kg bags	tonne	69.19
Coarse aggregates for concrete (20mm)	tonne	8.74
Sharp sand for concrete	tonne	8.54
Ready mixed concrete (10N/mm²)	m³	40.04
Ready mixed concrete (25N/mm²)	m³	42.68
Steel		
Mild steel reinforcement (12mm)	tonne	320.00
High tensile steel reinforcement (12mm)	tonne	320.00
Structural steel sections	tonne	384.00
Bricks and blocks		
Common bricks (215 x 102.5 x 65mm)	1,000	115.00
Good quality facing bricks (215 x 102.5 x 65mm)	1,000	315.00
Hollow concrete blocks (450 x 225 x 140mm)	1,000	820.00
Solid concrete blocks (450 x 225 x 100mm)	1,000	590.00
Precast concrete cladding units with exposed aggregate finish	m²	165.00
Timber and insulation		
Softwood sections for carpentry	m³	170.00
Softwood for joinery	m³	300.00
Hardwood for joinery (Iroko)	m³	690.00
Exterior quality plywood (18mm)	m²	10.74
Plywood for interior joinery (6mm)	m²	2.20
Softwood strip flooring (22mm)	m²	4.57
Chipboard sheet flooring (18mm)	m²	2.85
100mm thick quilt insulation	m²	2.16
100mm thick rigid slab insulation	m²	4.59
Softwood internal door complete with frames and ironmongery	each	67.00
Glass and ceramics		
Float glass (6mm)	m²	26.94
Sealed double glazing units	m²	40.00
Good quality ceramic wall tiles (198 x 64.5 x 6mm)	m²	18.58
Plaster and paint		
Plaster in 50kg bags (Carlite bonding)	tonne	101.81
Plasterboard (9.5mm thick)	m²	1.16

	Unit	Cost £
Emulsion paint in 5 litre tins	litre	2.53
Gloss oil paint in 5 litre tins	litre	3.18
Tiles and paviors		
Clay floor tiles (150 x 150 x 12.5mm)	m²	10.31
Vinyl floor tiles (300 x 300 x 2.5mm)	m²	5.00
Precast concrete paving slabs (200 x 100 x 65mm)	m²	5.52
Clay roof tiles (plain 265 x 165mm)	1,000	231.84
Precast concrete roof tiles (419 x 330mm)	1,000	654.43
Drainage		
WC suite complete	each	128.30
Lavatory basin complete (coloured)	each	70.51
100mm diameter clay drain pipes	m	2.96
150mm diameter cast iron drain pipes	m	26.05

Unit rates

The descriptions below are generally shortened versions of standard descriptions listed in full in section 4. Where an item has a two digit reference number (e.g. 05 or 33), this relates to the full description against that number in section 4. Where an item has an alphabetic suffix (e.g. 12A or 34B) this indicates that the standard description has been modified. Where a modification is major the complete modified description is included here and the standard description should be ignored. Where a modification is minor (e.g. the insertion of a named hardwood) the shortened description has been modified here but, in general, the full description in section 4 prevails.

The unit rates below are for main work items on a typical construction project in the Outer London area in the third quarter of 1995. The rates include all necessary labour, materials and equipment. Allowances to cover preliminary and general items and contractors' overheads and profit have been included in the rates. All the rates in this section exclude value added tax (VAT - see below).

		Unit	*Rate* £

Excavation

01	Mechanical excavation of foundation trenches	m³	2.91
02	Hardcore filling making up levels	m²	15.80
03	Earthwork support	m²	0.94

Concrete work

04	Plain insitu concrete in strip foundations in trenches 10N/mm²	m³	57.00
05	Reinforced insitu concrete in beds 20N/mm²	m³	61.76
06	Reinforced insitu concrete in walls 20N/mm²	m³	70.10
07	Reinforced insitu concrete in suspended floors or roof slabs 26N/mm²	m³	69.16
08	Reinforced insitu concrete in columns 20N/mm²	m³	81.53
09	Reinforced insitu concrete in isolated beams	m³	76.59
10A	Prestressed precast concrete slabs (100mm thick, 1200mm wide)	m²	20.46

Formwork

11	Softwood formwork to concrete walls	m²	18.77
12	Softwood or metal formwork to concrete isolated columns	m²	22.37
13	Softwood or metal formwork to horizontal soffits of slabs; 1.5-3m height to soffit not exceeding 200mm thick	m²	17.52

Reinforcement

14	Reinforcement in concrete walls (16mm)	tonne	599.11
15A	Reinforcement in suspended concrete slabs (16mm)	tonne	602.31
16	Fabric reinforcement in concrete beds (3.02kg/m²)	m²	1.99

Steelwork

17	Fabricate, supply and erect steel framed structure	tonne	1,137.75
18	Framed structural steelwork in universal joist sections	tonne	999.00
19A	Structural steelwork roof trusses; circular hollow sections	tonne	2,081.25

Brickwork and blockwork

20	Precast lightweight aggregate hollow concrete block walls (100mm thick)	m²	15.37
21A	Solid concrete blocks (100mm thick)	m²	13.88
22A	Solid (perforated) sand lime bricks (half brick thick)	m²	19.77
23	Facing bricks	m²	33.43

Roofing

24	Concrete interlocking roof tiles 419 x 380mm	m²	14.57
25	Plain clay roof tiles 265 x 165mm	m²	34.28

		Unit	Rate £
26	Fibre cement roof slates 600 x 300mm	m²	25.12
27A	Sawn softwood roof boarding to gutter bottom or sides	m²	15.03
28A	W.S. board roof covering (19mm t&g)	m²	12.49
29A	3 layers polyester based bitumen felt roof covering including chippings	m²	13.15
30	Bitumen based mastic asphalt roof covering	m²	9.59
31A	Glass-fibre mat roof insulation 60mm thick	m²	3.20
32A	Rigid sheet loadbearing roof insulation 50mm thick	m²	12.95
33	Troughed galvanized steel roof cladding	m²	12.91

Woodwork and metalwork

34	Preservative treated sawn softwood 50 x 100mm	m	2.53
35	Preservative treated sawn softwood 50 x 150mm	m	3.32
36A	Single glazed casement window in Meranti hardwood, size 630 x 900mm (including sills, ironmongery)	each	99.90
37A	Two panel glazed door in Afrormosia hardwood, size 838 x 1981 x 63mm (excluding glazing and ironmongery)	each	236.37
38A	Solid core half hour fire resisting hardwood internal flush door, size 826 x 2040 x 44mm	each	133.20
39A	Aluminium double glazed window, size 1200 x 1200mm (including glazing)	each	181.21
40A	Aluminium double glazed door, size 850 x 2100mm (including frame, sills and ironmongery)	each	1,198.80
41A	Hardwood skirtings (Afrormosia) 25 x 100mm	m	7.86

Plumbing

42A	UPVC half round eaves gutter (112mm)	m	5.79
43A	UPVC rainwater pipes (110mm)	m	8.78
44	Light gauge copper cold water tubing (15mm)	m	3.55
45A	Plastic waste pipes (32mm)	m	3.87
46A	Blue MDPE pipes for cold water distribution (50mm)	m	3.43
47	UPVC soil and vent pipes	m	8.54
48	White vitreous china WC suite	each	170.52
49A	Coloured vitreous china lavatory basin	each	97.86
50A	White glazed fireclay shower tray	each	135.42
51	Stainless steel single bowl sink and double drainer	each	133.20

Electrical work

52A	PVC insulated and PVC sheathed copper cable core and earth (1.5mm²)	m	2.59

		Unit	Rate £
53	13 amp 1 gang unswitched socket outlet	each	11.02
54A	Flush mounted 6 amp, 1 gang 1 way light switch	each	6.06

Finishings

55	2 coats gypsum based plaster on brick walls	m²	5.98
56	White glazed tiles on plaster walls	m²	22.99
57	Red clay quarry tiles on concrete floors	m²	21.28
58	Cement and sand screed to concrete floors 50mm thick	m²	7.80
59	Thermoplastic floor tiles on screed	m²	5.43
60	Mineral fibre tiles on concealed suspension system (suspension system included)	m²	18.80

Glazing

61A	6mm clear float glass; glazing to wood with putty	m²	26.64

Painting

62A	Emulsion on plaster walls (1 mist and 2 emulsion)	m²	1.94
63	Oil paint on timber (knot, 1 primer, 2 undercoats and 1 finish)	m²	4.43

Approximate estimating

The building costs per unit area given below are averages incurred by building clients for typical buildings in the United Kingdom as at the third quarter of 1995. They are based upon the total floor area of all storeys, measured between external walls and without deduction for internal walls.

Approximate estimating costs generally include mechanical and electrical installations but exclude furniture, loose or special equipment, and external works; they also exclude fees for professional services. The costs shown are for specifications and standards appropriate to the United Kingdom and this should be borne in mind when attempting comparisons with similarly described building types in other countries. A discussion of this issue is included in section 2.

Comparative data for countries covered in this publication, including construction cost data, are presented in Part Three.

Approximate estimating costs must be treated with caution; they cannot provide more than a rough guide to the probable cost of building. All the rates in this section exclude value added tax (VAT - see below).

	Cost m^2 £	Cost ft^2 £
Industrial buildings		
Factories for letting (including lighting, power and heating)	242	22
Factories for owner occupation (light industrial use)	313	29
Factories for owner occupation (heavy industrial use)	519	48
Factory/office (high tech) for letting (shell and core only)	325	30
Factory/office (high tech) for letting (ground floor shell, first floor offices)	519	48
Factory/office (high tech) for owner occupation (controlled environment, fully finished)	681	63
High tech laboratory (air conditioned)	1,395	130
Warehouses, low bay (6 to 8m high) for letting (no heating)	171	16
Warehouses, low bay for owner occupation (including heating)	251	23
Warehouses, high bay for owner occupation (including heating)	332	31
Cold stores/refrigerated stores	528	49
Administrative and commercial buildings		
Civic offices, non air conditioned	647	60
Civic offices, fully air conditioned	782	73
Offices for letting, 5 to 10 storeys, non air conditioned	558	52
Offices for letting, 5 to 10 storeys, air conditioned	690	64
Offices for letting, high rise, air conditioned	885	82
Offices for owner occupation 5 to 10 storeys, non air conditioned	647	60
Offices for owner occupation 5 to 10 storeys, air conditioned	841	78
Offices for owner occupation high rise, air conditioned	1,075	100
Prestige/headquarters office, 5 to 10 storeys, air conditioned	1,075	100
Prestige/headquarters office, high rise, air conditioned	1,390	129
Health and education buildings		
General hospitals	775	72
Teaching hospitals	750	70
Private hospitals	754	70
Health centres	528	49
Nursery schools	640	59
Primary/junior schools	604	56
Secondary/middle schools	576	54
University (arts) buildings	581	54
University (science) buildings	656	61
Management training centres	674	63

	Cost m^2 £	Cost ft^2 £
Recreation and arts buildings		
Theatres (over 500 seats) including seating and stage equipment	972	90
Theatres (less than 500 seats) including seating and stage equipment	713	66
Concert halls including seating and stage equipment	1,395	130
Sports halls including changing and social facilities	478	44
Swimming pools (international standard) including changing and social facilities	821	76
Swimming pools (schools standard) including changing facilities	585	54
National museums including full air conditioning and standby generator	1,710	159
Local museums including air conditioning	693	64
City centre/central libraries	702	65
Branch/local libraries	565	52
Residential buildings		
Social/economic single family housing (multiple units)	329	31
Private/mass market single family housing 2 storey detached/semidetached (multiple units)	325	30
Purpose designed single family housing 2 storey detached (single unit)	494	46
Social/economic apartment housing, low rise (no lifts)	393	37
Social/economic apartment housing, high rise (with lifts)	423	39
Private sector apartment building (standard specification)	389	36
Private sector apartment buildings (luxury)	629	58
Student/nurses halls of residence	460	43
Homes for the elderly (shared accommodation)	503	47
Homes for the elderly (self contained with shared communal facilities)	450	42
Hotel, 5 star, city centre	1,139	106
Hotel, 3 star, city/provincial	869	81
Motel	560	52

Regional variations

The approximate estimating costs are based on average UK rates. Adjust these costs by the following factors for regional variations:

Greater London	:	+12%	North West	:	-3%
South East	:	+2%	North	:	-2%
South West	:	-3%	Scotland	:	+2%
Midlands	:	-4%	Wales	:	-4%
East Anglia	:	-3%	Northern Ireland	:	-15%
Yorkshire and Humberside	:	-3%			

Value added tax (VAT)

The standard rate of value added tax (VAT) is currently 17.5%, chargeable on general building work.

EXCHANGE RATES AND INFLATION

The combined effect of exchange rates and inflation on prices within a country and price comparisons between countries is discussed in section 2.

Exchange rates

The graph below plots the movement of sterling against US dollar and 100 Japanese yen since 1985. The values used for the graph are quarterly and the method of calculating these is described and general guidance on the interpretation of the graph provided in section 2. The average exchange rate in the second quarter of 1995 were £0.63 to US dollar and £0.69 to 100 Japanese yen.

STERLING AGAINST US DOLLAR AND JAPANESE YEN

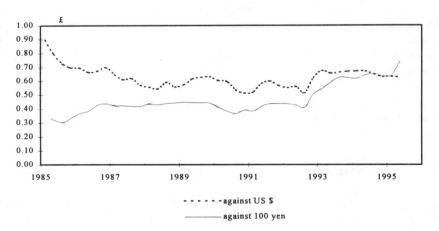

Price inflation

The table below presents retail price, building cost and tender price inflation in the United Kingdom since 1980. The basis of the first column is the official consumer price index. The other two indices have been produced by Davis Langdon & Everest: the building cost index provides an index of price movements in general building costs, and the tender price index indicates movements in general building prices in the Greater London area.

CONSUMER PRICE AND BUILDING COST AND PRICE INDICES

Year	Retail price index		Building cost index		Tender price index	
	average index	average change %	average index	average change %	average index	average change %
1980	100		100		100	
1981	112	12.0	112	12.0	102	2.0
1982	122	8.9	124	10.7	101	-1.0
1983	127	4.1	131	5.6	105	4.0
1984	133	4.7	139	6.1	111	5.7
1985	142	6.8	146	5.0	115	3.6
1986	146	2.8	154	5.5	121	5.2
1987	152	4.1	162	5.2	136	12.4
1988	160	5.3	172	6.2	163	19.9
1989	172	7.5	185	7.6	179	9.8
1990	189	9.9	198	7.0	163	-8.9
1991	200	5.8	209	5.6	138	-15.3
1992	207	3.5	215	2.9	128	-7.2
1993	210	1.4	219	1.9	124	-3.1
1994	216	2.9	225	2.7	133	7.3
1995	-	-	236F	4.9	139F	4.5

F = Forecast

USEFUL ADDRESSES

Public organizations

British Standards Institution
    389 Chiswick High Road
    London W4 4AL
    Tel: (0171) 629 9000
    Fax: (0181) 996 7400

Building Research Establishment
    Bucknalls Lane, Garston
    Watford
    Herts
    WD2 7JR
    Tel: (01923) 894040
    Fax: (01923) 664010

Department of the Environment
    2 Marsham Street
    London
    SW1P 3EB
    Tel: (0171) 212 3000
    Fax: (0171) 276 0818

Trade and professional associations

Building Employers Confederation
    82 New Cavendish Street
    London
    W1M 8AD
    Tel: (0171) 580 5588

Chartered Institution of Building Services Engineers (CIBSE)
    Delta House
    222 Balham High Road
    London
    SW12 9BS
    Tel: (0181) 675 5211
    Fax: (0181) 675 5449

Engineering Council
    Canberra House
    10-16 Maltravers Street
    London
    WC2 3ER
    Tel: (0171) 240 7891

Institution of Civil Engineers
    1-7 Great George Street
    London
    SW1P 3AA
    Tel: (0171) 222 7722
    Fax: (0171) 222 7500

Royal Institute of British Architects (RIBA)
    66 Portland Place
    London
    W1N 4AD
    Tel: (071) 580 5533
    Fax: (0171) 255 1541

Royal Institution of Chartered Surveyors (RICS)
    12 Great George Street
    London
    SW1P 3AD
    Tel: (071) 222 7000
    Fax: (0171) 222 9430

The Association of Consulting Engineers (ACE)
    Alliance House
    12 Caxton Street
    London
    SW1H 0QL
    Tel: (0171) 222 6557
    Fax: (0171) 222 0750

Transport and General Workers Union
    Transport House
    Smith Square
    London
    SW1P 3AJ
    Tel: (0171) 828 7788

Union of Construction and Allied Trades and Technicians
    UCATT House
    Abbeville Road
    London
    SW4 9RL
    Tel: (0171) 622 2442

Other organizations

British Board of Agrément (BBA)
    PO Box 195
    Bucknalls Lane
    Garston
    Watford
    Herts
    WD2 7JR
    Tel: (01923) 670844
    Fax: (01923) 662133

Building Centre Group (Building Centre)
    26 Store Street
    London
    WC1E 7BT
    Tel: (0171) 637 1022 (administration)
        (01344) 884999 (information)
    Fax: (0171) 580 9641

Building Cost Information Service (BCIS)
    85/87 Clarence Street
    Kingston-upon-Thames
    Surrey
    KT1 1RB
    Tel: (0181) 546 7554
    Fax: (0181) 547 1238

Construction Industry Research and Information Association
    6 Storey's Gate
    London
    SWIP 3AY
    Tel: (0171) 222 8891
    Fax: (0171) 222 1708

United States of America

KEY DATA

Population
Population	258.3mn
Urban population	76%
Population under 15	21.5%
Population over 65	12.9%
Average annual growth rate (1980 to 1993)	1.0%

Geography
Land area	9,809,000 km²
Agricultural area	47%
Capital city	Washington
Population of capital city (1990)	3.7 mn

Economy
Monetary unit	US dollar ($)
Exchange rate (average third quarter 1995) to:	
the pound sterling	$1.59
the yen x 100	$1.09
Average annual inflation (1980 to 1993)	3.8%
Inflation rate (1994)	2.6%
Gross Domestic Product (GDP) at market price	$6,343bn
GDP per capita	$24,557
Average annual real change in GDP (1990 to 1994)	2.2%
Private consumption as a proportion of GDP	68%
General government consumption as a proportion of GDP	17%
Gross domestic investment as a proportion of GDP	16%
Central government expenditure as a proportion of Gross National Product	24%

Construction
Gross value of construction output	$550bn
Net value of construction output	$234.7bn
Net value of construction output as a proportion of GDP	3.7%
Annual cement consumption (1991)	72mn tonnes

All data relate to 1993 unless otherwise indicated

THE CONSTRUCTION INDUSTRY

Construction output

The value of gross output of new construction work in 1993 was US$466.4 billion. Repair and maintenance is conservatively estimated at a further US$100 billion giving a total of approximately US$550 billion. Total construction output in 1993 was 8.7% of GDP. Net output was US$234.7 billion or 3.7% of GDP.

The value of gross output of new work in 1994 was US$506.3 billion. Repair and maintenance is conservatively estimated at a further US$100 billion giving a total of approximately US$600 billion. Total construction output in 1994 was 8.9% of GDP.

The level of new construction output (at current prices) has been improving since the end of 1993 following a downturn in US construction activity in the early 1990s. The table below shows the breakdown of output in 1993 and 1994.

OUTPUT OF CONSTRUCTION, 1993 AND 1994 (CURRENT PRICES)

Type of work	1993 US$ million	1993 % of total	1994 US$ million	1994 % of total
Private residential				
New housing units	144.5	30.7	167.5	33.1
Improvement	63.6	13.5	70.3	13.9
Total	208.1	44.3	237.8	47.0
Private commercial and				
industrial *	68.1	14.5	74.0	14.6
Other private	66.8	14.2	65.4	12.9
Total private	343.0	73.0	377.1	74.5
Federal, State and local	127.2	27.1	129.2	25.5
Total	470.1	100.0	506.3	100.0

* includes hotels and motels

Totals do not always sum exactly due to rounding

Source: Economic Indicators, May 1995, Washington 1995

Housing is a high proportion of total output partly because other construction work is still depressed. Civil engineering in 1991 was about 23% of total new work, of which two thirds was public and one third private.

Characteristics and structure of the industry

The construction industry has over a million firms employing about 3.5 million persons and has 15 million working partners or self-employed proprietors. Some states require contractors to be licensed, however this is rarely strictly administered. It is a way of gaining some revenue from the licence fee. About 40% of main contractors and trade contractors are union contractors which use union registered employees and negotiate wages with the unions. Open-shop contracting has grown significantly over the last 20 years, especially in housebuilding. This growth has moderated the behaviour and wage demands of unions. One adverse affect of the decline in union influence has been a fall in levels of training; the unions traditionally run good education programmes.

There are a large number of specialist trade contractors who carry out an important role on construction projects. They usually have to provide working drawings, organize and manage the work on site with little direction from the main contractor, and they often supply major items of plant and equipment. Labour-only subcontracting is rarely used.

Measured in terms of the value of contracts won, the USA was the base for six of the world's top ten contractors in 1993. The table overleaf shows the top US contractors in 1994.

The title of architect is protected in the USA and the regulations for registration vary from state to state. However, the National Council of Architectural Registration Boards grants a certificate to qualified architects which is usually recognized in all states. There are about 60,000 architects, mostly working in very small practices. The architect in the USA tends not to get involved in site operations and most of the detailed design is done by contractors. In the USA it is the architect who is principally concerned with the cost of the project and there are, therefore, very few quantity surveyors when compared with the UK. There are, however, construction cost consultants, who originally may have been architects or engineers, but are now increasingly being augmented by quantity surveyors. Contractors are often prepared to give cost advice to the architect.

TOP 10 US CONTRACTORS, 1994

Contractors	Revenue Total US$ billion	International US$ billion	Main types of work
Fluor-Daniel Inc, Calif	6.64	2.41	Industrial, petroleum
Bechtel Group Inc, Calif	6.55	1.60	Industrial, petroleum, power, transportation
Centrex Construction Group, Texas	3.17	-	General building
John Brown / Davy, Texas	2.93	1.33	Industrial, general building, petroleum
Brown and Root Inc, Texas	2.62	1.09	Industrial, general building, petroleum, transportation
Morrison Knudsen Corp, Idaho	2.52	0.68	Industrial, petroleum, transportation, hazardous waste
Raytheon Engineers and Construction Inc, Mass	2.44	0.77	Industrial, petroleum, power
The Turner Corp, NY	2.14	0.02	General building
Kiewit Construction Group Inc, Neb	2.04	0.28	Transportation, general building, power
Jacobs Engineering Group Inc, Calif	1.97	0.12	Industrial, hazardous waste, petroleum, manufacturing

Source : Engineering News Record 22 May 1995

Engineers have to be registered, which generally requires a recognized engineering degree and four years experience. There are a number of substantial multi-disciplinary practices in the USA. In the industry there are significantly more building engineers than architects (about 340,000 building engineers).

Client and finance

Over 70% of new construction is commissioned by the private sector and for housing the figure is nearly 100%. 55% of all housing units were owner occupied in 1950 but this rose to 64% by 1992. Private rented property accounts for the bulk of the remainder. Publicly provided housing known as 'project housing' is relatively unimportant. Most mortgages are now variable interest.

Selection of design consultants

In 1972, Congress established as federal law a policy to select architects and engineers on the basis of the highest qualification for each project and at a fair and reasonable price. For large public projects, invitations are published for interested architects and engineers (usually only in the state where the project is located) to indicate their interest and to submit detailed, specific information on their qualifications. A panel of private sector architects and engineers, who are not paid, recommends five firms. These five make presentations, attend interviews, and three are chosen. The most favoured of these enters into negotiations with the client. If these break down, the second negotiates, and so on. The process is costly to firms entering for a project.

Several states have followed the federal example and the American Institute of Architects (AIA) recommends the procedure for private clients. It is often followed by the large corporations, though sometimes in a form which gives earlier prominence to estimated construction prices and fees.

Contractual arrangements

The most usual methods of selecting a general contractor are by competitive bidding, by negotiation or by a combination of the two. There are two types of competitive bidding, 'open' and 'closed'. Open is the predominant type, where all contractors use the same proposal form. In the closed type, the competing contractors are required to submit their qualifications along with their bids and are encouraged to suggest cost saving proposals. There are numerous forms of negotiated contract, but most are of the cost-plus-fee type. Negotiated contracts are normally limited to privately financed work since competitive bidding is a legal requirement for most public projects.

Fixed price contracts are the most common. Tenders for buildings are customarily prepared on a lump sum basis, whereas engineering projects are generally bid as a series of unit prices. It is standard practice for contractors to prepare their own quantities which do not form part of the contract. With few exceptions, bids are accompanied by a bid bond guaranteeing that the contractor will enter into a contract if declared successful.

Standard contract conditions have been developed by various bodies, including the American Institute of Architects, the National Society of Professional Engineers, the Associated General Contractors of America and various federal, state and municipal governments. Where a contract provides for arbitration, most stipulate that it shall be conducted under the auspices of the Construction Industry Arbitration Association.

There has been an increasing use for large projects of management fee
or construction management arrangements, but often still retaining a
guaranteed maximum price. However, the tendency is now less apparent.
Design and build projects are also becoming more popular although there
are often other provisions for the contractor to offer advice at the design
stage.

Specialist trade contractors are usually invited to bid, often from a list
selected or approved by the architect. Eight to ten bidders are usual.
Nomination is virtually unknown.

The lien laws in the USA provide a large degree of protection for the
contractors and subcontractors working on a project. Under the provisions
a contractor can place a lien on the real property if he has not received
payment for goods and services provided. This lien is registered on the
title deed of the property and if not resolved can be a major impediment
for subsequent sale or mortgage financing on the property. The owner
is therefore obligated to ensure all payments are properly effected to each
supplier of goods or services. In the event that the employer has made
a payment to the general contractor, but the general contractor has not paid
his subcontractors, the subcontractors are entitled to place a lien on the
property. In this case the employer may have to pay for the works twice
to radiate (remove) the lien - unless he has a labour and material payment
bond in force in which case he can recover the double payment from the
bond company. Standard bond forms are available and in common use
throughout the USA. Employers and their agents need to monitor payments
carefully on projects to avoid lien actions.

Development control and standards

The planning process in the USA is known as planning control and zoning
control. It is very fragmented and every town has its own system. There
may be 50 separate zoning authorities in one state. There is normally a
Zoning Commission Board, a Zoning Board of Appeal and often a Planning
Commission or Board in each town. The ease with which development
zones of a town can be changed varies according to the attitude of the
town or the state.

There is no single national building code for the whole of the USA.
Approximately 19,000 municipalities are involved and many have their
separate codes. Nevertheless, various national codes have been prepared.
The most widely used is the *International Conference of Building Officials
(ICBO) Uniform Building Code*. Others are the *Building Officials and
Code Administrators International (BOCA)*, and the *Southern Building Code
Congress International (SBCC)*. There are also specialist codes for fire

safety, etc. The codes are basically performance codes rather than specifications for the form of construction. Several organizations are working on harmonization of codes, notably the National Institute of Building Sciences (NIBS), a non-governmental institution set up with representation from all parts of the building community.

The specific arrangements for obtaining planning permission and the statutory period for approval varies from state to state. Once the plans have been passed and construction has commenced, field inspection takes place. This is generally regarded as very important and the number of visits are often specified in the codes.

Standards are continually referred to in the building codes. They may be mandatory or discretionary. There are some 150 organizations which develop standards of which perhaps a dozen or so are important. These include the American Society for Testing and Materials (ASTM), the American National Standards Institute (ANSI) and the American Insurance Association (AIA).

Liability and insurance

The contractor is liable for damages caused by his own acts or omissions. He must therefore obtain comprehensive liability insurance to protect himself and his subcontractors.

The liability of designers and contractors varies with the contract used and from state to state. In the USA the architect or engineer has a contractual obligation to check the shop drawings of specialist trade contractors and this affects the liability. Normally, professional liability extends three to four years, but in some circumstances it can extend up to ten years.

Professional indemnity insurance covers the liability of parties involved in design, except that trade contractors may not be covered or, if they are, may be insufficiently so. Professional indemnity insurance is, in any case, very expensive in the USA. A survey of 1986 found that liability insurance was the major concern of the industry. Many companies in 1989 were paying double the insurance premiums of 1984, often with a reduced coverage.

CONSTRUCTION COST DATA

Cost of labour

The figures below are typical of labour costs in the Washington DC area
as at the third quarter of 1995. The wage rate is the basis of an employee's
income, while the cost of labour indicates the cost to a contractor of
employing that employee. The difference between the two covers a variety
of mandatory and voluntary contributions - a list of items which could be
included is given in section 2.

	Wage rate (per hour) US$	Cost of labour (per hour) US$	Number of hours worked per year
Site operatives			
Mason/bricklayer	25.90	40.70	2,000
Carpenter	25.20	40.25	2,000
Plumber	30.05	46.00	2,000
Electrician	29.30	44.20	2,000
Structural steel erector	27.85	52.15	2,000
HVAC installer	28.95	45.35	2,000
Semi-skilled worker	19.80	31.60	2,000
Unskilled labourer	19.25	30.65	2,000
Equipment operator	25.70	39.50	2,000
Watchmen/security	-	14.15	2,000
Site supervision			
General foreman	26.45	42.30	2,000
Trades foreman	27.95	44.70	2,000
	(per week)	*(per week)*	
Clerk of works	670	1,070	2,000
Contractors' personnel			
Site manager	1,150	1,835	2,000
Resident engineer	755	1,205	2,000
Resident surveyor	755	1,205	2,000
Junior engineer	565	900	2,000
Junior surveyor	565	900	2,000
Planner	670	1,070	2,000

Cost of materials

The figures that follow are the US national average costs for main construction materials, delivered to site in the Washington DC area, as incurred by contractors in the third quarter of 1995. These assume that the materials would be in quantities as required for a medium sized construction project and that the location of the works would be neither constrained nor remote.

	Unit	Cost US$
Cement and aggregate		
Ordinary portland cement in 50kg bags	bag	6.65
Coarse aggregates for concrete	tonne	11.75
Fine aggregates for concrete	tonne	12.30
Ready mixed concrete (mix 17MPa)	m^3	66.70
Ready mixed concrete (mix 21MPa)	m^3	68.66
Steel		
Mild steel reinforcement	tonne	573.00
High tensile steel reinforcement	tonne	632.00
Bricks and blocks		
Common bricks (8" x 2.67" x 4")	1,000	235.00
Good quality facing bricks (8" x 2.67" x 4")	1,000	290.00
Hollow concrete blocks (8" x 8" x 16")	1,000	950.00
Solid concrete blocks (4" x 8" x 16")	1,000	960.00
Precast concrete cladding units with exposed aggregate finish	m^2	98.50
Timber and insulation		
Exterior quality plywood (13mm)	m^2	7.58
Plywood for interior joinery (6mm)	m^2	4.95
Softwood strip flooring (25x102mm)	m^2	25.29
89mm thick unfaced fibreglass blanket	m^2	1.93
100mm thick rigid slab insulation	m^2	5.92
Softwood internal door complete with frame and ironmongery	m^2	214.00
Glass and ceramics		
Float glass (5mm)	m^2	28.30
Sealed double glazing units (16mm)	m^2	61.90
Good quality ceramic wall tiles	m^2	20.66

	Unit	Cost US$
Plaster and paint		
Plaster in 36kg bags	bag	16.00
Plasterboard (10mm thick)	m²	1.62
Emulsion paint in 5 litre tins	litre	2.20
Gloss oil paint in 5 litre tins	litre	4.50
Tiles and paviors		
Clay floor tiles (102 x 102 x 13mm)	m²	33.36
Vinyl floor tiles (305 x 305 x 3mm)	m²	19.91
Clay roof tiles	m²	51.12
Precast concrete roof tiles	m²	12.91
Drainage		
WC suite complete	each	385.00
Lavatory basin complete	each	320.00
100mm diameter clay drain pipes	m	4.92
150mm diameter cast iron drain pipes	m	38.71

Unit rates

The descriptions below are generally shortened versions of standard descriptions listed in section 4. Where an item has a two digit reference number (e.g. 05 or 33), this relates to the full description against that number in section 4. Where an item has an alphabetic suffix (e.g. 12A or 34B) this indicates that the standard description has been modified. Where a modification is major the complete modified description is included here and the standard description should be ignored; where a modification is minor (e.g. the insertion of a named hardwood) the shortened description has been modified here but, in general, the full description in section 4 prevails.

The unit rates below are US national average rates for main work items on a typical construction project as at the third quarter of 1995. The rates include all necessary labour, materials, equipment and allowances to cover preliminary and general items and contractors' overheads and profit.

	Unit	Rate US$
Excavation		
01 Mechanical excavation of foundation trenches	m³	5.75
02 Hardcore filling making up levels	m³	25.63
03 Earthwork support	m²	27.50

		Unit	*RateUS$*
Concrete work			
04	Plain insitu concrete in strip foundations in trenches	m³	199.00
05	Reinforced insitu concrete in beds	m³	175.00
06	Reinforced insitu concrete in walls	m³	294.00
07	Reinforced insitu concrete in suspended floors or roof slabs	m²	18.65
08	Reinforced insitu concrete in columns	m³	985.00
09	Reinforced insitu concrete in isolated beams	m³	875.00
10	Precast concrete slabs	m²	53.60
Formwork			
11	Softwood formwork to concrete walls	m²	26.15
12	Softwood or metal formwork to concrete columns	m	83.66
13	Softwood or metal formwork to horizontal soffits of slabs	m²	41.97
Reinforcement			
14	Reinforcement in concrete walls	tonne	1,215.00
15	Reinforcement in suspended concrete slabs	tonne	1,265.00
16	Fabric reinforcement in concrete beds	m²	41.97
Steelwork			
18	Framed structural steelwork in universal joist sections	tonne	1,735.00
19	Structural steelwork lattice roof trusses	tonne	1,735.00
Brickwork and blockwork			
20	Precast lightweight aggregate hollow concrete block walls	m²	48.00
21	Solid (perforated) concrete bricks	m²	71.58
22	Solid (perforated) sand lime bricks	m²	87.72
23	Facing bricks	m²	95.79
Roofing			
24	Concrete interlocking roof tiles 430 x 380mm	m²	39.28
25	Plain clay roof tiles 260 x 160mm	m²	76.42
29	3 layers glass-fibre based bitumen felt roof covering	m²	17.22
30	Bitumen based mastic asphalt roof covering	m²	1.65
31	Glass-fibre mat roof insulation 160mm thick	m²	7.96
32	Rigid sheet loadbearing roof insulation 75mm thick	m²	17.11
33	Troughed galvanized steel roof cladding	m²	21.52
Woodwork and metalwork			
36	Single glazed casement window in hardwood, size 650 x 900mm	each	225.00

		Unit	Rate US$
38	Solid core half hour fire resisting hardwood internal flush door, size 800 x 2000mm	each	228.00
39	Aluminum double glazed window, size 1200 x 1200	each	345.00
40	Aluminum double glazed door, size 850 x 2100mm	each	1,075.00

Plumbing

42	UPVC half round eaves gutter	m	11.87
43A	Rainwater pipes, 76mm DWC PVC	m	32.48
44A	Type L copper water tubing 13mm	m	20.17
45A	Plastic pipes for cold water distribution, Sch 80 CPVC, 76mm	m	86.94
46A	Plastic pipes for cold water distribution, Sch 40 CPVC, 38mm	m	49.70
47	Soil and vent pipes, 102mm	m	61.84
48	White vitreous china WC suite	each	700.00
49	White vitreous china lavatory basin	each	315.00
50	White glazed fireclay shower tray	each	690.00
51	Stainless steel single bowl sink	each	385.00

Electrical work

53	13 amp unswitched socket outlet	each	14.95
54	Flush mounted 20 amp, 1 way light switch	each	19.65

Finishings

55	2 coats gypsum based plaster on brick walls	m²	20.75
56	White glazed tiles on plaster walls	m²	53.28
57	Red clay quarry tiles on concrete floors	m²	85.03
60	Mineral fibre tiles on concealed suspension system	m²	9.04

Glazing

61	Glazing to wood	m²	81.50

Painting

62	Emulsion on plaster walls	m²	4.73
63	Oil paint on timber	m²	8.93

Approximate estimating

The building costs per unit area given below are US national averages incurred by building clients for typical buildings as at the third quarter of 1995. They are based upon the total floor area of all storeys, measured between external walls and without deduction for internal walls.

Approximate estimating costs generally include mechanical and electrical installations but exclude furniture, loose or special equipment, and external works; they also exclude fees for professional services.

The costs shown are for specifications and standards appropriate to the United States and this should be borne in mind when attempting comparisons with similarly described building types in other countries. A discussion of this issue is included in section 2. Comparative data for countries covered in this publication, including construction cost data, are presented in Part Three.

Approximate estimating costs must be treated with reserve; they cannot provide more than a rough guide to the probable cost of building.

	Cost m² US$	Cost ft² US$
Industrial buildings		
Factories for letting (including lighting, power and heating)	334	31
Factories for owner occupation (light industrial use)	484	45
Factories for owner occupation (heavy industrial use)	753	70
Factory/office (high tech) for letting (shell and core only)	764	71
Factory/office (high tech) for letting (ground floor shell, first floor offices)	969	90
Factory/office (high tech) for owner occupation (controlled environment, fully furnished)	1,216	113
High tech laboratory (air conditioned)	1,259	117
Warehouses, low bay (6 to 8m high) for letting (no heating)	258	24
Warehouses, low bay for owner occupation (including heating)	366	34
Warehouses, high bay for owner occupation (including heating)	560	52
Cold stores/refrigerated stores	538	50
Administrative and commercial buildings		
Civic offices, non air conditioned	710	66
Civic offices, fully air conditioned	861	80
Offices for letting, 5 to 10 storeys, non air conditioned	635	59
Offices for letting, 5 to 10 storeys, air conditioned	775	72
Offices for letting, high rise, air conditioned	764	71
Offices for owner occupation 5 to 10 storeys, non air conditioned	775	72
Offices for owner occupation, high rise, air conditioned	969	90
Prestige/headquarters office, 5 to 10 storeys, air conditioned	1,055	98
Prestige/headquarters office, high rise, air conditioned	1,216	113
Health and education buildings		
General hospitals	1,270	118
Teaching hospitals	1,496	139

	Cost m² US$	Cost ft² US$
Private hospitals	2,185	203
Health centres	936	87
Nursery schools	635	59
Primary/junior schools	775	72
Secondary/middle schools	807	75
University (arts) buildings	1,066	99
University (science) buildings	1,507	140
Management training centres	840	78

Recreation and arts buildings

Theatres (over 500 seats) including seating and stage equipment	807	75
Theatres (less than 500 seats) including seating and stage equipment	1,163	108
Concert halls including seating and stage facilities	1,163	108
Swimming pools (international standard) including changing facilities	1,744	162
Swimming pools (schools standard) including changing facilities	1,001	93
City centre/central libraries	1,249	116
Branch/local libraries	969	90

Residential buildings

Socail/economic single family housing (multiple units)	506	47
Private/mass market single family housing 2 storey detached/semidetached (multiple units)	538	50
Purpose designed single family housing 2 storey detached (single unit)	742	69
Social/economic apartment housing, low rise (no lifts)	506	47
Social/economic apartment housing, high rise (with lifts)	678	63
Private sector apartment building (standard specification)	689	64
Private sector apartment buildings (luxury)	840	78
Student/nurses halls of residence	1,055	98
Home for the elderly (shared accommodation)	689	64
Homes for the elderly (self contained with shared communal facilities)	926	86
Motel	667	62

Regional variations

The approximate estimating costs are based on US national average costs.
Adjust these costs by the following factors for regional variations:

Los Angeles, CA	: +13.3%	Providence, RI	: +7.9%
Hartford, CT	: +8.6%	Fort Worth, TX	: -15.9%
Miami, FL	: -12.6%	Columbia, SC	: -22.5%
New York, NY	: +36.1%	Seattle, WA	: +6.0%
Philadelphia, PA	: +9.7%	Dallas, TX	: -13.8%

EXCHANGE RATES AND INFLATION

The combined effect of exchange rates and inflation on prices within a
country and price comparisons between countries is discussed in section
2.

Exchange rates

The graph below plots the movement of American dollar against sterling
and 100 Japanese yen since 1985. The values used for the graph are
quarterly and the method of calculating these is described and general
guidance on the interpretation of the graph provided in section 2. The
average exchange rate at the second quarter of 1995 was US$1.59 to pound
sterling and US$1.09 to 100 Japanese yen.

US DOLLAR AGAINST STERLING AND JAPANESE YEN

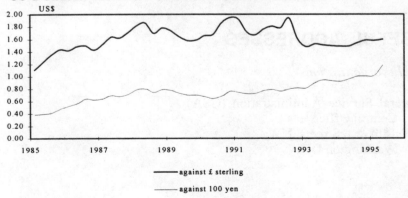

against £ sterling
against 100 yen

Price inflation

The table below presents the indices for consumer price and building cost inflation in the USA since 1980.

CONSUMER PRICE AND BUILDING COST INFLATION

Year	Consumer price inflation		Building cost index	
	average index	average change %	average index	average change %
1980	100		100	
1981	104	4.0	108	8.0
1982	117	12.5	115	6.5
1983	121	3.4	123	7.0
1984	126	4.1	125	1.6
1985	131	4.0	125	0.0
1986	133	1.5	128	2.4
1987	138	3.8	131	2.3
1988	143	3.6	134	2.3
1989	150	4.9	136	1.5
1990	159	6.0	139	2.2
1991	165	3.8	142	2.2
1992	170	3.1	146	3.0
1993	175	2.9	155	5.7
1994	180	2.6	160	3.5
1995	-	-	160	0.0

Source : Engineering News Record

USEFUL ADDRESSES

Public organizations

General Service Administration (GSA)
    Central Office
    18th & F Streets, NW
    Washington DC

For Regional Government Construction Ministries:
  Regional GSA Office in each state

Army Corps of Engineers
  20 Massachusetts Avenue, NW
  Washington DC 20314-1000

Department of Commerce, Office of Research and
Environmental Information
  14th Street between E Street and Constitution Avenue, NW
  Washington DC

Department of Housing and Urban Development Headquarters
(HUD)
  451 7th Street, SW
  Washington DC

Department of Transportation
  400 7th Street, SW
  Washington DC

National Academy of Science
  Building Research Advisory Board
  Army Corp of Engineers Research Laboratory

National Institute of Standards and Technology
  Gaithersburg
  Maryland 20899-0001
  Tel : 301 975 3058
  Fax: 301 9754032

National Statistics Organization
  Department of Commerce
  14th Street between E Street and Constitution Avenue, NW
  Washington DC

Small Business Administration
  1441 L Street, NW
  Washington DC

Trade and professional associations

AFL-CIO
  810 16th Street, NW
  Washington DC

American Association of Cost Engineers (AACE)
  Morgantown, West Virginia

American Institute of Architects (AIA)
  1735 New York Avenue, NW
  Washington DC

Associations of Building Contractors of America
(ABC - non-union)
  729 15th Street, NW
  Washington DC 20005

Associations of General Contractors (AGC - union)
  1957 E Street, NW
  Washington DC 20006

For Contractors Registration Board
  Respective county/city Chamber of Commerce

National Society of Professional Engineers (NSPE)
  1420 King Street
  Alexandria, Virginia

DAVIS LANGDON & SEAH INTERNATIONAL

Construction and Development in Vietnam

This report reviews the situation as regards construction and development in Vietnam. It can be used to identify opportunities for those involved in construction – developers, contractors, material producers and manufacturers, consultants and other construction professionals – and is aimed at attracting and encouraging their active involvement in Vietnam. It describes an emerging market in the midst of a flourishing region.

The 150 page report, illustrated with diagrams and maps, includes:

Authors' Introduction
Key Data
The National Context
The Construction Industry
Resources for Construction
Construction Markets
Construction Costs and Prices
Case Studies
Appendices

Vietnam

KEY DATA

Population
Population	71.3mn
Urban population	20%
Population under 15 (1989)	39%
Population 65 and over (1989)	5%
Average annual growth rate (1980 to 1993)	2.2%

Geography
Land area	332,000km²
Agricultural area	22%
Capital city	Hanoi
Population of capital city (1990)	2.2mn

Economy
Monetary unit	Vietnamese dong (D)
Exchange rate (average third quarter 1995) to:	
the pound sterling	D 17,479
the US dollar	D 11,028
the yen x 100	D 12,022
Inflation rate (1994)	14.4%
Gross Domestic Product (GDP) at market prices	D 136,571bn
GDP per capita	D 1,915,000
Average annual real change in GDP (1990 to 1994)	7.9%
Private consumption as a proportion of GDP	}84%
General government consumption as a proportion of GDP	}
Gross domestic investment as a proportion of GDP	21%

Construction
Gross value of construction output *	D 21,000bn
Net value of construction output	D 10,101bn
Net value of construction output as a proportion of GDP	7.4%
Annual cement consumption (1994) (estimated demand)	6.5mn tonnes

All data relate to 1993 unless otherwise indicated

* Author's estimate

THE CONSTRUCTION INDUSTRY

Construction output

The value of the new gross output of the construction industry is estimated by the authors to be 20,000 billion dong, equivalent to about US$2.0 billion, or about 15% of GDP. There may be say another 1,000 billion dong in repair and maintenance. The official figure for net construction output is 10,101 billion dong equivalent to US$1.0 billion, or 7.4% of GDP. In 1994 GDP grew by 8.8% and it would be expected that construction would also have increased.

The estimated breakdown by type of work for new construction output is shown in the table below.

ESTIMATE OF TOTAL CONSTRUCTION BY TYPE OF WORK, 1993
(BILLION DONG AT CURRENT PRICES)

Type of work	Total output	%
Housing and shop houses	3,250	16
Industrial buildings	6,100	30
Offices and other commercial buildings	2,550	13
Hotels	1,350	7
Schools and colleges	350	2
Health buildings	230	1
Agricultural and forestry buildings	1,550	8
Other buildings	270	1
Roads, railways and other civil engineering	4,350	22
Total	20,000	100

Source: Author's estimates

Estimated sources of funds were public 47.5%, official development assistance 5%, private foreign 25% *Viet Kieu* (Vietnamese abroad) 2.5% and private local 20%. Nearly two third of public funding was central, the remainder being from local authorities.

In the coming years, the construction industry is expected to grow steadily. The public sector demand will continue to grow especially in the area of infrastructure. It has been estimated that the expenditure for the country's transport needs including rehabilitation of roads, railways and ports would be around US$5.5 billion. Previously, the private sector construction demand amounted for a very small percentage of the total construction demand. However, with the implementation of the *Doi Moi* policy by the Vietnamese government, the private sector is increasingly playing a greater role in the industry. As a result, there is a massive increase in the number of private construction projects especially residential buildings. The increase in private sector construction demand is also fuelled by a steady inflow of foreign investments.

The regional distribution of local government construction work is shown in the table below and compared with the distribution of population.

DISTRIBUTION OF POPULATION AND LOCAL GOVERNMENT CONSTRUCTION WORK BY REGION, 1993

Region	Population 000 persons	%	Gross output billion dong	%
North Mountain and Midland	12,109	17	497	13
Red River Delta	13,809	19	716	19
Central Coast of Northland	9,517	13	282	7
Central Coast of Southland	7,375	10	416	11
Central Highland	2,904	4	157	4
North East of Southland	8,693	12	1,358	36
Mekong River Delta	15,532	22	361	10
All Vietnam	70,983	100	3,787	100

Source: Statistical Yearbook 1993 and 1994

The regional match is reasonably close with the notable exception of the North East of Southland - including Ho Chi Minh City and Vung Tau. Foreign private investment is concentrated in urban areas, particularly Hanoi and Ho Chi Minh City.

Characteristics and structure of the industry

The Ministry of Construction is responsible for all construction activities in Vietnam. The headquarters is located in Hanoi with a regional office in Ho Chi Minh City. The Ministry is divided into four key sections each under the jurisdiction of a Vice-Minister. These sections are: the Department of Construction Economics and Management; Science and Technology; Urban Management; Development of Construction Materials.

The Ministry is structured into departments, institutes and various construction related companies. Specific responsibilities of the four key sections are:

● Construction Economics and Management - sets guidelines on the costs of labour, materials and plant; to advise on bidding procedures and overhead, profit and taxation allowances for state projects.

● Science and Technology - approves Construction Standards and Regulations with particular attention to the environment.

● Urban Management - responsible for water supply and treatment, waste disposal, construction of low income housing and approval of each province's masterplan.

● Development of Construction Materials - promotes and gears foreign investment in domestic resources such as cement, brick, sanitary ware and roofing products in order to realize the benefits of the forecast increase in demand in products of an international standard both in Vietnam and for the potential export market.

All submissions and investment proposals related to construction activities must pass through the Ministry of Construction (as well as other Ministries) for approval before an investment licence can be issued for foreign/joint venture projects. Following design development further checks will be carried out by the Ministry on the technical content of the design.

Each province has a separate People's Committee whose responsibilities include determining the project's compliance with the appropriate development plan, evaluation of the project assets, financial status of the relevant parties, organization of utility supply of the project (if relevant) and determining land use ownership, rights and terms. All new Representative Offices must register with the People's Committee of the province in which the office will be located.

The Chamber of Commerce and Industry is an independent, non-government organisation whose functions are to promote trade and investment in Vietnam and abroad; to represent the Vietnamese business community for the promotion and protection of its interests in domestic and international relations; to serve as a forum for exchange of information between investment enterprises and the State on matters concerning the economic activity and business environment in Vietnam.

The Vietnamese Union of Architects is based in Hanoi and has branches throughout the country. The Union is a member of the International Union of Architects and, theoretically, has links with similar institutions around the world. Provincial branches of the Architects' Union are similarly organised and perform similar functions as the National Union in Hanoi. In Quang Nam-Da Nang provinces, the director of the Provincial Institute of Design and Planning (the Senior State Architect) is also an executive committee member of the Union. In the entire province there are around 100 architects and 45 are members of the Union. Non-members include those who are not practising and those who have not yet registered.

Clients and finance

Since initiation of Vietnam's economic reforms, some 44 countries have directly invested in the country's economy. There are more than 1,000 such projects belonging to some 700 companies. The investment value is around US$10.25 billion. Most of the investors are big corporations and institutions with their own source of finance.

Until late 1993, Vietnam was cut off from major international borrowing. Since the resumption of Official Development Assistance (ODA) to Vietnam in 1993, Vietnam is able to have access to international financial institutions including the International Monetary Fund (IMF), World Bank and the Asian Development Bank. The majority of this aid money is to be channelled into infrastructure development and improvement.

Selection of design consultants

There are no prescribed criteria or specific tender or selection procedures for the choice of design consultants in Vietnam. Foreign clients usually select the design consultants known to them or those who have a reputation for a specific type of building. These design consultants tend to come from their own countries.

There are relatively few private consulting firms in Vietnam. A principal reason appears to be the low level of official fee scales (2%-3% of the construction cost for all services). In addition, there is no tradition of private consultancy in the construction sector.

Contractual arrangements

Different forms of contract are used for the private projects. The forms of contract to be used will depend on the design consultants selected.

Development control and standards

The State Committee For Cooperation and Investment (SCCI) is the body responsible for control of all foreign investments in Vietnam and for issuing investment licences. The SCCI's role is to circulate investment licence applications among the various Ministries and relevant People's Committee for the region. The SCCI head office is in Hanoi with a representative office in Ho Chi Minh City. The various departments within the SCCI cover Project Evaluation, Investment Promotion, General Office, Information and Legislation.

The Project Evaluation Department's role is to determine whether an investment proposal is in accordance with the best interests of the State. During the evaluation process, which can take up to three months, questions from the various Ministries must be answered within a stipulated time frame which at the time of publishing is 45 days, after which the application is deemed to have lapsed. The SCCI provides pro-forma applications and documents and encourages reference to previously successful application to limit abortive time. After the evaluation process an Investment Licence is either issued or the application is rejected.

All foreign investors are required to register their financial accounting practices with the Ministry of Finance. Regular reports on the financial standing of an enterprise must be submitted. The Ministry of Finance also advises the SCCI on fiscal matters such as taxation levels, subsidies and incentives for the various forms of foreign investment.

CONSTRUCTION COST DATA

Cost of labour

The figures opposite are typical of labour costs in Vietnam as at the third quarter of 1995 for joint venture/international projects. Costs for third quarter of 1995 are not available at the time of publishing. The cost of labour indicates the cost to a contractor of employing that employee.

	Cost of labour (per day) US$	Number of hours worked per year
Site operatives		
Bricklayer	6.20	2,496
Carpenter	6.20	2,496
Plumber	7.50	2,496
Electrician	7.50	2,496
Structural steel erector	6.20	2,496
Welder	6.20	2,496
Labourer	3.50	2,496
Equipment operator	7.50	2,496

Cost of materials

The figures that follow are the costs of main construction materials, delivered to site in Vietnam, as incurred by contractors in the second quarter of 1995 (costs for third quarter of 1995 are not available at the time of publishing). These assume that the materials would be in quantities as required for a medium sized construction project and that the location of the works would be neither constrained nor remote.

	Unit	Cost US$
Cement and aggregate		
Ordinary portland cement in 50kg bags	tonne	115
Coarse aggregates for concrete	tonne	12
Fine aggregates for concrete	m³	15
Ready mixed concrete (Grade 30)	m³	80
Ready mixed concrete (Grade 20)	m³	70
Steel		
Mild steel reinforcement	tonne	450
High tensile steel reinforcement	tonne	500
Structural steel sections	tonne	550
Bricks		
Common bricks (220 x 105 x 60mm)	1,000	29
Good quality facing bricks (220 x 105 x 60mm)	1,000	40
Hollow concrete blocks (390 x 190 x 100mm)	1,000	600

	Unit	Cost US$
Timber and insulation		
Hardwood for joinery	m³	280
Exterior quality plywood (12mm)	m²	9
Plywood for interior joinery (12mm)	m²	8
50mm thick quilt insulation (16kg/m³)	m²	5
50mm thick rigid slab insulation (60kg/m³)	m²	8
Hardwood internal door complete with frames and ironmongery	each	300
Glass and ceramics		
Float glass (10mm)	m²	14
Plaster and paint		
Good quality ceramic wall tiles (300 x 300 x 8mm)	m²	25
Plasterboard (13mm thick) - gypsum	m²	14
Emulsion paint in 5 litre tins	litre	5
Gloss oil paint in 5 litre tins	litre	6
Tiles and paviors		
Clay floor tiles (100 x 200 x 8mm)	m²	10
Vinyl floor tiles (300 x 300 x 2mm)	m²	10
Clay roof tiles	1,000	56
Precast concrete roof tiles	1,000	70
Drainage		
WC suite complete	each	150
Wash hand basin complete	each	120
100mm diameter clay drain pipes	m	10
150mm diameter cast iron drain pipes (medium grade)	m	20

Unit rates

The descriptions below are generally shortened versions of standard descriptions listed in full in section 4. Where an item has a two digit reference number (e.g. 05 or 3), this relates to the full description against that number in section 4. Where an item has an alphabetic suffix (e.g. 12A or 34B) this indicates that the standard description has been modified. Where a modification is major the complete modified description is included here and the standard description should be ignored; where a modification is minor (e.g. the insertion of a named hardwood) the shortened description has been modified here but, in general, the full description in section 4 prevails.

The unit rates below are for main work items on a typical joint venture/ international project in the city area in the second quarter of 1995 (costs for third quarter of 1995 are not available at the time of publishing). The rates include all necessary labour, materials and equipment. An allowance of 12% has been added to the rates to cover preliminary and general items.

		Unit	Rate US$
Excavation			
01	Mechanical excavation of foundation trenches	m³	5.60
02	Hardcore filling making up levels; 150mm thick	m²	2.90
Concrete work			
04	Plain insitu concrete in strip foundations in trenches (Grade 20)	m³	100.80
05	Reinforced insitu concrete in beds (Grade 30)	m³	112.00
06	Reinforced insitu concrete in walls (Grade 30)	m³	112.00
07	Reinforced insitu concrete in suspended floors or roof slabs (Grade 30)	m³	112.00
08	Reinforced insitu concrete in columns (Grade 30)	m³	112.00
09	Reinforced insitu concrete in isolated beams (Grade 30)	m³	112.00
Formwork			
11A	Waterproof plywood formwork to concrete walls	m²	16.80
12A	Waterproof plywood formwork to concrete columns	m²	16.80
13A	Waterproof plywood formwork to horizontal soffits of slabs	m²	16.80
Reinforcement			
14	Reinforcement in concrete walls	tonne	784.00
15	Reinforcement in suspended concrete slabs	tonne	784.00
16	Fabric reinforcement in concrete beds	m²	6.70
Steelwork			
17	Fabricate, supply and erect steel framed structure	tonne	1,400.00
19	Structural steelwork lattice roof trusses	tonne	1,680.00
Brickwork and blockwork			
20	Precast lightweight aggregate hollow concrete block walls	m²	17.90
21A	Solid (perforated) concrete blocks	m²	20.15
23	Facing bricks (215mm thick)	m²	15.70
Roofing			
25	Plain clay roof tiles 260 x 160mm	m²	22.40
29	3 layers glass-fibre based bitumen felt roof covering	m²	24.60
33	Troughed galvanized steel roof cladding	m²	14.00

		Unit	*Rate US$*
Woodwork and metalwork			
34	Preservative treated sawn hardwood 50 x 100mm	m	11.20
35	Preservative treated sawn hardwood 50 x 150mm	m	12.90
37	Two panel glazed door in Kapur hardwood, size 850 x 2000mm	each	318.10
38	Solid core half hour fire resisting hardwood internal flush door, size 800 x 2000mm	each	672.00
39	Aluminium double glazed window, size 1200 x 1200mm	each	515.20
41	Hardwood skirtings	m	5.60
Plumbing			
42	UPVC half round eaves gutter	m	17.90
43A	UPVC rainwater pipes; 300mm diameter	m	33.60
44	Light gauge copper cold water tubing	m	16.80
45	High pressure plastic pipes for cold water supply	m	5.60
47	UPVC soil and vent pipes	m	28.00
48	White vitreous china WC suite	each	268.80
49	White vitreous china wash hand basin	each	224.00
51A	Stainless steel double bowl sink and double drainer	each	224.00
Electrical work			
52	PVC insulated and copper sheathed cable	m	4.50
53	13 amp unswitched socket outlet	each	24.60
54	Flush mounted 20 amp, 1 way light switch	each	42.60
Finishings			
55A	2 coats cement and sand (1:4) plaster on brick walls	m²	5.60
56	White glazed tiles on plaster walls	m²	39.20
57	Red clay quarry tiles on concrete floors	m²	28.00
58	Cement and sand screed to concrete floors	m²	4.50
59	Thermoplastic floor tiles on screed	m²	24.60
60	Mineral fibre tiles on concealed suspension system	m²	28.00
Glazing			
61	Glazing to wood	m²	22.40
Painting			
62	Emulsion on plaster walls	m²	3.40
63	Oil paint on timber	m²	4.50

Approximate estimating

The building costs per unit area given below are averages incurred by building clients for joint venture/international projects in Vietnam as at the second quarter of 1995 (costs for third quarter of 1995 are not available at the time of publishing). They are based upon the total floor area of all storeys, measured between external walls and without deduction for internal walls.

Approximate estimating costs generally include mechanical and electrical installations but exclude furniture, loose or special equipment, and external works; they also exclude fees for professional services. The costs shown are for specifications and standards appropriate to Vietnam and this should be borne in mind when attempting comparisons with similarly described building types in other countries. A discussion of this issue is included in section 2. Comparative data for countries covered in this publication, including construction cost data, is presented in Part Three.

Approximate estimating costs must be treated with caution; they cannot provide more than a rough guide to the probable cost of building.

	Cost m² US$	Cost ft² US$
Industrial buildings		
Factories for letting	550-650	51-61
Factories for owner occupation (light industrial use)	600-800	56-75
Factories for owner occupation (heavy industrial use)	800-1000	75-93
Factory/office (high tech) for owner occupation		
(controlled environment, fully finished)	800-1000	75-93
Warehouses, low bay (6 to 8m high) for letting	450-550	42-51
Warehouses, low bay for owner occupation	550-650	51-61
Warehouses, high bay for owner occupation	600-800	56-75
Administrative and commercial buildings		
Offices for letting, 5 to 10 storeys, non air conditioned	650-750	61-70
Offices for letting, 5 to 10 storeys, air conditioned	750-850	70-79
Offices for letting, high rise, air conditioned	850-950	79-89
Offices for owner occupation high rise, air conditioned	850-1000	79-93
Prestige/headquarters office, 5 to 10 storeys, air conditioned	950-1150	89-107
Prestige/headquarters office, high rise, air conditioned	1000-1200	93-112
Residential buildings		
Purpose designed single family housing 2 storey detached		
(single unit)	1000+	93+

	Cost m^2 US$	Cost ft^2 US$
Social/economic apartment housing, high rise (with lifts)	600-700	56-65
Private sector apartment building (standard specification)	650-750	61-70
Private sector apartment buildings (luxury)	850-950	79-89
Hotel, 5 star, city centre	1500+	140+
Hotel, 3 star, city/provincial	1100-1200	103-112

Regional Variations

The approximate estimating costs are based on projects in Hanoi. For other parts of Vietnam, adjust these costs by the following factors:

Ho Chi Minh City	: +9%
Northern Provinces	: -1%
Da Nang City and Central Provinces	: +3%

EXCHANGE RATES AND INFLATION

The combined effect of exchange rates and inflation on prices within a country and price comparisons between countries is discussed in section 2.

Exchange rates

The graph below plots the movement of the Vietnam dong against sterling, US dollar and 100 Japanese yen since 1985. The values used for the graph are quarterly and the method of calculating these is described and general guidance on the interpretation of the graph provided in section 2. The average exchange rates at the third quarter of 1995 was D 17,479 to pound sterling and D 11,028 to US dollar and D 12,022 to 100 Japanese yen.

THE VIETNAM DONG AGAINST STERLING, US DOLLAR AND
100 JAPANESE YEN

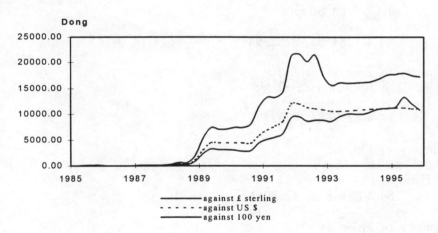

USEFUL ADDRESSES

Ministries

Ministry of Agriculture and Food Industry
    1 Bach Thoa Street
    Hanoi
    Tel : 84-4-8268161, 8252113

Ministry of Construction
    37 Le Dai Hanh Street
    Hanoi
    Tel : 84-4-8268571
    Fax : 84-4-8252153

Ministry of Culture and Sport
    51-53 Ngo Quyen Street
    Hanoi
    Tel : 84-4-8253231, 8253234

Ministry of Defence
    28 Dien Bien Phu Street
    Hanoi
    Tel : 84-4-8260084

Ministry of Education and Training
    49 Dai Co Viet Street
    Hanoi
    Tel : 84-4-8264795, 8262394

Ministry of Energy
    18 Tran Nguyen Han Street
    Hanoi
    Tel : 84-4-8257644, 8263725

Ministry of Finance
    8 Phan Huy Chu
    Hanoi
    Tel : 84-4-8264872, 8262061

Ministry of Fisheries
    57 Ngoc Khanh Street
    Hanoi
    Tel : 84-4-8256396, 8254714

Ministry of Foreign Affairs
    1 Ton That Dam Street
    Hanoi
    Tel : 84-4-8258201, 8258322

Ministry of Forestry
    123 Lo Duc Street
    Hanoi
    Tel : 84-4-8253236, 8253237

Ministry of Health
138A Giang Vo Street
Hanoi
Tel : 84-4-8264051, 8264416

Ministry of Heavy Industry
54 Hai Ba Trung Street
Hanoi
Tel : 84-4-8258311, 8267872

Ministry of Interior Affairs
15 Tran Binh Trong
Hanoi
Tel : 84-4-8268131, 8258624

Ministry of Irrigation
21 Lo Su
Hanoi
Tel : 84-4-8254785

Ministry of Justice
25A Cat Linh Street
Hanoi
Tel : 84-4-8254658, 8253395

Ministry of Labour, War Invalids and Social Affairs
2 Dinh Le Street
Hanoi
Tel : 84-4-8254728, 8255870

Ministry of Light Industry
7 Trang Thi Street
Hanoi
Tel : 84-4-8252852, 8253831

Ministry of Science, Technology and the Environment
39 Tran Hung Dao Street
Hanoi
Tel : 84-4-8252731

Ministry of Trade and Commerce
31 Trang Tien
Hanoi
Tel : 84-4-8262521, 8254950

Ministry of Transport and Communication
80 Tran Hung Dao Street
Hanoi
Tel : 84-4-8252079, 8254012
Fax : 84-4-8267291

State committees

National Committee for Population and Family Planning
56 Quoc Tu Giam Street
Hanoi
Tel : 84-4-8260020

National Committee for Protection and Care of the Child
55 Tran Phu Street
Hanoi
Tel : 84-4-8233342

State Committee for Cooperation and Investment
56 Quoc Tu Giam
Hanoi
Tel : 84-4-8253666
Fax : 84-4-8259271

State Committee for Ethic and Mountainous Regions
82 Phan Dinh Phung Street
Hanoi
Tel : 84-4-8258261

State Planning Committee
8 Hoang Dieu
Hanoi
Tel : 84-4-8254363

People's committees

People's Committee of Ho Chi Minh City
  86 Le Thanh Ton
  District 1
  Ho Chi Minh City
  Tel : 84-8-8290739

People's Committee of Hanoi Chief Architect's Office
  9B Cat Linh Street
  Hanoi
  Tel : 84-4-8234634

Chamber of commerce

Chamber of Commerce and Industry of Vietnam
  33 Ba Trieu Street
  Hanoi
  Tel : 84-4-8266235
  Fax : 84-4-8256446

4. Amplified descriptions of construction items

Excavation

(Assume excavation in firm soil)

1   Mechanical excavation of foundation trenches; starting from ground
    level (including removal of excavation material from site); over 0.30m
    wide, not exceeding 2.00m deep.

2   Hardcore filling in making up levels; hard brick, broken stone (or sand
    where appropriate); crushed to pass a 100mm ring 150mm deep.

3   Earthwork support; sides of trench excavation; distance between opposing
    faces not exceeding 2.00m; maximum depth 2.00m.

Concrete work

(Formwork and reinforcement measured separately)

4   Plain insitu concrete in strip foundations in trenches 20N/mm²; ordinary
    portland cement, 20mm coarse aggregate; size 500mm wide x 300mm
    thick.

5   Reinforced insitu concrete in beds 20N/mm²; ordinary portland cement,
    20mm coarse aggregate; 200mm thick.

6   Reinforced insitu concrete in walls 20N/mm²; ordinary portland cement,
    20mm coarse aggregate; 200mm thick.

7   Reinforced insitu concrete in suspended floor or roof slabs 20N/mm²;
    ordinary portland cement, 20mm coarse aggregate; 150mm thick.

8   Reinforced insitu concrete in columns 20N/mm²; ordinary portland
    cement, 20mm coarse aggregate; size 400 x 400mm.

9   Reinforced insitu concrete in isolated beams 20N/mm²; ordinary portland
    cement, 20mm coarse aggregate; size 400 x 600mm deep.

10 Precast concrete slabs (including reinforcement as necessary); contractor
   designed for total loading of 3N/mm²; 5.00m span.

Formwork

(Assume a simple repetitive design which allows three uses of formwork)

11 Softwood or metal formwork to concrete walls; basic finish; (one side
   only).

12 Softwood or metal formwork to concrete columns; basic finish; columns 1600mm girth.

13 Softwood or metal formwork to horizontal soffits of slabs; basic finish; slabs 150mm thick, not exceeding 3.50m high.

Reinforcement

14 Reinforcement in concrete walls; hot rolled high tensile bars cut, bent and laid, 16mm diameter.

15 Reinforcement in suspended concrete slabs; hot rolled high tensile bars cut, bent and laid, 25mm diameter.

16 Fabric (mat) reinforcement in concrete beds (measured separately); weight approximately 3.0 kg/m²; laid in position with 150mm side and end laps.

Steelwork

17 Fabricate, supply and erect steel framed structure; including painting all steel with one coat primer.

18 Framed structural steelwork in universal joist sections; bolted or welded connections, including erecting on site and painting one coat at works.

19 Structural steelwork lattice roof trusses; bolted or welded connections, including erecting on site and painting one coat at works.

Brickwork and blockwork
(Assume a notional thickness of 100mm for bricks and blocks. Rates should be for the nearest standard size to 100mm)

20 Precast lightweight aggregate hollow concrete block walls; gauged mortar; 100mm thick.

21 Solid (perforated) clay or concrete common bricks (priced at .... per m² delivered to site); gauged mortar; 100mm thick walls.

22 Solid (perforated) sand lime bricks (priced at .... per m² delivered to site); gauged mortar; 100mm thick walls.

23 Facing bricks (priced at .... per m² delivered to site);   gauged mortar, flush pointed as work proceeds; half brick thick walls.

Roofing

24 Concrete interlocking roof tiles 430 x 380mm (or nearest equivalent); on and including battens and underfelt; laid to 355mm gauge with 75mm laps (excluding eaves fittings or ridge tiles).

25 Plain clay roof tiles 260 x 160mm (or nearest equivalent);   on   and including battens and underfelt; laid to 100mm lap (excluding eaves fittings or ridge tiles).

26 Fibre cement roof slates 600 x 300mm (or nearest equivalent);   on and including battens and underfelt;   laid flat or to fall as coverings for roofs.

27 Sawn softwood roof boarding, preservative treated 25mm thick; laid flat or to fall.

28 Particle board roof coverings with tongued and grooved joints 25mm thick; laid flat or to fall.

29 Three layers glass-fibre based bitumen felt roof covering; finished with limestone chippings in hot bitumen; to flat roofs.

30 Bitumen based   mastic   asphalt   roof   covering   in   two layers; on and including sheathing felt underlay, with white chippings finish; to flat roofs.

31 Glass-fibre mat roof insulation 160mm thick; laid flat between ceiling joists.

32 Rigid sheet resin-bonded loadbearing glass-fibre roof insulation 75mm thick; laid on flat roofs.

33 0.8mm troughed galvanized steel roof cladding in single spans of 3.00m with loading of 0.75 KN/m²;   fixed to steel roof trusses with bolts;   to pitched roofs.

Woodwork and metalwork
(Hardwood should be assumed to be of reasonable exterior quality)

34 Preservative treated sawn softwood; size 50 x 100mm; framed in partitions.

35 Preservative treated sawn softwood; size 50 x 150mm; pitched roof members.

36 Single glazed casement window in (.............) hardwood including hardwood frame and sill; including steel butts and anodized aluminium espagnolette bolt; size approximately 650 x 900mm with 38 x 100mm frame and 75 x 125mm sill.

37 Two panel door with panels open for glass in (.............) hardwood including hardwood frame and sill; including glazing with 6mm wired polished plate security glass fixed with hardwood beads and including steel butts, anodized handles and push plates and security locks; size approximately 850 x 2000mm with 38 x 100mm frame and 38 x 150mm sill.

38 Solid core half hour fire resisting hardwood internal flush door lipped on all edges; unpainted, including steel butts, anodized handles and push plates and mortice lock; size approximately 800 x 2000mm.

39 Aluminium double glazed window and hardwood sub-frame; standard anodized horizontally sliding double glazed in (..............) hardwood sub-frame and sill; including double glazing with 4mm glass, including all ironmongery; size approximately 1200 x 1200mm with 38 x 100mm sub-frame and 75 x 125mm sill.

40 Aluminium double glazed door set and hardwood sub-frame; standard anodized aluminium, double glazed in (..............) hardwood sub-frame and sill; including double glazing with 4mm glass, including all ironmongery; size approximately 850 x 2100mm with 38 x 100mm sub-frame and 75 x 125mm sill.

41 Hardwood skirtings. Wrought (...............) hardwood; fixed on softwood grounds; size 20 x 100mm.

Plumbing
(Sizes of sanitary installations and pipes are indicative)

42 UPVC half round eaves gutter; screwed to softwood at 1.00m centres; 110mm external diameter (excluding bends, outlets etc.).

43 UPVC rainwater pipes with pushfit joints; screwed to brickwork at 1.50m centres; 100mm external diameter (excluding bends, outlets etc.).

44 Light gauge copper cold water tubing with compression or capillary fittings; screwed to brickwork horizontally at 1.00m centres; 15mm external diameter.

45 High pressure polypropylene, polythene or UPVC (as appropriate) pipes for cold water supply; fixed horizontally to brick walls at 1.00m centres; 15mm external diameter, complete with fittings.

46 Low pressure polypropylene, polythene or UPVC (as appropriate) pipes for cold water distribution; with plastic compression fittings 20mm external diameter, laid in trenches.

47 UPVC soil and vent pipes with solvent welded or ring seal joints; fixed vertically to brickwork with brackets at 1.50m centres; 100mm external diameter.

48 White vitreous china WC suite with black plastic seat and cover and plastic low level cistern, 9 litre capacity; complete with ball valve and float and flush pipe to WC suite; fixed to concrete.

49 White vitreous china lavatory basin with 2 No. chrome plated taps (or medium quality chrome plated mixer taps); including plug, overflow and waste connections (excluding trap); size approximately 560 x 400mm, fixed to brickwork with concealed brackets.

50 Glazed fireclay shower tray; including overflow and waste (excluding trap); size approximately 750 x 750 x 175mm, fixed to concrete.

51 Stainless steel single bowl sink and double drainer (excluding taps); including plug, overflow and connections (excluding trap); size approximately 1500 x 600mm, fixed to softwood sink unit (excluding sink base).

Electrical work

52 PVC insulated and copper sheathed cable, 450/750 volt grade, twin core and ECC 6mm² cross section area; fixed to timber with clips.

53 13 amp, 2 gang flush mounted white, unswitched socket outlet; including 6.0m of 2.5mm² concealed PVC insulated copper cable (excluding conduit); flush mounted to brickwork including all fittings and fixing as necessary.

54 Flush mounted 20 amp, 2 gang, 1 way white light switch; including 6.0m of 1.5mm² concealed mineral insulated copper cable (excluding conduit); flush mounted to brickwork including all fittings and fixings as necessary.

Finishings

55 Two coats gypsum based plaster on brick walls 13mm thick; floated finish.

56 White glazed tiles on plaster walls size 100 x 100 x 4mm; fixed with adhesive and grouted between tiles.

57 Red clay quarry tiles on concrete floors size 150 x 150 x 16mm; bedded and jointed in mortar.

58 Floor screed; cement and sand screed to concrete floors 1:3 mix; 50mm thick; floated finish.

59 Thermoplastic floor tiles on screed 2.5mm thick; fixed with adhesive.

60 Suspended ceiling system; fissured mineral fibre tiles size 300 x 300 x 15mm; on galvanized steel concealed suspension system; fixed to concrete soffits with 500mm drop (excluding lamp fittings).

Glazing

60 Glazing to wood; ordinary quality 4mm glass; softwood beads.

Painting

61 Emulsion on plaster walls; one coat diluted sealer coat and two coats full vinyl emulsion paint.

62 Oil paint on timber; one coat primer and two coats oil based paint.

PART THREE
COMPARATIVE DATA

5. Introductory notes

Part Three brings together data from a variety of sources but mainly Part Two, and presents them in the form of tables to allow rapid comparison among the countries included in the book. This also helps place countries, their main statistical indicators and their construction costs in an international context.

There are twenty five tables derived from Part Two arranged in three sections:

Key national indicators
- Population
- Geography
- The economy

Construction output indicators
- Construction output
- Construction output per capita

Construction cost data
- Mason/bricklayer and unskilled labour costs
- Site manager and qualified architect labour costs
- Material costs - Cement and concrete aggregates
- Material costs - Ready mixed concrete and reinforcing steel
- Material costs - Common bricks and hollow concrete blocks
- Material costs - Softwood for joinery and quilt insulation
- Material costs - Sheet glass and plasterboard
- Material costs - Emulsion paint and vinyl floor tiles
- Approximate estimating - Factories and warehouses
- Approximate estimating - Offices
- Approximate estimating - Housing
- Approximate estimating - Hospitals and schools
- Approximate estimating - Theatres and sports halls
- Approximate estimating - Hotels

The first five tables are based on the Key data sheets at the beginning of each country section, the remainder are drawn from the Construction cost data in each country section. Each table is prefaced by explanatory notes. There are inherent dangers in attempting to compare international data, particularly where two sets of data are used (e.g.construction output and population) and, even more so, when exchange rates are used. While these tables can provide useful initial comparisons between countries they should, nevertheless, be used with caution.

6. Key national indicators

POPULATION

The table below summarizes population statistics for all seventeen countries included in this book. The table highlights not only the differences in total population among the countries but also variations in the distribution of population between age groups within countries, in population growth rates and in the proportion of the population living in urban areas.

The table includes the most populous country in the world (China) and three others from the top ten most populous countries (the United States, Indonesia and Japan). The developed countries generally have high rates of urbanisation though so also do the two city states of Hong Kong and Singapore. The developed countries also have relatively low proportions of population under 15 and relatively high populations over 65. Interestingly the population of working age (between 15 and 65) does not vary by so much; it is between 56% (Vietnam) and 72% (Hong Kong) with the figures for the rest of the countries in the range of 60%-70%.

Population growth rates vary from less than 1% per annum in the UK, New Zealand, Taiwan and Japan to over 2% in Philippines, Vietnam and Malaysia.

| | Population | | | | |
| | Total | Urban | Under 15 | Over 65 | Growth |
Country	(m)	%	%	%	% pa
Australia	17.6	85.0	22.0	11.0	1.5
Brunei	0.3	n.a.	n.a.	n.a.	n.a.
China	1,178.4	29.0	27.0	7.0	1.4
Hong Kong	5.8	95.0	19.0	9.0	1.1
Indonesia	187.2	33.0	35.0	3.0	1.7
Japan	124.8	77.0	17.2	13.1	0.5
Malaysia	19.0	52.0	36.0	4.0	2.5
New Zealand	3.5	86.0	23.0	11.0	0.9
Philippines	64.8	52.0	37.0	4.0	2.3
Singapore	2.8	100.0	23.0	7.0	1.1
South Korea	44.1	78.0	25.0	6.0	1.1
Sri Lanka	17.9	22.0	32.0	4.0	1.5
Taiwan	21.1	52.0	25.0	11.0	0.9
Thailand	58.1	19.0	33.0	2.0	1.7
UK	57.9	89.0	19.0	16.0	0.3
USA	258.3	76.0	21.5	12.9	1.0
Vietnam	71.3	20.0	39.0	5.0	2.2

THE ECONOMY

This table summarizes economic data for the countries included in this book. In the country sections Gross Domestic Product (GDP) figures are given in national currencies; here they have been converted to US dollars using the average exchange rate for the appropriate year - usually 1993. The table contains the two wealthiest nations in the world - the US and Japan - and some of the poorest. As with population density, GDP per capita is a more helpful measure of national wealth than total GDP. Again, the US and Japan have amongst the highest GDPs per capita in the world. Brunei has one of the highest GDP per capita in the world while total GDP is less than a tenth of neighbouring Malaysia.

The GDP growth rates are perhaps more interesting indicators of potential wealth. The growth rates are real, that is the effects of inflation are excluded. South Korea, China, Thailand and Hong Kong have all doubled or more than doubled their GDP in the past decade. With the exception of Sri Lanka and the Philippines, average annual inflation 1980-1993 in all countries is below 10%, often well below.

Country	1993 GDP US$ bn	GDP per capita US$	1980-1993 GDP Growth (real) % pa	Inflation average % pa
Australia	279.55	15,883.54	3.1	6.1
Brunei	4.00	14,445.81	n.a.	-5.1.
China	543.25	461.02	9.6	7.0
Hong Kong	116.19	20,032.53	6.5	7.9
Indonesia	159.40	851.50	5.8	8.5
Japan	4,325.31	34,741.00	2.5	1.5
Malaysia	64.48	3,392.89	6.2	2.2
New Zealand	43.17	14,509.03	1.5	8.5
Philippines	54.91	847.33	1.4	13.6
Singapore	54.80	19,575.12	6.9	2.5
South Korea	331.19	7,509.97	9.1	6.3
Sri Lanka	10.32	576.71	4.0	11.1
Taiwan	215.52	10,214.31	6.8	3.9
Thailand	124.40	2,141.06	8.2	4.3
UK	952.38	16,448.98	2.5	5.6
USA	6,343.00	24,557.00	2.2	3.8
Vietnam	12.92	181.22	7.9	n.a.

GEOGRAPHY

The table below summarizes geographical statistics for the countries included in this book. As with population the table highlights the differences between countries. It includes two out of the four largest countries in the world (China and the US); it also includes two of the smallest (Hong Kong and Singapore).

The figures for population density and the percentage of national population in the largest city are perhaps more helpful indicators of land use than total area. As might be expected the table shows that the country with one of the largest areas in the world (Australia) has almost the lowest population density, while Hong Kong with over 5,000 persons per km² has one of the highest population densities in the world. The percentage of national population in the largest city gives an indication of the relative importance of that city - usually the capital.

| Country | Land area | | Population | Largest city | |
	Total 000 km²	Agriculture area %	per km²	000's	% of total
Australia	7,713.00	63	2.3	3,500	19.9
Brunei	5.77	2	47.9	46	16.8
China	9,561.00	42	123.3	11,000	0.9
Hong Kong	1.08	8	5,390.3	n.a.	n.a.
Indonesia	1,905.00	18	98.3	9,200	4.9
Japan	378.00	14	330.2	11,900	9.5
Malaysia	330.00	39	57.6	1,340	7.1
New Zealand	271.00	53	12.9	886	25.3
Philippines	300.00	24	216.0	8,500	2.8
Singapore	0.64	2	4,381.8	n.a.	n.a.
South Korea	99.00	23	445.5	10,400	23.6
Sri Lanka	66.00	36	271.2	2,000	11.2
Taiwan	36.00	25	586.1	2,700	12.8
Thailand	513.00	41	113.3	7,000	12.0
UK	245.00	76	236.3	6,700	11.6
USA	9,809.00	47	26.3	3,700	1.4
Vietnam	332.00	22	214.8	2,200	3.1

7.Construction output indicators

CONSTRUCTION OUTPUT

The table below summarizes construction output statistics from the country Key data sheets. On the Key data sheet for each country an output figure is given in national currency and the year to which it relates is noted.

In this summary table, figures in national currency are listed and, in addition, in order to facilitate (crude) comparisons, US dollar, pound sterling and yen equivalents are presented for each figure. The currency conversions have been carried out using appropriate exchange rates. As noted earlier, construction statistics, including those for construction output, are notoriously unreliable and, in addition, national definitions of construction output vary widely. It would, therefore, be unwise to draw too many conclusions from this table.

Country	National unit of currency	Construction output National currency	UK£	US $	billions Yen
Australia	A$	28.60	12.77	19.32	2,102.94
Brunei	B$	0.60	0.24	0.37	40.27
China	Rmb	210.50	24.11	36.42	3,971.70
Hong Kong	HK$	41.50	3.54	5.35	583.68
Indonesia	Rp	19,790.00	6.45	9.57	1,175.88
Japan	¥	48,560.00	294.75	445.50	48,560.00
Malaysia	RM$	11.60	2.98	4.51	491.53
New Zealand	NZ$	3.20	1.15	1.74	189.35
Philippines	P	79.60	1.96	2.96	284.18
Singapore	S$	6.60	2.69	4.07	442.95
South Korea	Won	21,250.00	17.53	26.50	2,889.19
Sri Lanka	Rp	36.00	0.50	0.75	81.67
Taiwan	NT$	319.20	7.98	12.07	1,315.75
Thailand	Bt	217.20	5.67	8.58	935.00
UK	£	33.40	33.40	50.61	5,475.41
USA	US$	234.70	155.43	234.70	25,510.87
Vietnam	Dong	10,101.00	0.63	0.96	104.19

CONSTRUCTION OUTPUT PER CAPITA

This table is based on the previous one, but has each figure for construction output divided by the population of that country. Despite the uncertainty of both construction and population data and the limitations of exchange rates, the table reveals some useful indicators of construction activity. Japan has the highest by far construction output per capita - almost 300 times greater than the lowest in the table (Vietnam). Like Vietnam, China and Sri Lanka, Indonesia and the Philippines have output per capita of less than US$100. The remainder of the Asia Pacific countries are spread over the range from Thailand (US$148) to Hong Kong (US$923). The UK and the US are similar to Hong Kong; Australia and Singapore are higher.

Country	National unit of currency	Construction output per capita			
		National currency	UK£	US$	Yen
Australia	A$	1,625	725.45	1,097.97	119,485.29
Brunei	B$	1,232	502.81	760.42	82,676.78
China	Rmb	179	20.46	30.91	3,370.42
Hong Kong	HK$	7,155	611.03	923.25	100,635.34
Indonesia	Rp	105,716	34.48	51.10	6,281.39
Japan	¥	389,103	2,361.78	3,569.75	389,102.56
Malaysia	RM$	611	156.95	237.56	25,869.76
New Zealand	NZ$	914	328.88	496.89	54,099.75
Philippines	P	1,228	30.26	45.73	4,385.56
Singapore	S$	2,357	962.10	1,455.03	158,197.51
South Korea	Won	481,859	397.57	600.82	65,514.54
Sri Lanka	Rp	2,011	27.69	41.86	4,562.55
Taiwan	NT$	15,128	378.39	571.95	62,357.63
Thailand	Bt	3,738	97.66	147.65	16,092.91
UK	£	577	576.86	874.03	94,566.66
USA	US$	909	601.74	908.63	98,764.50
Vietnam	Dong	141,669	8.87	13.41	1,461.26

8. Construction cost data

MASON/BRICKLAYER AND UNSKILLED LABOUR COSTS

This table summarizes hourly labour costs for a mason/bricklayer and for unskilled labour in each country as at third quarter of 1995. The figures in national currency are taken from each country's construction cost data and have been converted into pound sterling, US dollar and yen equivalents using third quarter of 1995 exchange rates. As indicated earlier, the cost of labour is the cost to a contractor of employing that employee; it is based on the employee's income but also includes allowances for a range of mandatory and voluntary contributions which vary from country to country.

It is probable that the definitions of skilled and unskilled and what is included in labour costs varies between countries, thus these figures should not be taken as strictly comparable. The ranking and relative level of labour costs are broadly similar to the GDP per capita figures though there are interesting detailed differences in ranking.

Country	Mason/bricklayer National Currency	UK£	US$	hour Yen	Unskilled labour National Currency	UK£	US$	hour Yen
Australia	27.00	12.50	19.85	1,824	24.00	11.11	17.65	1,622
Brunei	n.a.				n.a.			
China	9.80	0.74	1.18	108	3.95	0.30	0.48	44
Hong Kong	93.90	7.65	12.13	1,113	62.15	5.07	8.03	736
Indonesia	1,125	0.32	0.50	46	625	0.18	0.28	26
Japan	n.a.				n.a.			
Malaysia	7.50	1.92	3.04	279	3.90	1.00	1.58	145
New Zealand	n.a.				n.a.			
Philippines	31.25	0.77	1.22	112	22.65	0.56	0.88	81
Singapore	7.10	3.18	5.04	464	n.a.			
South Korea	7,000	5.79	9.17	860	4,167	3.45	5.46	512
Sri Lanka	46.90	0.58	0.93	85	33.15	0.41	0.65	60
Taiwan	53.15	1.25	1.99	182	35.40	0.84	1.32	121
Thailand	n.a.				23.00	0.58	0.92	85
United Kingdom	5.90	5.90	9.37	855	4.95	4.95	7.86	717
United States	40.70	25.60	40.70	3,734	30.65	19.28	30.65	2,812
Vietnam	8,600	0.49	0.78	72	n.a.			

SITE MANAGER AND QUALIFIED ARCHITECT LABOUR RATES

This table is from the same source as the previous and is presented in the same way. Site managers and qualified architects are representative of staff rather than site labour.

Country	Site manager National Currency	UK£	US$	hour Yen	Qualified architect National Currency	UK£	US$	hour Yen
Australia	60.00	27.78	44.12	4,054	65.00	30.09	47.79	4,392
Brunei	35.30	15.83	25.04	2,307	32.35	14.51	22.94	2,114
China	n.a.				n.a.			
Hong Kong	180.00	14.67	23.26	2,133	271.60	22.14	35.09	3,218
Indonesia	n.a.				n.a.			
Japan	n.a.				n.a.			
Malaysia	39.30	10.05	15.91	1,461	28.60	7.31	11.58	1,063
New Zealand	n.a.				n.a.			
Philippines	105.50	2.59	4.11	377	49.65	1.22	1.93	177
Singapore	41.10	18.43	29.15	2,686	34.05	15.27	24.15	2,225
South Korea	11,285	9.33	14.79	1,387	12,075	9.99	15.83	1,484
Sri Lanka	309.40	3.85	6.11	560	140.65	1.75	2.78	255
Taiwan	n.a.				n.a.			
Thailand	n.a.				n.a.			
United Kingdom	20.95	20.95	33.25	3,036	16.25	16.25	25.79	2,355
United States	47.70	30.00	47.70	4,376	n.a.			
Vietnam	n.a.				n.a.			

MATERIALS COSTS - CEMENT AND CONCRETE AGGREGATES

The table below summarizes costs per tonne for cement and costs per m³ for concrete aggregates as at third quarter of 1995. The figures in national currency are taken from each country's construction cost data and converted into US dollar, pound sterling and yen equivalents using third quarter of 1995 exchange rates. Converted figures have been rounded to the nearest whole number.

Costs are as delivered to site in a major - usually the capital - city. They assume that the materials are in quantities as required for a medium sized construction project and that the location of the works would be neither constrained or remote. Material costs generally exclude value added or similar taxes.

Despite the fact that there are internationally recognized standards of quality for cement and that it is one of the few internationally traded construction materials, the variation in cost between countries is remarkably large (from US$60 to US$210 per tonne). This may well be a result of controlled prices or of import protection or of undervalued or overvalued currencies. The variation in aggregate costs is less surprising; quality and availability can be expected to vary widely within, let alone between, countries and a large proportion of aggregate costs can be in their transportation.

Country	Cement National Currency	UK£	US$	tonne Yen	Aggregate for concrete National Currency	UK£	US$	m³ Yen
Australia	n.a.				n.a.			
Brunei	190	85.20	134.75	12,418	40.00	17.94	28.37	2,614
China	500	37.97	60.17	5,519	65.00	4.94	7.82	717
Hong Kong	675	55.01	87.21	7,998	85.00	6.93	10.98	1,007
Indonesia	200,000	56.25	89.15	8,177	31,500	8.86	14.04	1,288
Japan	16,000	110.05	174.42	16,000	5,700	39.20	62.14	5,700
Malaysia	192	49.10	77.73	7,138	46.20	11.82	18.70	1,717
New Zealand	315	132.35	210.00	19,325	79.00	33.19	52.67	4,847
Philippines	2,725	66.90	106.03	9,729	500.00	12.28	19.46	1,785
Singapore	150	67.26	106.38	9,804	17.50	7.85	12.41	1,144
South Korea	65,000	53.76	85.19	7,987	14,000	11.58	18.35	1,720
Sri Lanka	5,200	64.77	102.67	9,417	1,000	12.46	19.74	1,811
Taiwan	3,200	75.51	119.67	10,978	320.00	7.55	11.97	1,098
Thailand	1,660	42.12	66.75	6,123	300.00	7.61	12.06	1,107
United Kingdom	69.20	69.20	109.84	10,029	8.75	8.75	13.89	1,268
United States	133	83.65	133.00	12,202	11.75	7.39	11.75	1,078
Vietnam	12,860,200	72.56	115.00	10,549	132,300	7.57	12.00	1,100

MATERIALS COSTS - READY MIXED CONCRETE AND REINFORCING STEEL

The table below summarizes costs per m³ for ready mixed concrete and costs per tonne for reinforcing steel as at third quarter of 1995. The figures in national currency are taken from each country's construction cost data and converted into US dollar, pound sterling and yen equivalents using third quarter of 1995 exchange rates.

Costs are as delivered to site in a major - usually the capital - city. They assume that the materials are in quantities as required for a medium sized construction project and that the location of the works would be neither constrained or remote. Material costs generally exclude value added or similar taxes.

The range of costs for reinforcing steel is rather less than that for cement or for ready mixed concrete; from a low of US$343 per tonne in Japan to a high of US$933 per tonne in New Zealand.

Country	Ready mixed concrete			m³	Mild steel reinforcement			tonne
	National Currency	UK£	US$	Yen	National Currency	UK£	US$	Yen
Australia	132	61.11	97.06	8,919	1,000	462.96	735.29	67,568
Brunei	185	82.96	131.21	12,092	600	269.06	425.53	39,216
China	n.a.				3,100	235.38	373.04	34,216
Hong Kong	550	44.82	71.06	6,517	2,900	236.35	374.68	34,360
Indonesia	170,000	47.81	75.78	6,950	835,000	234.84	372.21	34,137
Japan	13,400	92.17	146.08	13,400	31,500	216.66	343.40	31,500
Malaysia	148	37.85	59.92	5,502	1,120	286.45	453.44	41,636
New Zealand	182	76.47	121.33	11,166	1,400	588.24	933.33	85,890
Philippines	2,690	66.04	104.67	9,604	14,778	362.83	575.02	52,760
Singapore	101	45.29	71.63	6,601	600	269.06	425.53	39,216
South Korea	42,800	35.40	56.09	5,259	280,000	231.60	366.97	34,404
Sri Lanka	4,900	61.04	96.74	8,874	35,000	435.97	691.02	63,383
Taiwan	2,200	51.91	82.27	7,547	n.a.			
Thailand	1,590	40.35	63.93	5,865	11,500	291.80	462.40	42,420
United Kingdom	42.70	42.70	67.78	6,188	320	320.00	507.94	46,377
United States	52.50	33.02	52.50	4,817	573	360.38	573.00	52,569
Vietnam	882,200	50.47	80.00	7,338	4,962,600	283.92	450.00	41,279

MATERIALS COSTS - COMMON BRICKS AND HOLLOW CONCRETE BLOCKS

The table below summarizes costs per 1,000 for bricks and blocks as at third quarter of 1995. The figures in national currency are taken from each country's construction cost data and converted to US dollar, pound sterling and yen equivalents using third quarter of 1995 exchange rates.

Costs are as delivered to site in a major - usually the capital - city. They assume that the materials are in quantities as required for a medium sized construction project and that the location of the works would be neither constrained or remote. Material costs generally exclude value added or similar taxes.

The costs of bricks and blocks vary by the availability of raw materials and the national practices in walling construction. Where brick-making clays are not readily available, for example, the cost of bricks may be relatively high. It is probably reasonable to assume that brick dimensions are broadly similar; the dimensions of concrete blocks, however, can and do vary widely.

| Country | Common bricks | | | 1,000 | Hollow concrete blocks | | | 1,000 |
	National Currency	UK£	US$	Yen	National Currency	UK£	US$	Yen
Australia	380	175.93	279.41	25,676	132	61.11	97.06	8,919
Brunei	170	76.23	120.57	11,111	450	201.79	319.15	29,412
China	265	20.12	31.89	2,925	2,000	151.86	240.67	22,075
Hong Kong	870	70.90	112.40	10,308	4,000	326.00	516.80	47,393
Indonesia	100,000	28.12	44.58	4,088	380,000	106.87	169.39	15,536
Japan	80,000	550.24	872.12	80,000	244,000	1,678	2,660	244,000
Malaysia	250	63.29	101.21	9,294	1,430	365.73	578.95	53,160
New Zealand	970	407.56	646.67	59,509	2,300	966.39	1,533	141,104
Philippines	4,300	105.57	167.32	15,352	6,700	164.50	260.70	23,920
Singapore	250	112.11	177.30	16,340	750	336.32	531.91	49,020
South Korea	40,000	33.09	52.42	4,915	500,000	413.56	655.31	61,436
Sri Lanka	1,750	21.80	34.55	3,169	14,100	175.64	278.38	25,534
Taiwan	n.a.				n.a.			
Thailand	550.00	13.96	22.11	2,029	3,750	95.15	150.78	13,833
United Kingdom	115	115.00	182.54	16,667	820	820.00	1,302	118,841
United States	235	147.80	235.00	21,560	950	597.48	950.00	87,156
Vietnam	320,000	18.31	29.02	2,662	6,617,000	378.57	600.02	55,041

MATERIALS COSTS - SOFTWOOD FOR JOINERY AND QUILT INSULATION

The table below summarizes costs per m³ for softwood for joinery and costs per m² for 100mm thick quilt insulation as at third quarter of 1995. The figures in national currency are taken from each country's construction cost data and converted to US dollar, pound sterling and yen equivalents using third quarter of 1995 exchange rates.

Costs are as delivered to site in a major - usually the capital - city. They assume that the materials are in quantities as required for a medium sized construction project and that the location of the works would be neither constrained or remote. Material costs generally exclude value added or similar taxes.

Country	Softwood for joinery			m³	Quilt insulation 100mm			m²
	National Currency	UK£	US$	Yen	National Currency	UK£	US$	Yen
Australia	1,200	555.56	882.35	81,081	9.00	4.17	6.62	608
Brunei	2,350	1,054	1,667	153,595	7.00	3.14	4.96	458
China	1,600	121.49	192.54	17,660	50.00	3.80	6.02	552
Hong Kong	1,700	138.55	219.64	20,142	45.00	3.67	5.81	533
Indonesia	1,200,000	337.49	534.92	49,060	31,000	8.72	13.82	1,267
Japan	103,000	708.44	1,123	103,000	n.a.			
Malaysia	450	115.09	182.19	16,729	9.00	2.30	3.64	335
New Zealand	900	378.15	600.00	55,215	10.00	4.20	6.67	613
Philippines	16,526	405.75	643.04	59,000	342.00	8.40	13.31	1,221
Singapore	n.a.				6.00	2.69	4.26	392
South Korea	687,700	568.82	901.31	84,500	5,100	4.22	6.68	627
Sri Lanka	n.a.				n.a.			
Taiwan	6,500	153.37	243.08	22,298	n.a.			
Thailand	14,000	355.24	562.93	51,641	150.00	3.81	6.03	553
United Kingdom	300	300.00	476.19	43,478	2.20	2.20	3.49	319
United States	n.a.				n.a.			
Vietnam	n.a.				110,300	6.31	10.00	917

MATERIALS COSTS - SHEET GLASS AND PLASTERBOARD

The table below summarizes costs per m² for sheet or float glass and for plasterboard as at third quarter of 1995. The figures in national currency are taken from each country's construction cost data and converted to US dollar, pound sterling and yen equivalents using third quarter of 1995 exchange rates.

Costs are as delivered to site in a major - usually the capital - city. They assume that the materials are in quantities as required for a medium sized construction project and that the location of the works would be neither constrained or remote. Material costs generally exclude value added or similar taxes.

Country	Sheet/float glass National Currency	UK£	US$	m² Yen	Plasterboard 9-12mm National Currency	UK£	US$	m² Yen
Australia	32.00	14.81	23.53	2,162	4.60	2.13	3.38	311
Brunei	35.00	15.70	24.82	2,288	7.00	3.14	4.96	458
China	36.00	2.73	4.33	397	18.00	1.37	2.17	199
Hong Kong	80.00	6.52	10.34	948	110.00	8.96	14.21	1,303
Indonesia	42,000	11.81	18.72	1,717	14,900	4.19	6.64	609
Japan	1,990	13.69	21.69	1,990	150.00	1.03	1.64	150
Malaysia	43.00	11.00	17.41	1,599	18.00	4.60	7.29	669
New Zealand	130	54.62	86.67	7,975	16.00	6.72	10.67	982
Philippines	475	11.66	1.58	16.96	672.00	16.50	26.15	2,399
Singapore	86.00	38.57	60.99	5,621	4.00	1.79	2.84	261
South Korea	5,400	4.47	7.08	664	1,290	1.07	1.69	159
Sri Lanka	450	5.61	8.88	815	n.a.			
Taiwan	n.a.				n.a.			
Thailand	450	11.42	18.09	1,660	55.00	1.40	2.21	203
United Kingdom	26.95	26.95	42.78	3,906	1.20	1.20	1.90	174
United States	28.30	17.80	28.30	2,596	1.65	1.04	1.65	151
Vietnam	154,400	8.83	14.00	1,284	154,400	8.83	14.00	1,284

MATERIALS COSTS - EMULSION PAINT
AND VINYL FLOOR TILES

The table below summarizes costs per litre for emulsion paint and costs per m²
for vinyl tiles as at third quarter of 1995. The figures in national currency are
taken from each country's construction cost data and converted to US dollar,
pound sterling and yen equivalents using third quarter of 1995 exchange
rates.

Costs are as delivered to site in a major - usually the capital - city. They
assume that the materials are in quantities as required for a medium sized
construction project and that the location of the works would be neither
constrained or remote. Material costs generally exclude value added or
similar taxes.

Country	Emulsion paint National Currency	UK£	US$	litre Yen	Vinyl floor tiles National Currency	UK£	US$	m² Yen
Australia	n.a.				17.75	8.22	13.05	1,199
Brunei	9.00	4.04	6.38	588	16.00	7.17	11.35	1,046
China	5.00	0.38	0.60	55	30.00	2.28	3.61	331
Hong Kong	22.00	1.79	2.84	261	45.00	3.67	5.81	533
Indonesia	7,000	1.97	3.12	286	10,000	2.81	4.46	409
Japan	335.00	2.30	3.65	335	10,000	68.78	109.02	10,000
Malaysia	11.00	2.81	4.45	409	28.50	7.29	11.54	1,059
New Zealand	7.50	3.15	5.00	460	30.00	12.61	20.00	1,840
Philippines	52.80	1.30	2.05	189	290.00	7.12	11.28	1,035
Singapore	3.50	1.57	2.48	229	6.00	2.69	4.26	392
South Korea	5,460	4.52	7.16	671	3,340	2.76	4.38	410
Sri Lanka	200.00	2.49	3.95	362	n.a.			
Taiwan	n.a.				n.a.			
Thailand	59.40	1.51	2.39	219	160.00	4.06	6.43	590
United Kingdom	2.55	2.55	4.05	370	5.00	5.00	7.94	725
United States	2.65	1.67	2.65	243	19.90	12.52	19.90	1,826
Vietnam	55,100	3.15	5.00	458	110,300	6.31	10.00	917

APPROXIMATE ESTIMATING - FACTORIES AND WAREHOUSES

This table summarizes approximate estimating costs per square metre for factories and warehouses. Approximate estimating costs are averages as incurred by building clients for typical buildings in major - usually capital - cities in the third quarter of 1995. They are based upon the total floor area of all storeys, measured between external walls and without deduction for internal walls. Approximate estimating costs generally include mechanical and electrical installations but exclude furniture, loose or special equipment, and external works; they also exclude fees for professional services. Where a range of costs has been given, the mid point is shown. The figures in national currency are taken from each country's construction cost data and converted to US dollar, pound sterling and yen equivalents using third quarter of 1995 exchange rates.

It must be borne in mind that even where costs are given under the same description in one or more countries, this is not to say that they are identical, or even physically similar. Approximate estimating costs for a particular country are for the normal standards prevailing in that country. Quality and technical standards vary widely and there are differences between countries in what is, and is not, included. The table, therefore, should be used with care.

Country	Factories for owner occupation (light industrial use)			m^2	Warehouse,low bay (6-8m high) for letting (no heating)			m^2
	National Currency	UK£	US$	Yen	National Currency	UK£	US$	Yen
Australia	470	217.59	345.59	31,757	350	162.04	257.35	23,649
Brunei	720	322.87	510.64	47,059	690	309.42	489.36	45,098
China	n.a.				n.a.			
Hong Kong	5,400	440.10	697.67	63,981	5000	407.50	646.00	59,242
Indonesia	650,600	182.98	290.00	26.599	560,850	157.74	250.00	22,929
Japan	n.a.				170,000	11,170	1,853	170,000
Malaysia	700	179.03	283.40	26,022	n.a.			
New Zealand	410.00	172.27	273.33	25,153	400	168.07	266.67	24,540
Philippines	11,300	277.44	439.69	40,343	7,500	184.14	291.83	26,776
Singapore	950	426.01	673.76	62,092	850	381.17	602.84	55,556
South Korea	611,000	505.38	800.79	75,075	343,000	283.71	449.54	42,145
Sri Lanka	9,500	118.34	187.56	17,204	n.a.			
Taiwan	n.a.				n.a.			
Thailand	n.a.				n.a.			
United Kingdom	313	313.00	496.83	45,362	171	171.00	271.43	24,783
United States	484	304.40	484.00	44,404	258	162.26	258.00	23,670
Vietnam	7,720,000	441.67	700.04	64,216	5,514,000	315.46	500.00	45,866

APPROXIMATE ESTIMATING - OFFICES

This table summarizes approximate estimating costs per square metre for two different types of office buildings. Approximate estimating costs are averages as incurred by building clients for typical buildings in major - usually capital - cities in the third quarter of 1995. They are based upon the total floor area of all storeys, measured between external walls and without deduction for internal walls. Approximate estimating costs generally include mechanical and electrical installations but exclude furniture, loose or special equipment, and external works; they also exclude fees for professional services. Where a range of costs has been given, the mid point is shown. The figures in national currency are taken from each country's construction cost data and converted to US dollar, pound sterling and yen equivalents using third quarter of 1995 exchange rates.

It must be borne in mind that even where costs are given under the same description in one or more countries, this is not to say that they are identical, or even physically similar. Approximate estimating costs for a particular country are for the normal standards prevailing in that country. Quality and technical standards vary widely and there are differences between countries in what is, and is not, included. The table, therefore, should be used with care.

Country	Offices for letting, 5-10 storeys air conditioned			m^2	Prestige/headquarters office high rise, air conditioned			m^2
	National Currency	UK£	US$	Yen	National Currency	UK£	US$	Yen
Australia	1,150	532.41	845.59	77,703	2,100	972.22	1,544	141,892
Brunei	1,150	515.70	815.60	75,163	1,570	704.04	1,113	102,614
China	n.a.				9,141	694.08	1,100	100,894
Hong Kong	8,000	652.00	1,034	94,787	12,500	1,019	1,615	148,104
Indonesia	1,346,000	378.56	600.00	55,029	1,963,000	552.08	875.03	80,253
Japan	n.a.				380,000	2,614	4,143	380,000
Malaysia	1,400	358.06	566.80	52,045	2,153	550.64	871.66	80,037
New Zealand	1,750	735.29	1,167	107,362	2,400	1,008	1,600	147,239
Philippines	17,500	429.66	680.93	62,478	28,000	687.45	1,090	99,964
Singapore	1,600	717.49	1,135	104,575	2,300	1,031	1,631	150,327
South Korea	918,000	759.31	1,203	112,797	1,071,000	885.86	1,404	131.597
Sri Lanka	28,700	357.50	566.63	51,974	32,300	402.34	637.71	58,493
Taiwan	n.a.				n.a.			
Thailand	n.a.				20,000	507.49	804.18	73,774
United Kingdom	690	690.00	1,095	100,000	1,390	1,390	2,206	201,449
United States	775	487.42	775.00	71,101	1,216	764.78	1,216	111,560
Vietnam	8,823,000	504.78	800.05	73,390	12,131,000	694.03	1,100	100,907

APPROXIMATE ESTIMATING - HOUSING

This table summarizes approximate estimating costs per square metre for housing. Two types of housing have been taken: private sector, single family houses and medium quality, medium rise apartments. In countries where housing types did not match exactly these descriptions, the nearest equivalent has been taken.

Approximate estimating costs are averages as incurred by building clients for typical buildings in major - usually capital - cities in the third quarter of 1995. They are based upon the total floor area of all storeys, measured between external walls and without deduction for internal walls. Approximate estimating costs generally include mechanical and electrical installations but exclude furniture, loose or special equipment, and external works; they also exclude fees for professional services.

Where a range of costs has been given, the mid point is shown. The figures in national currency are taken from each country's construction cost data and converted to US dollar, pound sterling and yen equivalents using third quarter of 1995 exchange rates.

It must be borne in mind that even where costs are given under the same description in one or more countries, this is not to say that they are identical, or even physically similar. Approximate estimating costs for a particular country are for the normal standards prevailing in that country. Quality and technical standards vary widely and there are differences between countries in what is, and is not, included. The table, therefore, should be used with care.

Country	Single family housing private, detached, semi detached			m^2	Private sector apartment building (standard specification)			m^2
	National Currency	UK£	US$	Yen	National Currency	UK£	US$	Yen
Australia	600	277.78	441.18	40,541	1,100	509.26	808.82	74,324
Brunei	950	426.01	673.76	62,092	1,100	493.27	780.14	71,895
China	n.a.				n.a.			
Hong Kong	7200	586.80	930.23	85,308	5,700	464.55	736.43	67,536
Indonesia	n.a.				1,402,100	394.33	625.00	57,322
Japan	n.a.				n.a.			
Malaysia	646	165.22	261.54	24,015	850	217.39	344.13	31,599
New Zealand	850	357.14	566.67	52,147	1,800	756.30	1,200	110,429
Philippines	7,200	176.77	280.16	25,705	16,500	405.11	642.02	58,908
Singapore	1,800	807.17	1,277	117,647	1,300	582.96	921.99	84,967
South Korea	688,000	569.07	901.70	84,536	611,000	505.38	800.79	75,075
Sri Lanka	10,760	134.03	212.44	19,486	31,850	396.74	628.83	57,678
Taiwan	n.a.				n.a.			
Thailand	12,500	317.18	502.61	46,108	13,500	342.55	542.82	49,797
United Kingdom	325	325.00	515.87	47,101	389.00	389	617.46	56,377
United States	538	338.36	538.00	49,358	689	433.33	689.00	56,377
Vietnam	n.a.				7,720,000	441.67	700.00	64,216

APPROXIMATE ESTIMATING - HOSPITALS AND SCHOOLS

This table summarizes approximate estimating costs per square metre for general hospitals and secondary or middle schools. Approximate estimating costs are averages as incurred by building clients for typical buildings in major - usually capital - cities in the third quarter of 1995. They are based upon the total floor area of all storeys, measured between external walls and without deduction for internal walls. Approximate estimating costs generally include mechanical and electrical installations but exclude furniture, loose or special equipment, and external works; they also exclude fees for professional services. Where a range of costs has been given, the mid point is shown. The figures in national currency are taken from each country's construction cost data and converted to US dollar, pound sterling and yen equivalents using third quarter of 1995 exchange rates.

It must be borne in mind that even where costs are given under the same description in one or more countries, this is not to say that they are identical, or even physically similar. Approximate estimating costs for a particular country are for the normal standards prevailing in that country. Quality and technical standards vary widely and there are differences between countries in what is, and is not, included. The table, therefore, should be used with care.

Country	General hospitals National Currency	UK£	US$	m² Yen	Secondary/middle schools National Currency	UK£	US$	m² Yen
Australia	1,750	810.19	1,287	118,243	1,000	462.96	735.29	67,568
Brunei	1,730	775.78	1,227	113,072	1,160	520.18	822.70	75,817
China	n.a.				n.a.			
Hong Kong	11,000	896.50	1,421	130,332	5,000	407.50	645.99	59,242
Indonesia	n.a.				n.a.			
Japan	450,000	3,095	4,906	450,000	270,000	1,857	2,943.42	270,000
Malaysia	n.a.				538	137.60	217.81	20,000
New Zealand	2,400	1,008	1,600	147,239	1,100	462.18	733.33	67,485
Philippines	30,700	753.74	1,195	109,604	13,300	326.54	517.51	47,483
Singapore	1,750	784.75	1,241	114,379	1,100	493.27	780.14	71,895
South Korea	1,334,000	1,103	1,748	163,912	688,000	569.07	901.70	84,536
Sri Lanka	16,300	203.04	321.82	29,518	n.a.			
Taiwan	n.a.				n.a.			
Thailand	n.a.				n.a.			
United Kingdom	775	775	1,230	112,319	576	576.00	914.29	83,478
United States	1,270	798.74	1,270	116,514	807	507.55	807.00	74,037
Vietnam	n.a.				n.a.			

APPROXIMATE ESTIMATING - THEATRES AND SPORTS HALLS

This table summarizes approximate estimating costs per square metre for theatres and sports halls. Approximate estimating costs are averages as incurred by building clients for typical buildings in major - usually capital - cities in the third quarter of 1995. They are based upon the total floor area of all storeys, measured between external walls and without deduction for internal walls. Approximate estimating costs generally include mechanical and electrical installations but exclude furniture, loose or special equipment, and external works; they also exclude fees for professional services. Where a range of costs has been given, the mid point is shown. The figures in national currency are taken from each country's construction cost data and converted to US dollar, pound sterling and yen equivalents using third quarter of 1995 exchange rates.

It must be borne in mind that even where costs are given under the same description in one or more countries, this is not to say that they are identical, or even physically similar. Approximate estimating costs for a particular country are for the normal standards prevailing in that country. Quality and technical standards vary widely and there are differences between countries in what is, and is not, included. The table, therefore, should be used with care.

Country	Theatres including seating and stage equipment, over 500 seats			m^2	Sports halls including changing and social facilities			m^2
	National Currency	UK£	US$	Yen	National Currency	UK£	US$	Yen
Australia	2,100	972.22	1,544	141,892	1,000	462.96	735.29	67,568
Brunei	3,320	1,489	2,355	216,993	1,780	798.21	1,262	116,340
China	n.a.				n.a.			
Hong Kong	12,500	1,019	1,615	148,104	n.a.			
Indonesia	n.a.				n.a.			
Japan	520,000	3,577	5,669	520,000	n.a.			
Malaysia	n.a.				969	247.83	392.31	36,022
New Zealand	1,500	630.25	1,000	92,025	1,300	546.22	866.67	79,755
Philippines	25,200	618.71	980.54	89,968	16,300	400.20	634.24	58,194
Singapore	2,800	1,256	1,986	183,007	1,200	538.12	851.06	78,431
South Korea	1,529,000	1,265	2,004	187,872	1,334,000	1,103	1,748	163,912
Sri Lanka	n.a.				n.a.			
Taiwan	n.a.				n.a.			
Thailand	n.a.				n.a.			
United Kingdom	972	972.00	1,543	140,870	478	478.00	758.73	69,275
United States	807	507.55	807	74,037	n.a.			
Vietnam	n.a.				n.a.			

APPROXIMATE ESTIMATING - HOTELS

This table summarizes approximate estimating costs per square metre for two
types of hotels. Approximate estimating costs are averages as incurred by
building clients for typical buildings in major - usually capital - cities in the
third quarter of 1995. They are based upon the total floor area of all storeys,
measured between external walls and without deduction for internal walls.
Approximate estimating costs generally include mechanical and electrical
installations but exclude furniture, loose or special equipment, and external
works; they also exclude fees for professional services. Where a range of
costs has been given, the mid point is shown. The figures in national currency
are taken from each country's construction cost data and converted to US
dollar, pound sterling and yen equivalents using third quarter of 1995
exchange rates.

It must be borne in mind that even where costs are given under the same
description in one or more countries, this is not to say that they are identical,
or even physically similiar. Approximate estimating costs for a particular
country are for the normal standards prevailing in that country. Quality and
technical standards vary widely and there are differences between countries in
what is, and is not, included. The table, therefore, should be used with care.

	Hotel, 5 star, city centre			m^2	Hotel, 3 star city/provincial m^2			
Country	National Currency	UK£	US$	Yen	National Currency	UK£	US$	Yen
Australia	2,200	1,019	1,618	148,649	1,800	833	1,324	121,622
Brunei	3,420	1,534	2,426	223,529	2,760	1,238	1,957	80,392
China	14,376	1,092	1,730	158,679	9,141	694	1,100	100,894
Hong Kong	13,600	1,108	1,757	161,137	11,500	937	1,486	136,256
Indonesia	3,028,500	852	1,350	123,814	2,187,300	615	975	89,424
Japan	450,000	3,095	4,906	450,000	370,000	2,545	4,034	370,000
Malaysia	3,229	826	1,307	120,037	2,260	578	915	84,015
New Zealand	2,800	1,176	1,867	171,779	2,200	924	1,467	134,969
Philippines	34,000	835	1,323	121,385	32,000	786	1,245	114,245
Singapore	2,800	1,256	1,986	183,007	2,100	942	1,489	137,255
South Korea	1,334,000	1,103	1,748	163,912	1,147,000	949	1,503	140,935
Sri Lanka	73,100	911	1,443	132,380	35,875	447	708.29	64,967
Taiwan	n.a.				n.a.			
Thailand	31,250	793	1,257	115,271	23,250	590	935	85,762
United Kingdom	1,139	1,139	1,808	165,072	869	869	1,379	125,942
United States	n.a.				n.a.			
Vietnam	16,542,000	946.39	1,500	137,598	12,683,000	725.61	1,150	105,498

Index